FERAL CITY

FERAL CITY

On Finding Liberation in Lockdown New York

JEREMIAH MOSS

W. W. NORTON & COMPANY
Independent Publishers Since 1923

CONTENTS

PART FOUR

PART FIVE

PART ONE

1.

THE BEFORE TIME
(SOMEWHERE IN 2019)

The mothers are coming up the stairs, holding the hands of adult children, asking, "Is the neighborhood safe?" The real-estate agent replies, "The East Village used to have quite a reputation, but now it's totally safe." Or did he say *tame*? As in domesticated, subjugated, a wild horse broken. I'm listening from inside my apartment, looking through the peephole to see who my new neighbors might be, knowing they'll be the same as all the rest. Young and funded, they belong to a certain type: utterly unblemished, physically fit and clean-cut, as bland as skim milk and unsalted Saltines. One shouts, "I work on Wall Street!" The agent replies, "Awesome!"

They didn't use to come here. They were intimidated by the city's bois-terous diversity, its blunt embrace. Then New York, long discredited by the Heartland—for being too Jewish, Black, and queer, too dirty, sexual, and untamed—emerged from the dust of September 11 as a symbol of American patriotism. The New People got the idea that the city needed them to save it and they came running, missionaries to the heathen wil-derness, spreading good, clean, suburban normalization.

I call them New People, but this is misleading. Their newness is not the problem. The city has always attracted newcomers. I was new once, a queer refugee from a working-class town, a place since fallen to Trump flags and Dollar Stores, streets littered with mini liquor bottles and failed lottery tickets, telephone poles tacked with signs offering Suboxone Treatment and Cash for Diabetic Test Strips. I ran to the city for the reasons queers have always run to cities—to be free and find my people. When I say *New* People, I don't mean recent. I mean a new *type* of person, fiercely devoted to the normative order—the dominant standard that dictates what we should (and should not) think, say, and do. The New People are hyper-normal. With all the alienation that comes with it.

The city has long held space for the non-normative, the weird and unwanted, but some say this is no longer necessary. You have the Internet, they say; you don't need bars, bookstores, unpoliced public parks. You don't need cities. Suburban America, they say, is a welcoming place, as in: "My cousin in Ohio has a nonbinary child who goes by they/them and they're doing fine." Meanwhile, the kid is cutting themself with an Exacto knife and dreaming of the day they can flee to the city. I know because, when they do escape, they come to me for psychotherapy and roll up their sleeves.

In the early 1990s I was a young, queer, transsexual poet, and where else would I run but to the East Village with its hundred years of anarchists, feminists, beatniks, and punks? I came armed with a pair of combat boots, a pocketknife, and an education from an elite college where I went on scholarship and work-study, served food to the descendants of US presidents, and failed to grasp entitlement. I cleaned rich New Yorkers' apartments, got fired when a client accused me of sticking hair to her bathroom ceiling, and took another job that involved picking up dog shit and getting yelled at. The East Village was full of people who were bruised like I was bruised, trying to make something of life, and I belonged here, sinking into a space that felt like home, a longed-for destination.

Home for a trans person can be hard to find. Normal spaces are straightened spaces, orderly, policed, and filled with risk, from soft erasure to murder. The trans body, too, doesn't always feel like home. No matter what alterations it employs, it often remains an uncanny dwelling. Such slantedness can become a kind of home, and a trans person might seek disorderly spaces occupied by other Others. The city used to be full of slanted people and unstraightened spaces. This was sanctuary.

For twenty-five years I'd been living securely in my apartment, a rent-stabilized walk-up with leaky ceilings, crooked linoleum floors, and walls as thin as communion wafer, when the landlord sold the building to a nameless corporate entity. Until then, the New People were kept outside, roaring down the sidewalks in packs, body-slamming us with their shoulders, getting drunk at bottomless brunches and attacking us while screaming, "My dad owns half of fucking Manhattan!" My changeless tenement was a holdout full of old-school New Yorkers, but that was not to last.

To attract New People, the new owners installed a doorbell system linked to smartphones, though not my smartphone, because I resist having one, so I can't always buzz people in. (When I complained, the manager said, "Maybe now you'll buy an iPhone! It's great for getting packages! You can be all the way in Kansas and still let people in!" What would I be doing in *Kansas*?) When they installed cameras in the halls, trained on our doors to catch us in eviction-worthy acts, my old neighbors and I stood on the street, outside the landlord's net of surveillance, and debated whether or not the cameras were dummies, duping us into good behavior. The Panopticon Effect in action. I've never vandalized the hallways and never would, but since the cameras came, I think about how much I would like to but can't because they might be watching, so I stop myself from thinking about vandalizing the hallways. The cameras incited a thought in my mind and then censored that thought. Sometimes it's hard to know, in the presence of the cameras, which thoughts belong to me and which ones belong to them.

Every year there's a new batch of New People in the building. It's a constant revolving door. Before they arrive, teams of hired hands prepare the Insta-partments. First come the cleaners, sending up the chlorine tang of bleach, followed by the movers with their tidy plastic totes. Professional unpackers assemble and arrange new furniture, kitchen knives gleaming in wooden blocks, salt mills prefilled with chunks of pink salt mined from the Himalayas. The New People are outsourcers and completists. If they don't hire furnishers, they order entire apartments through the mail. A generic catalog spread, the decor is as tedious and temporary as the people.

A New York apartment used to take time to coalesce, forming around you as you evolved into a New Yorker. I furnished my place from the bounty of the streets. A midcentury modern chair from the trash on Twenty-Third Street. A vintage lamp in the shape of a panther for 50 cents from a homeless woman on Third Avenue. Recently, a friend said my apartment smells like the nineties, like a wooden house, something alive.

I never intended to stay between these walls. I thought other options would open, apartments with exposed brick, worn wood floors, and quiet, but the rents skyrocketed around me and my income did not keep up. I do alright now, but can't shake my sense of precarity. Sometimes I think I'll die here, my corpse found when the smell troubles the neighbors. I doubt the New People worry about dying that kind of death. If times get tough, if a plague descends or rising seas swallow the city, they have other places to go. But if you don't worry like New Yorkers worry, can you dream like New Yorkers dream? While they sleep, do the walls of their apartments open into extra rooms like they do for us, or have they got all the space they need? Hashtag abundance. Hashtag gratitude.

When my elderly downstairs neighbor died, a police officer asked for his last name. I couldn't remember. Because of the mailboxes. Our last names used to be printed on each box, never changing because no one ever left. I saw them every day, a reminder of the people I lived among, names conjuring neighborhood history, Jewish and Ukrainian syllables redolent with sour pickle and pierogi steam. When the new owners covered our names with anonymous numbers, I thought: They want us to forget.

I only know the New People's names because they appear on packages that accumulate in the hall where there never used to be packages. Now I'm always tripping over boxes. Sometimes I kick the boxes. Amazon, Amazon, Amazon. Sephora. Vineyard Vines with the smiling, pink, preppie whale. Kick, kick, kick.

The New People don't introduce themselves so I read their names on the packages and google them, sifting through Instagram and YouTube, trips to Bali and brunch. This sounds creepy, but instead of some Dostoevskian fiend (my former psychoanalyst used to say, "You're like Raskolnikov, skulking through the streets"), I think of Gladys Kravitz, the watchful neighbor on *Bewitched*. She suffered from a Cassandra complex, certain something strange was going on, but forever disbelieved. "The Cassandra woman," wrote Jungian analyst Laurie Layton Schapira, "may blurt out what she sees, perhaps with the unconscious hope that others might be able to make some sense of it. But to them her words sound meaningless." Doomed to be dismissed as a hysteric.

Since the New People came into the building, I've developed an irritable bowel. I go to doctors, take tests, rule out celiac and Crohn's. I get a microbiome test kit, ship a stool sample through the mail, learn the names of my gut bacteria. I try elimination diets, cutting out cruciferous vegetables, but nothing helps. The IBS is a hysterical symptom but I can't prove it because the one irritant I can't eliminate is the New People.

While the rest of us schlep to the laundromat, the renovated market-rate apartments enjoy washer/dryers. The tenement is too flimsy, however, and when the machines spin, my apartment vibrates, the stove rattling so hard I brace for a gas explosion. The New People do their laundry every day. How clean do they need to be? When their garbage fills, they dump the odorous bags in the hall for the rest of us to trip over.

The New People are expulsive. Everywhere they go becomes unbearably loud. In the 1990s I slept with the windows open. Then I slept with the windows closed, and then with earplugs, and then with earplugs and a white-noise machine. New York has always been noisy, but this is different. A popular outdoor restaurant can hit 90 decibels, as loud as a lawn mower (yes, I've walked around with a sound meter), and this noise is charged with social status. For example, the laughter. The New People laugh more intensely, but not because they are more joyful. They are taking space with "dominant laughter," the kind that researchers describe as louder, faster, and typically deployed by aggressors.

I am fascinated by their power of invasion, the way they expand into every space, apparently believing their lifestyle belongs everywhere. Spaces of queerness. Spaces of Blackness. Spaces of otherness. Spaces of *This is our little scrap of somewhere, can't you just let us have it, oh you who have everywhere?* This is ontological expansiveness, philosopher Shannon Sullivan's term for the unconscious habit of people with social privilege (race, gender, class) to assume that "all spaces are rightfully available for the person to enter comfortably." The ontologically expansive person expects to enjoy total psychological comfort in every space, and if anything makes him uneasy, it is "an unjust violation of his basic right to be and feel welcomed wherever he chooses."

Pasteurized and homogenized, the New People look like a J.Crew catalog, ultra-white and monied, everything new and polished, not a speck

of human messiness. Their apartments display the algorithmic placeless-
ness of what Kyle Chayka calls AirSpace, "the anesthetized aesthetic"
of a globalized sameness in which everything is white and blank, a frictionless homogeneity for the "vanilla tourist" who seeks comfort in the
uncomfortable diversity of the city. "Among the phenomenon's consequences," says Chayka, "is depersonalization, in the psychiatric sense: 'a
state in which one loses all sense of identity.'"

I confess: In my queer adolescence I wanted to be a smooth and golden
Mayflower WASP. To be supremely normal, not just straight but straight-
haired, skinny, gender-correct, rich, even whiter than the whiteness I
possessed. I didn't want to be Italian and Irish, ethnicities I thought
would hold me back. I got rid of my gold chain and working-class accent,
took up field hockey, made pilgrimages to L.L.Bean. Any blue-blooded
Anglo-Saxon could see I was faking, but they didn't see me. I saw them.
On my way to Catholic school, I would pass their leafy boarding school,
gaze upon their abundance, and feel my lack. Being close to what you
don't have can make you angry.

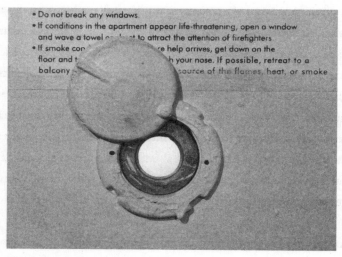

Peephole, looking out from inside

When the newest New People move in next door they look like all the
New People who've come before, blond, glossy and glowing, dressed in
white, with identical Maison Goyard bags, white AirPods plugged in
their ears. I google them. One is a teenage heiress. The other is an Instagram influencer with a page full of beige. Here she is in the Hamptons. Here she is in Starbucks. Here she is in a video about everything
she bought at Whole Foods. (I dip a toe down the "haul" video rabbit
hole and watch another hauler, identical to my neighbor, unpack bags
from Trader Joe's, turning herself into an advertisement as she says, "I
feel like I'm blending into the walls." Existential dread? She explains, "I
wear white a lot and also my home is white.")

I have a doormat made to say, "Welcome to New York: Now Go Home,"
slogan of the 1990s city. I don't, however, have the heart to place it in
the hall, so I drop it at my kitchen sink, where I am the only person it
urges to leave.

The New People are always forgetting things. They leave their apartments, slamming the doors, and drift down the hallway absently staring at phones. When they pause in front of my peephole to adjust their
AirPods, I am Gladys Kravitz holding her breath, trying not to sneeze.
Through the murky, fish-eye lens, they look lost as they drift down the
stairs and then come trudging back for whatever they forgot. Umbrella.
Wallet. They slam the door, slam it again, stare and drift, down and
down. Sometimes this routine happens two or three times. So much
forgetting. The minds of the New People are elsewhere. They don't know
where they are or what they have.

As a psychoanalyst, I am attuned to variations in the psychic field, but
anyone paying attention can feel a person's psyche in close proximity. You
feel if it runs shallow or deep, elegant or jumbled. What I feel from the
New People is an absence of mind. They are tightly compressed knots,

blank spots inside buzzy clouds of agitated distraction. Of course, this is impossible to measure, so you'll have to trust me when I say: They aren't really here. Caught in the trap of being the New People, they are alienated from *here*. All that absence makes the city a lonelier place. I miss the New York mind.

Even on uncrowded sidewalks I am constantly getting hit by the New People. They refuse to perform what sociologist Erving Goffman called "civil inattention," the act of glancing at a stranger just long enough "to demonstrate that one appreciates that the other is present (and that one admits openly to having seen him)," and then making space. Masters of unseeing, the New People erase the rest of us, giving us the "nonperson treatment." In our buildings, they don't say hello. When I greet them, they look through me with empty eyes. Am I a ghost? I feel spectral, barely embodied, in their presence. When I do manage to get their attention, they appraise me with suspicion and contempt, like a plate of food gone moldy. Do you know what the New People call us? The Leftovers. As in, "I love the East Village, but there's, like, still too many Leftovers."

The New People are the same everywhere, colonizing cities with a mass-produced, globalized state of mind. When essayist Dodie Bellamy encountered troops of them in San Francisco, she noted, "All these clean, clean people—I stare at them trying to crack the mystery of how they do it, walk down the street impeccable as a doll wrapped in plastic. Person after person bumps into me without saying sorry." Seattle author Mattilda Bernstein Sycamore calls their absent look "the gentrified gaze, the suburban imagination in the urban environment, the white picket fence in the eyes." Why come to a city if you're afraid of contact with strangers? I remember being eighteen and talking to a friend who moved to Greenwich Village, into an apartment next to a retired Rockette. It became my fervent New York dream to be neighbors with a salty old-lady dancer who'd sit around in her leotard, smoking long cigarettes and recalling the time she had a threesome with Peter Lawford and JFK. To the New People she'd be just another Leftover.

Why *do* they come? Because they are a valuable commodity (Influencers, especially, help to increase gentrification and raise commercial rents) and New York has been remade just for them, a curated Immersive Experience to consume and toss away. For the fulfillment of their latest cravings, we've become a disposable city.

While I'm watching the New People, my new landlords are watching me, waiting for transgression. I'm less valuable than the hyper-normals. As a queer, this is not an unfamiliar feeling. In the isolation of the 1980s, when I first understood I was trans, I saw myself as an outlaw. How would I make a living? Where would I live? Who would love me? I did not understand society's capacity for change, how time and transition would render me into something (conditionally) respectable, and while it has enabled my survival, that respectability also chafes, an itchy sweater against the skin. Sometimes I want to shrug it off. But how will I make a living? Where will I live? Who will love me?

I find a mirror in the trash. It looks brand new, but my Influencer neighbor bought an extra-new mirror and tossed this one out. I drag it to the sidewalk for someone to take. We used to do this all the time, leaving items for fellow scavengers, giving back as we had taken. Sometime in the 2000s, this habit stopped—maybe it was too anti-capitalist, too messy—and putting out the mirror now feels like a minor act of rebellion.

I watch the Influencer's latest video. Here she is drinking a matcha latte. Here she is smiling into a Sweetgreen salad. Here she is giving a tour of her renovated apartment behind my crummy kitchen with its broken stove and leaky sink. I look for books, paintings, some sign of a creative and uncontrolled life, conflict and imperfection, but there is nothing.

She has one green plant, a housewarming gift from the landlord (the New People get gifts?). Everything else is white. The couch is white. The pillows are white. The curtains are white. The bed, sheets, and blankets are white. The desk is white. The dining set is white. The rug is white. The new mirror, the one that replaced the old white mirror, has a blond wood frame that looks almost white. The Influencer loves the blond wood because, she says, "Everything's white, so I needed, like, some texture."

I tell myself the Influencer is not a bad person, she just doesn't know what texture is. Maybe she's afraid of texture. I once knew a woman who only ate white food. She'd experienced a horrible trauma and didn't want anything entering her body that didn't signify purity and cleanliness. Maybe the Influencer had a horrible trauma. Maybe the normativity of America is the trauma, complex and repressed, and all that whiteness is there to keep her safe, holding her together so she doesn't fly apart. Maybe the New People hope that living here will give them some texture. But not too much.

I agree with author Sarah Schulman when she says, "No one is inherently problematic as a city-dweller because of his/her race or class. It is the ideology with which one lives that creates the consequences of one's actions on others." I wonder: How might the ideology of *normal* traffic in race/class dominance?

I keep thinking about the attachment to white. Do the white walls, furniture, and clothing point to white skin? Do they deflect from (and thereby reveal) white anxiety in urban space? Claudia Rankine says blondness "points to white power and its values as desirable, whether the thought enters one's head or not." She wonders if "white women are trapped inside the machinery that insists on the authenticity of whiteness." Do the New People feel trapped in all that white and blond? When Rankine asks if blond is "an investment that increases one's value," I wonder if the color also signifies a self steeped in capitalism, self as consumer product. Blondes make more money and attract richer husbands. Everyone told me to be that girl but I couldn't pull it off.

In their expansiveness, their presumption of total comfort and security, the New People don't lock their apartment doors. Out in the hall, the Influencer calls friends on the phone and shouts, loud enough for anyone to hear, "You can hang out at my place! I left the door unlocked!" Later, when she comes up the stairs with a group of boys, I look through the peephole to see her stop short, point at my door, and say with disdain, "Why do they have a *padlock* on their door?" Padlock? She doesn't know what a dead bolt is, doesn't recognize this basic domestic protection. Her use of *they* is odd, too, since I live alone and I doubt she means it in the nonbinary sense. I remain unknown to her, an ambiguous spectral someone she hasn't perceived. After staring at my dead bolt a moment longer, mouth open in a performance of incredulity, she declares with contempt, "It's so *extra*," excessive and unnecessary. The Alpha Boy of the group says, in a mocking doofusy voice, "Welcome to New Yo-o-ork," and the crowd laughs, having decided I'm a hysteric, like this city, a Cassandra waiting for something bad to happen when bad things never happen. Not to them.

I think about moving. I look at my savings account, twenty-five years of scrimping and squirreling, and wonder if I could buy a small place at the edge of the East Village, away from the screaming crowds. The new owners offered me money to leave so they can replace me with more New People. It's not enough. When I complain to friends about the neighborhood, they get impatient and say, "Move to Brooklyn," as if that borough could bring relief. I feel dyspeptic and misunderstood. The East Village is still here, I insist, underneath the static. This is my home and I won't let it be taken. Raised by pushy, controlling people, I have a highly resistant personality, rooted and intractable. The more I'm pushed, the more I dig in. You know the game adults play with groups of children, *Let's see who can sit still and be quiet the longest?* I always won.

The Influencer has friends over, including the Alpha Boy, who adds a jolt of malice. I'm trying to write, but they keep going in and out, slamming the door and shouting in the hall. There's a thump against my window, a whinny of male laughter, as the boys take the fire escape. Sitting on my sill, they are almost inside, an intrusion too far. I knock on the glass and make the gesture for "get off." As the boys take their time, grumbling, I know: I am now the enemy. Minutes later, the Influencer bursts into the hall with a girl friend and sets up a photo shoot. She's never done this and I suspect the Alpha Boy put her up to it. They are by my door, taking photos for Instagram, and they are loud. "I like this shot best because it's the most white," the Influencer says, meaning the walls, which are painted white, and her clothing, which is always white. Alpha Boy leans out from her apartment door and shouts, "Can you keep it down? Other people are living here! I pay good money to live here!" He's using a put-on voice, an imitation of a whiny neighbor. It's supposed to be me. "Shut up," the Influencer says, like she's saying it to me. Alpha Boy shouts again in the neighbor voice and the girls ignore him, playing out the act of ignoring me, and I understand there is nothing I can do without becoming the ridiculed thing they're performing, a joke that looks like Gladys Kravitz. "Take another picture," the Influencer insists. "This time, get more white."

They escalate, leaving their door open with music blaring, trying to flush me out, setting me up for abuse. The girl with the camera tries seduction, coaching the Influencer like a sly pornographer. "Yeah, like that," she says. "That is so your vibe, with the white wall, like, so cute! Lift your shirt. Higher. More belly. Yeah, like that." I've had enough. I step into the hall and glare. "Are we being loud?" the Influencer asks. She is grinning, performing cute. "Yeah," I say, not seduced. "I'm trying to write." Alpha Boy leaps into view. This is his moment. In a white T-shirt, white baseball cap turned backward, he gives me the hang loose sign and waggles his tongue. In a mocking tone, barely holding back mean-boy laughter, he shouts, "Go for it, bro! Good luck with that *writing*!" I say nothing. The Influencer looks up and down my body, measuring and judging, before she settles on my slippers and lets a wisp of contempt crinkle her mouth. I wait, feeling all the bullied feelings, the Carrie-covered-in-pig-blood feelings, and then I light them on fire with my mind. Still burning, they go inside. Still burning, I go inside. When they leave, snickering down the hall, I watch through the peephole. Alpha Boy stops at my door, bites his lip, and flips me the finger. He doesn't know I'm watching, thinks I can't see, and that's the point. He's the kind of boy who sticks it to you when your back is turned. Everyone who's ever been a girl knows this boy. He never does it to your face.

"The ten most popular kids from every high school in the world are now living in New York City," downtown performance artist Penny Arcade once said. "Those are the people who most of us who came to New York came here to get away from." The popular kids want to push us out, but I'm not leaving. I'm good at sitting still. I will outwait them. One day the tide will shift and New York will change, as it always does. That, as people like to say, is the one thing you can count on in this town.

PART TWO

2.

EMPTINESS GIVES PERMISSION

J ust like that, the New People abandon New York. On the weekend before lockdown, the bars are packed. Young hyper-normals go roving past in drunken mobs, grabbing a last hurrah—and a dose of coronavirus. On Monday, March 16, 2020, I wake to a ghost town, the streets gone tumbleweed quiet. No cars, no people, my building relaxed into stillness. All the market-rate tenants have gone. While the rest of us were stocking up on toilet paper and hand sanitizer, the heiress vanished, along with the downstairs people who leave bags of garbage in the hall. The Influencer has taken refuge at her family's home in a master-planned gated community with its own private airport. On her Instagram she puts up photos of palm trees and golf courses, complains about the dark roots in her quarantined hair, and styles a poolside picnic with Moët rosé, baguette, and brie. Hashtag blessed.

As soon as the New People leave, the Amazon packages stop coming. Doors stop slamming. Washing machines stop shivering the timbers of the building. No more screeching in the halls. No more Instagram photo shoots. No more Alpha Boys giving me the finger. And it's not just my building. Friends across social media say it's happening everywhere— the New People have fled. At night, when I look from my windows to the windows of other buildings, half have gone dark. Everyone is supposed to be home, sheltering in place, but no one is home. Except for the Remainders. The Leftovers. We stay, taking our temperatures and waiting for the virus to find us. As for the rest, it's as if they've been raptured away.

A velvet drape of silence falls across the neighborhood. Along the avenue, traffic evaporates, turning a thundering river into a noiseless canyon. Living above a clamorous intersection, I have wished for such quiet, but this is plague quiet and it unsettles me. There is nothing human out there. A police car drifts by, blaring its dystopian recording: "Due to the current health emergency, members of the public are reminded to keep a safe distance of six feet from others while in public places to reduce the spread of the coronavirus." The voice is digitized, dropping into the uncanny valley somewhere between real and hyperreal. This is where we live now.

"Millennials cooped up by the coronavirus head back home," the *Times* announces. They're not afraid of getting sick; they just don't want to be bored, stuck in New York with nothing to do. They want to be "comfortable," they say, to play "childhood board games" and "watch TV" with their parents. At their age, the last place I wanted to be was back in my mother's house, playing Candyland and watching *Wheel of Fortune*. When terrorism shook the city on 9/11, I didn't consider going home. New York was home. I came as a fugitive and don't relate to the desire to return. This is not generational. When the *Times* says "millennials," they don't mean *all* the millennials. They don't mean the immigrant and working-class millennials, the restaurant deliveryman, laundromat washerwoman, grocery cashier, ER nurse millennials. They don't mean the queer artist black sheep of the family millennials, the punk-rock millennials, the diehard New York, in sickness and in health millennials. They don't mean the native-born, nowhere-else-to-go millennials either. To freely choose to "go home" requires another place in which you feel *at home*. For others, belonging is bound up in New York.

We who remain worry about our laundry. Should we sit in the laundromat, breathing its deadly air? Or drop it off and take a different chance, the virus offloading from the washerwoman's well-intentioned hands? As my dirty clothes pile up, as laundromats close and my friends take to scrubbing underwear in buckets, I think about the washer/dryer in the abandoned apartment next door. The fire escape window is probably unlocked. I could slip right in.

Twice a day, I check my temperature and clip my finger into a pulse oximeter. I try not to slide into the darkest dark of pandemic panic. It's like treading water, sinking down, and fighting back to the surface. Some of the people I love get sick. Some of the people I love lose people they love. The numbers of the dead keep rising. Hundreds a day. I develop a dry cough with a sore throat. Is this it? There's no way to get tested and I wish for a mild case, just to get it over with.

I am fortunate to work from home, seeing patients over video. Some leave the city and some stay. Some are untroubled by the virus while others worry about the water supply turning toxic, the food running out, the plague exterminating most of humanity and sending the rest of us to Mad Max Thunderdome. Those who left feel guilty about leaving and wonder: Did I do the right thing? Those who stayed feel regretful about staying and wonder: Did I do the right thing? Some get the virus and fall sick with fever. They want to know if I'm safe. Did they infect me when we last met face to face? In another time, I would have analyzed that fear, traced its history, uncovered the wish to infect, to be taken in by the other, but now I only reassure. *I'm okay.* Some want to know where I am. Did I leave or stay? *I am here*, I say, following up with the analyst's eternal question: *What does that mean to you?* The ones who've stayed say, "I'm glad you're here because it feels like we're going through this together. You know what it's like." When I see my own therapist over video, away in his country house, I'm glad for his safety but feel distant. A barrier has risen that keeps me inside while he's out there, protected and free. I see the forest outside his windows, ventilated and clean, and when he gives me advice on how to survive the plagued city, I say, "You don't know what it's like to be here," a statement I've been making my entire life.

My upstairs neighbors get sick. They walk the stairs, gasping for breath. From behind my door the coughs sound lethal, glutinous and Cronenbergian. The virus, experts say, lingers in the air for hours, aerosolized clouds of death I walk through when I go to check the mail, though the mail doesn't come anymore. I cover the gaps around my door with weather sealing tape. I worry about the man upstairs who lives alone. I haven't heard his piano in days, but I'm too afraid to knock.

When corona first hit, building management posted a notice: "We take this matter very seriously. We will maintain extra cleanings throughout the season of this virus." For a week, maybe two, they kept their promise, filling the halls with the reassuring bite of bleach. But when the more valuable market-rate people left, the cleanings stopped. Sometimes I think we have been left here to die.

Not all who left are bored millennials gone back to the suburbs. Many are the superrich, skipped to the Hamptons. Others are middle-class professionals like myself, but with modest country houses in upstate New York and New England. Some are my friends. On Facebook, I see photos of their gardens and trees, the spacious kitchens where they bake sourdough bread like American pioneers. Is there a word for envying what you do not want? These are people I love, and their lives in exile look pleasant enough, but I'm not built that way. Sometimes, I wish I were. Life, I am told, would be soft and breezy. And yet the last thing I want is a country house. It would require leaving the city every weekend and I don't like to leave the city. I don't want to go hiking and I don't want to bake bread. Whenever I go on vacation, I get a little depressed.

In a country house I might disappear, succumbing to daytime television and mild suicidal ideation. So, when I ask myself, "If I had someplace to go, would I leave New York?" the answer is clear.

Given the choice, what makes one person stay and another go? Maybe it comes down to attachment. How attached are you to New York? How deeply are the tendrils of the city intertwined with your nervous system? When you're away, do you go into withdrawal? Do you experience anxiety, nausea, fatigue, malaise? If you can leave New York and freely enjoy the pleasures of the countryside, the quiet spaciousness of a house, consider yourself lucky. Call it pathological, but for some of us, the affect of the city mirrors our own and it's the only environment where we feel functional. New York has ruined other places for me. Even when I visit other cities, I feel off. The light is wrong, the bricks are wrong, the air is tinted an entirely wrong color and my body feels wrong moving through it. Like an ocean-dwelling fish dropped in fresh water, I miss the salt, that bitter grit. This appetite requires a certain disposition, the sort that some call "cranky," a descriptor often thrown at me. And Fran Lebowitz. When *The New Yorker* asks if she would ever flee the city, especially now, Lebowitz replies, "Never. It didn't even occur to me." She finds it shocking that anyone would want to leave during a disaster. "I'm not leaving. In fact, I feel that I am like the designated New Yorker. Everyone else can leave."

At the pizza place on the corner, I am the only customer. The pizza man in his greasy apron is delighted, desperate to make contact with another human. "Hello, my friend!" he calls. "How are you? Isn't this crazy? Fucking crazy." Behind my mask, I agree, "fucking crazy," as he heats up my slice. He does not wear rubber gloves. "Buddy," he says, "if this goes on much longer, you should buy a gun. We're all gonna need guns. The crime will go up!" I'm more concerned about his bare hands on my slice. After eating this pizza, I will have to count fourteen days, corona's incubation period, to see if I have COVID. If I die for this pizza, I will feel regretful, but at least I will die a New Yorker.

Has the East Village ever been so quiet? In the silence after 9/11, I heard crickets on the street, but it didn't last. The quarantine quiet goes on and on, permitting the softer sounds that usually go unheard. The screech of a hawk. The squeaky wheel on a homeless person's cart. A sigh. A yawn. A tugboat's horn resounding from the East River. Every day, every hour, feels like Sunday morning. Sunday morning in a snowstorm, muffled and fleecy. I play Morrissey, singing of Armageddon, "Every day is like Sunday. Every day is silent and grey."

I can't sleep. My head aches. I expend a great deal of energy trying not to think about death. After spending half the day in bed, I pull on dirty jeans and walk to Tompkins Square Park. This changes everything. The New People are really gone, their absence like an atmosphere, the sky clear after a storm, and the park is sparsely populated with ordinary folks, working-class locals, and diehard East Village types—oddballs, gray-haired anarchists, junkies, hobos, young hippies, poets. An older man is performing spoken word about a goth girl breathing on him, sharing sweat and virus, *so what the hell*. From an open window at Vazac's Horse-shoe Bar, a tattooed woman is serving drinks to go in plastic cups. She has one customer, a grizzled barfly, and me. I order a cocktail to drink in the sunshine of the park where everyone is getting drunk or high. *It's the end of the world as we know it and I feel fine*. The guy who rides his bike while blasting hip-hop is sitting on a bench, blasting hip-hop while a few hippie girls dance, their hands in blue rubber gloves. Everyone is masked, six feet apart, yet we feel more connected, more human, less alone.

Most of the neighborhood has vanished, I'm sure of it, a hunch confirmed weeks from now by the *Times*: "Hundreds of thousands of New

York City residents, in particular those from the city's wealthiest neighborhoods, left as the coronavirus pandemic hit." The vanishing first
makes itself known to the Department of Sanitation, who are collecting
a third less trash from rich neighborhoods. Then the smartphone data
comes in, tracking human movement as people scatter outward. By some
estimates, half a million people, mostly upper-class, white Manhattanites, will skip town this spring in another white flight, and the largest
exodus is from the East Village, where the population has dropped by
more than half.

Throughout the plagues of history, people with means have fled cities.
In Boccaccio's *Decameron*, the wealthy run from the Black Death to
their country estates, "as though the wrath of God . . . was meant to
harry only those remaining within their city walls." Pampinea, one of
the storytellers, believes the plague will be less distressing in the beauty
of nature. "The heavens may be scowling at us," she says, "but they still
won't refuse us their glimpse of eternal beauty—and that's a great deal
more beauty than we'll ever find staring at the empty buildings in the
city!" I disagree. The empty buildings of the city are beautiful, and after
one week of quarantine, I rush out to meet them. The governor's stay-at-
home order allows us to venture out as long as we are alone. I am alone.
I put on a mask and walk far, through the cold, on sunny days and rainy
days, for hours. The pandemic offers a profound accidental experiment.
What happens to New York when its least tenaciously attached residents
are suddenly gone?

■ ■ ■

MANHATTANITES ARE LOOKING AT EACH OTHER AGAIN, THE WAY WE
used to on the streets. A miracle happens: No one is looking at phones.
We who remain slip back into our old rhythm. Awake and watchful,

wary of the virus, we move the way we used to, giving space on the sidewalk, cooperating in a time of mutual risk. We nod in solidarity. *I see you. I won't hurt you. We're here together.* Among these New Yorkers, I am again a human being with a body, a ghost returning to matter.

The slogan "New York Tough" appears around town, pointing to us, the ones who've stayed. We are meant to feel fortified, to remember how this city used to require toughness more than money. To come here, you had to be hungry. You had to need it.

In a seeming paradox, a number of my patients feel better. Their anxieties, depressions, and psychosomatic symptoms disappear. The melancholics feel less melancholic because "now the outside matches my inside." I find myself feeling the same. My irritable bowel stops being irritable—and so does the rest of me. My inner Cassandra, my Chicken Little, can finally relax. The sky has fallen—and I'm not the only one who sees it. I have a Zoom call with my friend Jake, an indigenous trans man and homeopath, who understands this minority emotional experience, the taboo of feeling better when the world is so much worse. He tells me about the suspension of chronic disease conditions during epidemics, how a communally shared acute disease can bring relief from the larger collective, persistent problem. "However," Jake says, "that relief is temporary. Throughout history, the acute eventually recedes and the chronic always returns." I don't want to hear this. I want the pandemic to change the world—and me—for good. For the better.

On WNYC, Rebecca Solnit is talking about disaster and how it bestows a "violent gift" that "throws people into the present and sort of gives them this supersaturated immediacy that also includes a deep sense of connection. . . . You're close to mortality in a way that makes you feel more alive. You're deeply in the present and can let go of past and future. . . . You have shared an experience with everyone around you."

For two minutes, at 7:00 each night, the city erupts in applause. We clap for the caregivers, first responders, and essential workers. And for ourselves. For still being alive. As my neighbors emerge from windows, one woman appears with a pot and spoon, banging them together like it's New Year's Eve. Men holler and whistle. The few passing cars honk their horns. A delivery woman stands by her scooter and cheers the delivery men rolling down the bike lane, calling, "We made it another day! That's right!" A young man climbs onto his fire escape to play "The Star-Spangled Banner" on a blue electric guitar, a nod to Jimi Hendrix, who played it in wartime. When the applause is over, people linger, leaning on windowsills the way New Yorkers used to, connecting above the concrete, until the woman with the pot and spoon calls out, "Goodnight everyone, see you tomorrow," and the streets settle back to their hush. I break into sobs, clashing joy and grief, because everywhere is death yet it feels so alive.

As the Leavers flee to forty-eight different states, they aren't going empty-handed. Geneticists who track viral mutation signatures will find that most cases of COVID across the country are linked to New York, what one epidemiologist calls "the Grand Central Station for this virus." Across New England, people with New York license plates are accosted in parking lots by finger-waggers shouting, "Shame!" State troopers in Rhode Island hunt down New Yorkers, stopping cars and conducting house-to-house searches for escapees. The city becomes again, in the American imagination, the stigmatized Other, the diseased Rotten Apple. Calling back the 1970s, Trump tells us to drop dead.

We the Remainders expand our sense of civic pride, a tough New Yorker mythos around staying put. We know many people left for compelling reasons, for compromised immune systems, debilitating anxiety, and lost jobs, for elderly parents and young children. We know some were leaving anyway and this just hastened the process. We focus our indignation on the kind of Leaver who becomes the Archetypal Deserter, the ones who skip out when times are tough because they're easily bored and New York is only a product to consume, a shopping mall, an Instagrammable moment. We tell ourselves that those Leavers are weak and we, the Remainders, are New York Tough. This defensive maneuver is what New Yorkers have always done in difficult times. The New York attitude, the swagger and boast of exceptionalism, is a way of coping—not just with the difficult city, but with the difficult life that attaches you to the city, a life that might crush you if you weren't so goddamned *resilient*. It's an attitude that has not collectivized in a long time. As we begin again to think of ourselves as rugged survivalists in the urban dystopia, my Twitter feed fills with *Escape from New York* memes, Snake Plissken growling, "Oh, you mean I can't count on you?" Months from now, there will be T-shirts: "We Stayed & We Don't Miss You."

The deserted streets are beautiful in their vacancy, an empty stage made more quiet by the memory of noise. I can hear the ambient tone of the city, a soft blanket of nothing much. When Sartre said, "Hell is other people," he meant that we are trapped by the gaze of the other, judged and interpreted. The unoccupied city fulfills the fantasy: What if there were no others? What if there was no dominating gaze?

I move freely on the sidewalks, breathing deep, and my body expands, or my soul, something, stretches out. I unclench, joint by joint, a glad unfolding. I wave my arms in circles, taking up space, not caring how I look because there is no one to see. It's a sunny Saturday on Broadway in SoHo, where there's always a crush of shoppers, but not a single person passes. No car, no truck. No push, no shove. Nothing but asphalt and brick, sunlight and air, the rough gray lungs of the city audibly breathing. Emptiness gives permission. My body remembers how the quieter city of the past gave me space, and I linger for a long while on an empty corner, Lafayette and Prince, enjoying the loose-limbed, criminal pleasure of loitering. I'm doing something shady, something queer. A loitering trans body is an illegal body, and while my transness is mostly invisible, it gives off a vibe. Here comes a cop car, slowing down to look at me. I talk out loud to myself, the way I used to but stopped when New York changed into a place where the New People would shoot you dirty looks, but now they're gone and, anyway, no one sees your lips moving behind a mask. A man comes along. He, too, has seized the moment, waving his arms and taking space. I recognize a kindred soul, similarly unfolding.

People keep saying New York has become unrecognizable in the pandemic, not itself, but that depends on which New York you're attached to. There are missing layers, the obvious stuff, but I'm not interested in the obvious. Listen. Without all the noise, you can hear the signal. We're getting down to the marrow of this town, dark and succulent. Something is shifting in the warp and woof of New York's fabric. Something has torn and, through that rupture, other elements slip. On a bone-deep level, beyond the restaurants, shops, and crowds, New York feels more like itself than it has in twenty years. Not everyone feels this. Not everyone *wants* to feel this. But for many of us, it's like catching the scent of a lost perfume, the madeleine that makes memory bloom, and we go tumbling back through time.

The East Village has instantly refilled with homeless people. They didn't just become unhoused, they've been here, unseen in the crowds, constantly pushed out, but the cops aren't hassling them now that the valuable New People and tourists have left, so the unhoused are permitted to exist once more on the gentrified streets. A man shakes a beggar's cup tied to the end of a stick, a supple branch ripped from a tree. It's the second social-distancing stick I've seen in two days, necessity giving birth to collective invention.

In Chinatown, on what is usually a busy corner, a freakishly large flock of pigeons has massed in a rumbling gray cloud. I stop to stare at the avian marvel, made possible by the absence of people. Around the world, shutdown cities are rewilding, taken over by lions, peacocks, Kashmir goats. In New York, the pigeons and rats are organizing, forming armies to gather what scraps of food they can find. (Without humans, there are no pizza crusts or restaurant trash, and the rats are resorting to cannibalism and infanticide.) This period of global lockdown will be called anthropause, the temporary slowing of human activity, a deceleration of industrialist capitalism and its profound effect on the environment. Satellite imagery reveals air pollution levels dropping around the globe. As the skies clear of nitrogen dioxide and other particulates, the snowy peaks of the Himalayas come into view for the first time in decades and the smoggy dome over Los Angeles turns crystal blue. In a phenomenon scientists will call the great seismic quiet period, the earth's upper crust goes still, unrattled by the pounding of cars, trains, and other human vibrations. "Nature is healing," say the memes, tongue in cheek. "We are the virus."

As the pandemic takes, it also gives, showing us what other ways of life are possible. In empty New York, a feral energy is returning to the streets. The word *feral* does not mean wild, but rewild, a creaturely life once free and then tamed, confined, and broken free again. Cities, too, have their nature. A left-alone city is a forest, while an overmanaged city is a farm, and New York, like many globalized cities after the neoliberal turn in the 1970s, has been farmed, landscaped, and policed to yield profits for big business, real estate, and tourism. This tamed city attracted a tamed population. But now, as that population has removed itself, the resilient city is changing back. And so am I.

The more I walk, the more I drop into a subterranean feeling I used to experience all the time, a connection to vibrating threads, an image I took from the poet Hart Crane, who took it from the philosopher P. D. Ouspensky, who wrote about using poetry to get below the surface phenomenon of the street to the "infinite noumenon," the invisible grid. There's a second city under the static. I lived there until the New People came to jam the atmosphere with frazzled energies and psychic vacancies. I lost touch but kept looking for my city, hunting around with a camera, trying to capture remnants, to get my fingers on the invisible strings and feel the thrum of their music. When I fell out from the poetry of the streets, I thought it was me. I had gotten older, more constricted. But here it is again. Has it been here all along? Is it the absence of the New People, the spaciousness they've left behind, or the closeness of death that puts me in touch with this poetical deportment?

Poetical deportment is how E. B. White described the gift given to the city by newcomers, the ones who came, as I did, with the excitement of first love. How is it that tragedy would make me fall in love with the city again? I am troubled by this unexpected joy in the presence of so much suffering. Is my euphoria a by-product of mass trauma, a neurological state of hyperarousal that comes from living with ambient death? Is it the pleasure of being a New Yorker among New Yorkers again? Feeling a certain shame in my joy, I consult the poets. Mary Oliver, what should I do? "If you suddenly and unexpectedly feel joy," she replies, "don't hesitate." Langston Hughes chimes in, "Sometimes a crumb falls from the tables of joy." Should I grab it? "Joy is not made to be a crumb," Mary counters. But what if that's all I'm allowed? Well, she sighs, "don't be afraid of its plenty."

The pandemic, saturated by a communal consciousness of death, brings with it a profound anti-alienation effect. Maybe this is the source of its enigmatic joy. Others feel it, too. Like this woman in a surgical mask, strutting down Avenue A looking like Joni Mitchell, white hair streaming from a black beret. She flaps her arms and yells, "Woo-hoo! We're still alive!" She takes up space the way I take up space, arms flapping, signaling the existence of a body among other bodies. Here we are. She sees me see her. As we take each other in, she calls, "We're still alive!" And I reply, "So far!"

. . .

HERE IN THE EPICENTER, THE NUMBERS KEEP GOING UP—*THE numbers*, we say, to forget they are people, to forget they could be us— and the air is fractured by sirens. Every hour of the day and night, ambu- lances go tearing up the avenue to Bellevue and Mount Sinai. I look out my window to see two jockeying side by side, lights aflame, racing each other to the ER. I hold my breath and wish: *Be well, be well, be well.*

When the refrigerator trucks arrive, I counterphobically go to find them between the pigeon-fouled FDR overpass and the old Bellevue Psychiatric Hospital, the looming brick building where Valerie Sola- nas stayed after shooting Andy Warhol and Mark David Chapman went after killing John Lennon. It is not a pleasant spot, but this is a makeshift morgue and there's nothing pleasant about it. A dozen white trailers fill the lot, each fitted with a cooling unit embossed with the word *Whisper,* a reminder to keep our voices down, here in New York's dismal funeral parlor. The trucks, parked all over town, have been repurposed by the U.S. Department of Defense, their various com- pany logos painted over in white, but the paint jobs are slapdash and the ghosts show through. One truck carries the Walmart logo and the words "Save money. Live better." Inside are stacked the bodies of peo- ple who could not be touched by their loved ones, not kissed goodbye. Some are wrapped in bedsheets because the city has run out of body bags. I say a wish for the dead and another for myself: *Please don't let me end up in a Walmart truck.*

As I stare at the trucks, I feel indecent, like a gawker. Weegee, the famed New York street photographer of murder victims, tenement fires, and car wrecks, called such onlookers "the curious ones," but looking at death is more than morbid curiosity. As Nora Ephron wrote, "Death happens to be one of life's main events." Should we turn away? Later, I'll confess my shame to my friend Liz, sheltering at her half-demolished home on Cape Cod, where she has invested in chickens for eggs and a machete for self-defense. "Of course you went to see the trucks," she'll say. Fellow Cassandras, we've been friends since high school and know each other's difficult histories. She'll tell me she went to visit a local crematorium for the same reason. She sat outside, gazing at the smokestack, thinking of ashes and virus, getting close to what she fears, because "we have to look." It's impossible to know a thing if you refuse to see it.

The newspapers overwhelm us with photos of bodies, too many, too fast, piled in bags in hallways, scattered naked in parking lots, spilling from U-Haul trucks outside a Brooklyn mortuary. "I ran out of space," the funeral director says. "Bodies are coming out of our ears." We see aerial shots of mass graves on Hart Island, workers in Hazmat suits stacking and burying pine boxes in a deep trench. I am haunted

April 2020 (wheatpaste posters by Jeremyville and Dysturb)

by images of bodies in bags, so each time I see a bag of trash slumped on the sidewalk, I flinch, as if the bodies are everywhere. Because the bodies are everywhere.

Black and Latinx New Yorkers are dying disproportionately from COVID. Low-income neighborhoods in the outer boroughs are hit hard while wealthy, white Manhattan is another country, a boat lifted on the uneven tide of racial capitalism.

Those of us outside the worst of this disaster have the privilege of looking away, changing the channel, clicking another link. We sail on, like the helmsman of the ship in W. H. Auden's "Musée des Beaux Arts," the one who sees Icarus fall from the sky but does not stop. Suffering, says the poet, takes place while the rest of us are going about our lives. Is it better to look or not look? Regarding the pain of others, Susan Sontag wrote, "One can feel obliged to look," but "One should feel obliged to think about what it means to look."

After making myself look at the refrigerator trucks, I cross under the overpass to the East River greenway where people are jogging, not wearing masks. I avoid them and come upon a gray-haired man tap dancing on a derelict wooden stage in front of a shack. How are these crummy old structures still here, in gleaming, affluent New York? It feels like a dream, the past transported to the present—an increasing phenomenon I will come to think of as the Pandemic Space-Time Vortex. Watching the man, I reconnect to aliveness, and when he takes a break, I call out my thanks. He modestly replies, "Oh, I'm just a beginner," and I have to stop myself from crying, thinking of this man, in the gray phase of life, in the fierce proximity of death, starting something joyfully new.

I lie on my bed and wish for someone to comfort me. My wish conjures Susan Sontag. With that shock of white hair, dressed in slacks and dark sweater circa 1975 (in a photograph by Peter Hujar), she appears on my bed and spoons me, saying everything will be alright. While I suspect she was not the most maternal of mothers in real life, she is doing a fine job of it here, today, in the unreal life.

■ ■ ■

I START RIDING MY BIKE. IT GIVES ME BIG GULPS OF FREEDOM, CAR- rying me for miles up and down Manhattan, a powerful sensation that makes me feel as though the city belongs to me. There's no one else here. Central Park is almost empty. Inside the arcade of Bethesda Terrace, I break the rules, riding in lazy circles around the man who plays classical guitar, just the two of us in his music. I find a steady peace in Times Square's cavernous silence, so quiet I can hear the electric billboards humming just to me. On the Brooklyn Bridge, under a stone tower, I sprawl on the soft wooden boards like a single person luxuriating in a king-size bed, reading a copy of Hart Crane's *The Bridge*. I used to do this all the time, before the 65 million tourists crowded us out, but now they're gone and we are free again to enter this sacred space, the bridge a cathedral, a harp in the sky. I count the many minutes in which I don't see another human being, and then nod to the few passing locals seeking respite from quarantine in cramped apartments. "Out of some subway scuttle, cell or loft," wrote Crane, "A bedlamite speeds to thy parapets." Lifted up on this *harp and altar*, suspended in its *choiring strings*, I feel closer to the celestial, the euphoric vault of blue that bears the soul aloft. You know that feeling in your belly when you're thrown into the sky? When the bridge opened in 1883, New Yorkers had never been so high, the elevation made them fizzy, seagulls flying beneath their feet.

Plagues have a disinhibiting effect. As the normal order is suspended, the repressive force of civilization lifts and our rules fall away, shifting the boundaries of society and psyche. In Defoe's *Journal of the Plague Year*, the gentry flee the city and the people left behind go wild, running naked, seeing apparitions, taking the streets. With the restraining upper classes gone from New York, the city begins to sing. On my block, a woman walking her dogs is singing Fleetwood Mac, "Oh, I've been afraid of changing." A man in Central Park sings the Smiths, "In the midst of life we are in death, etcetera." A hippie-punk troubadour plays guitar and sings the Ramones, "I wanna be sedated." Strung together, the words tell a story of our collective feeling.

Sailing on my bike through lowermost Manhattan, down the very center of empty Broadway, I belt out Cole Porter, "I happen to like New York," my voice caroming through the hollow canyon of the sleeping Financial District—such acoustics! Dreams of Judy Garland at Carnegie Hall, how I always wanted to be a belter—'cause "I like the sight and the sound and even the *stink* of it," and there's no place I'd rather live and die.

On walls and light poles, people put up signs declaring their hope and dread, anger and longing: Take One Last Breath, Spread No Virus, Don't Panic, Don't Be Afraid, Wash Your Hands, Don't Throw Your Gloves in the Street, Put On a Fucking Mask, Keep Going, Don't Give Up, Eat the Rich, Look Out For Each Other, Spread Love, (Is It Time to Eat the Rich Yet?), Make a New Reality.

Along the lustrous corridors of SoHo and Fifth Avenue, some luxury chain stores—Club Monaco, Aritzia, Coach—have boarded their windows, turning their backs to us, the Remainders, after their upscale customers have fled. This is an example of "elite panic," the anxious belief among people in power that the underclasses will become violent during natural disasters. In reality, disaster more often brings people together, but elite panic, as Rebecca Solnit explains, "presumes that we are all easily activated antisocial bombs waiting to go off." Sociologist Kathleen Tierney lists features of the panic: "fear of social disorder; fear of poor, minorities, and immigrants; obsession with looting and property crime;

willingness to resort to deadly force." The luxury shops have yet to use deadly force, but their plywood feels like a slap in the face, and their violent fantasy turns into a prophecy that yearns for self-fulfillment. The plywood incites in me thoughts of insurrection. I want to throw a brick. I want to *be* a brick.

I'm not the only one who thinks about breaking into my neighbor's abandoned apartment to use the washing machine. The fantasy surfaces on Facebook, in comments hushed and criminal, a collective longing for trespass. My friend Tank confesses she has taken the fantasy into reality. The market-rate New People have left her building and not one locked their doors behind them, so Tank just walks in and does her laundry. To keep it interesting, she uses different apartments, even though "they all look just the same."

It is hard to admit to the pleasures of this terrible time. My patients whisper them in the virtual confession booth of therapy. Many describe feeling less pressured and more connected. Released from social competition, they're more relaxed in their imperfect bodies, less concerned with status. Some notice that their inner critics, those endlessly chattering voices, have shut up. Some don't want lockdown to end. This is not the appropriate American affect. In Finland, the happiest country in the world, 23 percent of survey respondents admit to feeling that lockdown has improved their lives. A psychologist in Helsinki explains, "In Finnish culture we are not that highly sociable. We like to be on our own and be a bit isolated." Similarly, for American introverts, the lockdown brings a sense of peace, while the extroverts take their turn with social pain. But it's not just the loners and Finns who find relief. It's the Cassandras, too. I'll have an email conversation about this with feminist psychoanalyst Naomi Snider. As we trade thoughts, she'll write: "the reason that the Cassandras feel better when things are bad is not some sort of *Schadenfreude*, but rather, with the onset of 'bad times' comes the hope that other people will finally acknowledge the painful or dangerous realities that have hitherto been denied, and thus the Cassandras' feelings of being crazy and alone, of absolute despair, are relieved. Once the wound is seen and acknowledged *en masse*, hope in the possibility of repair is reignited."

The singing doesn't stop and in the singing there is hope. A Facebook friend shares a video of his Harlem street at midnight, where five Black men gather, making an affable commotion from which rises one voice singing Sam Cooke's "A Change Is Gonna Come," 1964 anthem of the civil rights movement. The men call, *come on, come on now*, urging the singer into the heights, empowering his voice as it grows stronger and more certain. When he sings, "It's been too hard living, but I'm afraid to die," the other men join him, amplifying the words in one booming voice, singing like they believe, this time, change is on the way.

When I imagine breaking into the abandoned apartment next door to do my laundry, I extend the criminal fantasy by looking around for something to steal. I've never been much of a thief, but I feel this urge like an invitation. I know everything inside the apartment because the Influencer has shown it all on Instagram. I decide it's the houseplant that needs liberating. The only living thing in the apartment, it must be dying, so long unwatered, its leaves dropping to the glossy hardwood floor. If a leaf falls in a renovated, market-rate apartment and no one is around to hear it, does it make a sound?

"New Yawk! Where you at? New Yawk City! Come on out! Don't be scared of the virus!" The man is shouting on the avenue, his voice echoing like a cry in a desert canyon. It is night. Other men shout back from windows, "Shut up!" I haven't been outside at night in weeks and when I venture into it, the air is softly altered, throbbing with disobedience. The man is Black and bearded, wearing a patterned sweater and carrying a bottle of booze. A white man with a gray ponytail joins him and brings the music, a boom box playing the Sugarhill Gang's "Rapper's Delight," conceived in 1979 just blocks from here, and again I have fallen through time. The men are giddy, dancing in traffic, though there isn't much. "New Yawk! Come on out! Don't be scared! It's Friday night! New Yawk City! The greatest city on planet Earth!" I dance at a distance, hoping the cops never come, wishing we were in the kind of movie where people pour out of their tenements and start dancing, stripping out of quarantine sweatpants to reveal shimmering leotards as a disco ball lowers from the sky, splashing glittery joy. This does not happen. The police arrive. The Black man leaps up and down in front of the flashing cruiser, shouting, "New Yawk! New Yawk!" The white man gets in front and reasons with the officer, white man to white man, and the cops let them go. They slip into the night, leaving us to our silent solitude, spiced with the possibility of a dance party, the city cracking open with echoes of *you don't stop the rock it to the bang-bang boogie, say up jumped the boogie to the rhythm of the boogie, the beat.*

The rush of sirens begins to slow. The curve is flattening. My neighbors have recovered and I hear the music of the man upstairs. He is playing piano again, after a long silence. It is Chopin's *Berceuse*, the French word for lullaby.

■ ■ ■

ON THE FIRST WEEKEND IN MAY, THE TEMPERATURE JUMPS INTO THE 70s, and after six weeks of lockdown, clusters of New People resurface, emerging like locusts stimulated by the warm sun. Are they back from their suburban getaways or have they been sequestered here all along? They cover every patch of grass from the Hudson River to Brooklyn's gentrified waterfront, sprawling close together to guzzle cans of White Claw. The rest of us are still masked and social distancing outdoors, afraid of the air, and this feels like an invasion of madness. Photos of the crowded, unmasked picnics appear online. "This can't be real," people say, accusing the photographers of creating a hoax.

In the East Village, I watch a police officer gently shoo young white people from the lawns of Tompkins Square Park. "What are we supposed to do," one girl argues, "sit on the hard concrete?" Pouting, the New People gather their blankets and White Claws, walk off grumbling, and return when the coast is clear. Meanwhile, two blocks away on Avenue D, cops are grabbing people of color outside a corner market, tackling them to the sidewalk in a "social distancing enforcement action." When a bystander, a Black man, intervenes, one of the officers punches him in the head, slams him to the sidewalk, and kneels on his neck, pressing his face into the hard concrete.

CBS2 News will soon obtain leaked data on the NYPD's record of enforcing rules in the first weeks of lockdown. The social distancing arrests break down: 68 percent Black, 24 percent Hispanic, 7 percent white.

Crowds of New People keep disappearing and reappearing in patterns I cannot decipher, though their collective chronobiological rhythm seems to coincide with sunny days above 72 degrees. Clouds keep them sequestered indoors. This will go on for months. Now, as white flight intensifies, the "panic moving" begins and sales of houses in Connecticut, Long Island, and New Jersey skyrocket. All over town, New People walk with flattened cardboard boxes under their arms, rolls of packing tape in hand. Moving trucks jam the streets. In the East Village, they park four and five to a block, and all the people leaving look the same, same clothes, same bodies. I ask the movers where they're headed. Kentucky, they say. Virginia, South Carolina, Michigan. Rents come down as apartments sit empty. I feel hopeful for a more open city and can't stop singing "So Long, Farewell" from *The Sound of Music* each time I pass a moving truck. The *Times* editorial board wrings its hands about the departure of white people with money. "The pandemic has prompted some affluent Americans to wonder whether cities are broken for them," they write. "It has suspended the charms of urban life while accentuating the risks." An op-ed at the *Daily News* takes a different tone: "Thinking of Fleeing NYC After COVID? Good Riddance."

A handwritten sticker, stuck to a mailbox, says: "Real New Yorkers had to stay."

Between one moving truck and another, I settle onto a bench outside a shuttered artisanal ice-cream shop ($5.75 for one scoop made of black charcoal) to watch a pair of bros pack their car. They're moving out of what used to be a funeral home. Now it's "a first-class boutique residential building" with "the feeling of LUXURY in a very hip downtown location." The basement, where bodies were embalmed, rents for $4,950. The penthouse goes for $8,925—or $14,000 fully furnished. The bros' car is packed tight, but they're determined to cram in one last item—a bag of golf clubs, that ubiquitous symbol of the suburbanized city.

At the next building, a young couple stands on the fire escape chatting with a middle-aged woman leaning on her windowsill. They talk about leaving. The older woman, with spiked yellowy hair and a vague European accent, says she will never leave. "With New York," she says, "it is a love-hate relationship." When the young woman says, "We've been here six *years* already," the older woman replies, "That's not long at all. That's no time." This is not what the young woman wants to hear. They talk about the suburbs, where life might be more comfortable. The young man says he prefers the country to the suburbs, to which the young woman makes a comment I can't hear, but which must be sarcastic, because the man responds by threatening to push her off the fire escape. "You're going over the edge," he says, making her shriek. The older woman closes her window, calling, "Maybe you do need to make a change. Maybe it's time to go." Next door, amid the hustle of moving trucks, the bros take a break from trying to force the golf bag into the car. One pulls out a club. In the middle of the street, he swings, as if he is driving a ball, watching it fly west, over Greenwich Village, the Hudson River, and into the sunset, all the way to the greener pastures of the rest of America.

As the population shifts, the power dynamic shifts with it and the New York attitude reasserts itself. My friend Rosella DMs me on Facebook: "Tonight is officially marking the turn in the neighborhood! This group of old-school East Villagers were hanging out on their stoop, drinking and chatting, when a young white woman yelled down at them to keep quiet and this woman below went off! She started screaming back, and this is a direct quote, 'You come down here and tell me that to my face. You wanna pay $3,000 a month to live here? This is *my* street. Born and raised. I'm Puerto Rican. Fuck outta here! I'm gonna keep yelling until you come down here and tell me to my face to be quiet. Fuck you!'"

Welcome to New Yawk.

JUST BEFORE THE REVOLUTION,
A CERTAIN ATMOSPHERE ARISES

Pandemic time is strange time, a slippery temporality that stretches days into weeks and weeks into months. When, exactly, are we? For the people staying inside, time can feel endlessly empty, marked by little change, but for those of us in the streets, time becomes endlessly full. So much is about to happen, it will have to be told in episodes, fragmented and tangential. I don't know how else to tell it. The days unfold in phases, unsteady states that refuse linearity. In the handful here, the week or so surrounding Memorial Day, something tremendous is revving up. It's as if the past nine weeks of lockdown lasted nine months, a gestational period to ferment a new form of life, one that expands and billows into many elements. After weeks of pressing, the city is about to break free.

Everything lines up to drive this flowering. By mid-May, the city's new cases of COVID drop from thousands to hundreds. I'm still worried about fomites, bleaching my doorknob and swabbing groceries with Clorox wipes, but science says being outside is safer than we thought. The city's public spaces, abandoned by white flighters and tourists, open to wild possibilities. People out of work, buoyed by unemployment insurance, find free time. People working from home take free time. Conspicuous consumption has vanished from the streets—the stores are closed, no one rushes around with shopping bags, and neglected advertisements fade in the sun. People stroll without hurry. A gap has opened. Sometimes, all you need for transformation is a gap. In Manhattan, there are two public spaces that have utterly unspooled: Washington Square and Times Square. It's between these magnetic poles that the center of the city starts to quake—and my life boomerangs, up and down, bicycle propelling me back through time and into the future.

■ ■ ■

LIKE MOST NEW YORKERS, I USUALLY AVOID TIMES SQUARE. BEFORE lockdown, it had become a master-planned phantom zone, a plastic theme park climate-controlled for people who are afraid of cities. As Samuel Delany observed, redeveloped Times Square was constructed to *look safe* to tourists suffering from the "small-town terror of cross-class contact." Designed to suppress connection, it imposed the rule: "Never speak to strangers." That is not its natural state.

In the 1990s, I loved Times Square. Walking the streets with my camera, taking moody pictures of crumbling marquees and faded signs, I felt at home. The Square's louche, off-kilter charms mirrored something inside me when, as a young transsexual, I was an outlaw who needed to be around other outlaws. I'd go for hot dogs at the Grand Luncheonette, perched on a greasy swivel stool under a hand-lettered sign that read: "No Loitering. No Spitting. No Water. No Ice." I'd walk Forty-Second Street, looking at objects in the windows of the smoke shops and joke shops: Spanish fly, corncob pipes, brass knuckles, samurai swords, dirty magazines, handbooks with titles like *How to Pick Up Girls*, *How to Create a New Identity*, *How to Build Your Own Bazooka*. Men called from doorways, "One-dolla, one-dolla, one-dolla, live nude girls." One asked, "Hey big guy, you looking for a fake ID?" I looked younger than I was, fresh on testosterone, like a teenage boy. I shook my head. "Some fine Hawaiian weed? How about some nice spicy aftershave?" Ready to connect me to anything a heart might desire, he wagged his finger, a canny look in his eye, and said, "I know you're looking for *something*." He was right. I occupied a transitional body, trying to figure out how to be a legible person, and I sensed Times Square had what I needed. Before I could find it, Rudy Giuliani and the real-estate developers bulldozed the place, replacing old brick buildings with sugarcoated glass towers full of Mickey Mouse, banks, and global chains. They chased the nude girls and boys away. Mike Bloomberg erased Broadway, paving the Great White Way with pedestrian plazas that attracted tourists and repelled locals. Still, for years, I felt Times Square calling, a visceral, ringing bell that summoned, *Come, come, it's here if you look hard enough.* Year after year, as more disappeared, I stopped listening, letting the bell's echo recede from the chambers of my heart. But today, in the middle of a plague, Times Square is calling again.

Forsaken by tourists and office workers, the stores shuttered, the square has filled with a giddy, lawless feeling. I bike through the pedestrian plazas illegally, retracing the lost path of Broadway, as if my wheels could undam the river. Cops are here, but they don't care. I figure-eight up and down Seventh Avenue, gliding in wide-open air. There is no traffic, no construction, and the Square is silent except for a low hum rising from a subway grate. You could mistake it for a mechanical drone, part of the underground apparatus, but it's an installation planted by composer Max Neuhaus in 1977. Titled *Times Square*, the sound work remains unmarked and, usually, it is stifled by crowds. I have never noticed it. Now the tone fills the ghost town, deep and spectral, reaching up from underground. No one is looking. I get on my hands and knees and put my ear to the grate to feel the subterranean thrum. Neuhaus said sound provides a "direct channel to the unconscious," and that's what rewilded Times Square feels like during the plague, dropping from the manifest to the latent. Like a dream. A place where time has warped, letting past leak into present. Attempting to remove sound from time, Neuhaus described his piece as a spatialized texture that resembles "the after ring of large bells." Maybe this is the sound of Times Square I've been hearing, calling from the past. I'm not the only one who receives it. The place exerts a gravitational pull, and during the pandemic it again attracts its rightful people, the hustlers, freaks, and oddballs who were drowned out or swept away.

Barbie stands in the center, dressed in a grimy glitter dress and bunny slippers, her hair a long, woolly Niagara of matted ropes the color of wheat bread, reaching past her knees. She's a homeless white woman, beyond middle age, and bears a resemblance to one of my maternal aunts, making her feel like family. She wears clotted blue eye shadow and red lipstick, rolls her own smokes, and performs a spectacle that transfixes me. Carrying a busted guitar she whangs with a fist, Barbie opens her mouth wide and thrusts to the sky a yodeling howl of pain and joy, wordless and without tune, the cry of being human in an animal body. The howl consists of two sounds, Oh and Ay, so it goes, "Oh, oh, oooooh" and "Ay, ay, aaaaaay," and "Oh, ay, oh, ay, oh, aaaaay!" Where one vowel collides with another, there's a glottalization, a throaty throttle deep in the vocal cords that makes the sound stagger as Barbie sings herself hoarse, hurling her barbaric yawp over the rooftops of the world. *I too am not a bit tamed*, Walt Whitman. *I too am untranslatable.* Barbie's sound is a preverbal callback from the earliest phase of life, and it grabs me, mirroring my own suppressed yawp. I put money in her box and listen. Day after day, we greet each other, bowing with hands to hearts to say something like gratitude, and each time I hear Barbie's sound, it reverberates inside, like the after ring of a large bell, so I find myself bellowing, too, "Oh, ay, oh, ay, oh, ay," echoing the echolalia of another time and place.

Philosopher Giorgio Agamben, writing on old cities, speaks of urban specters, "those signs, ciphers, or monograms that are etched onto things by time." Signatures read by the flaneur, these specters also appear to beggars and rats—to those who drift through the latent content of the city's dreams. People, too, can be specters, traces of memory reverberating on sub-frequencies, calling to anyone who will hear. In this space, I reunite with the specter of my past self, a part I had to leave behind in order to survive.

There are other outsiders who've come to heed the call of Times Square. There's the man with a sign that says THE END IS NEAR and another who carries a crucifix and rings a brass bell. There's the woman who sings to pigeons and the man who meditates in a ratty sackcloth. There's a transgender girl dancing ecstatically, her chubby belly bare as she waves to me, and a ballerina in toe shoes and tutu, spinning pirouettes down the deserted street. The Naked Cowboy and Cowgirl are here, along with an odd woman who walks around topless in a straw hat and hot-pink thong, her butt spattered with bruises. Usually the Square is filled with cartoon characters, but the only ones these days are machismo Batman, a swaggering dude in stacked black boots, and his diminutive sidekick, El Chapulín Colorado, the Red Grasshopper, from 1970s Mexican television. Now and then, if I am lucky, I'll catch sight of a man made of muscle, his monumental chest bare and glistening with oil, sweatpants hanging low to show a dark thatch of pubic hair. In the shadows of scaffolds, wearing an evil clown mask, he uses the street to build his body. I see him in the doorway of a shuttered Walgreens, bicep curling a metal barricade. I find him doing push-ups with a rubber demon baby chained to his back and a boom box playing "Rapper's Delight," that song again, echoing from the past. (Months from now, he'll tell me his name is Silk, because when he was a stripper, *back in the day*, they called him Silky Smooth. We'll bond over Chick-O-Sticks, a favorite childhood candy, and discuss the possibility of humanlike androids walking among us.)

As the weather warms and the virus recedes, working-class Black and brown New Yorkers fill the Square, families, couples, and teenagers dining out on McDonald's. Groups of boys come to breakdance for their own pleasure, not for money, no tourist gaze falling upon their bodies. In packs of hundreds, bicycle riders stream through the plazas, popping wheelies, colorful spokes spinning jubilation. A Brooklyn motorcycle crew shows off their burnout skills, churning clouds of smoke, and a Mexican lowrider club rolls in from the Bronx, candy-painted Cutlass Supremes bouncing on hydraulics. Day by day, New Yorkers are reclaiming Times Square.

· · ·

WHATEVER PARANOIA THE PLAGUE IGNITES, IT BOILS OVER IN WASH-ington Square Park. A woman who looks like a Dust Bowl photograph by Dorothea Lange, her face gray and harrowed, walks up to the fountain holding a cardboard sign on which she has neatly printed:

HR6666
DOOR-TO-DOOR TESTING
FORCED ISOLATION AND QUARANTINE
MANDATORY VACCINATION
PATENT 060606
BILL GATES OF HELL NANOTECHNOLOGY
IN HUMAN BODY-HIVE MIND

And on the flip side:

MELINDA GATES OF HELL ON TODAY SHOW
WEARING SATANIC INVERTED CROSS
MAY 8 2020

Attracted to the magnet of her madness, a small group gathers to talk about Bill Gates and the tracking technology they believe he will insert into a future COVID vaccine. As they come to the agreement that drinking orange juice is enough to keep the virus away, the Plandemic people show up and unfurl their sign:

Plandemic (planned event)
Bitchute/Spiro/Event 201
Corona is Bio and Psychological Warfare
Against Humanity by the World State

A man in a gray ponytail sets up a microphone for whoever wants to talk about George Soros, Jeffrey Epstein, and the pedophilic plan to control the leaders of the free world by taking pictures of them having sex with girls on a private island in the Caribbean Sea. A young man takes the mic to say the coronavirus was invented by America's leaders to decrease the global population and save the world from climate catastrophe, a bleak eco-fascist conspiracy theory with a hopeful ending.

Across the fountain, a woman in a skirt made from today's *Times* is constructing an actual tinfoil hat. It's the first I've seen in decades and it seems, again, like the past leaking into the present, repressed New York coming back to mess with the regulated new city. Nearby, the man who chalks surfaces with the slogan "Rents to high" (it'll be weeks before he learns to spell *too*) is handing out flyers asking people to help the unhoused. I take the flyer and give him a couple of bucks. He pushes a wheelchair decorated with a banner listing twenty things to worry about:

1. RENT RANSOM
2. HOME INVASION
3. SOCIAL ABDUCTION
4. LATENT VIOLENCE
5. RE VICTIMIZATION
6. COHERSION

7. FOOD TAMPERING

8. FORCED ASSOCIATION

9. EVICTORY

10. SEX TORTION

11. FORCED TRAFFIC

12. CRIMINALIZE

13. RENT EXTORTION

14. END HOMLESSNESS

15. GAS ASSAULTS

16. SLEEP MARE-DEPRIVED

17. MASTER-MIND-BATION

18. NO RETREAT

19. TICKET PAROLE

20. VOICE BOX

"Music is ambient everywhere outside," Lucy Sante recalls of 1981 New York. "And all the music around you is in the process of becoming one music, a great river of groove." The city's beat went silent in the Walkman Effect, an urban strategy to avoid interaction with strangers, but now it's coming back. More and more, people appear with vintage boom boxes and retro Bumpboxxes, chunky Bluetooth speakers evoking the '80s. Soon they'll be hauling luggage carts with extra-large party boxes, speakers that flash colorful lights and pump out beats so loud you feel them dance inside your chest. We're tuned to the same psychic radio, a salty current resurfaced from underground, so the Bee Gees' "Night Fever" glides down St. Mark's Place from an open car window and, hours later, tumbles along a Christopher Street pier in a handheld speaker, finally winding through Washington Square from a rolling boom box. In this river of groove we turn back to one another and re-attune.

Around the fountain, a pair of middle-aged Black men in satin jackets, the words SK8MAFIA HIGHROLLERS printed in gold letters on the back, are roller-skating to funk, dancing on gritty wheels, joined by an older white woman dressed in head-to-toe purple, including her skates, made of velvet the color of grape soda. The air is fragrant with weed smoke. No one—not one single person—is posing for a selfie in front of the Washington Arch. We are all New Yorkers. This public space, dulled and whitewashed by the Bloomberg years, swerves into profusion, becoming Blacker and browner than I've ever seen it. In the dry basin of the fountain, skateboarders of all colors whirl, their hair in shades of pink and blue, mohawked, locked, ratted, and spiked. A girl takes out her ukulele. A boy in John Lennon glasses reads Plutarch, *The Rise and Fall of Athens*. In the fountain's hub, on the platform where water usually spouts, a queer young man finds his place. He is Jesus of Washington Square, but no one knows that yet. He has just received his calling, the voice of God speaking through cannabis haze. Soon he'll be famous, but now he's just a lost-looking white boy in a dirty Irish-knit sweater, sneakers held together with duct tape, notebook in hand as he claims the center of the center.

■ ■ ■

ON EVERY TRIP BETWEEN WASHINGTON SQUARE AND TIMES SQUARE, there are more Jesus preachers, plague-time doomsayers come out of the woodwork to tell us it's time to repent. In Herald Square, a Korean woman is preaching behind a plastic face shield while the Black Isra-elites, with their golden crowns and dashikis, posters of lynchings and mushroom clouds, shout about white cracker devils. One of the Israelites starts a fight with the Korean woman and they face off with Bibles in hand, arguing about who possesses the true word of God. At Fifty-First and Broadway, the King James Bible Baptist Church commandeers the block with racks of Chick tracts, little comic books of damnation. Stacked haphazardly under tables, placards bear slogans like REPENT WHORES. One lists all the people who will go to Hell, including:

Rebellious Women, Gangster Rappers, Pot Smoking Little Devils, Homos, Thieves, and Sports Nuts. The preacher calls, "Help yourself," and a random passerby takes him up on it, hoisting a sign over her head to shout about Jesus while people wait for the sermon to begin. The parishioners are an odd bunch. One man is draped in plastic sheets. A woman carries a sign that reads, "I am a Jew—Prey of NYPD Porn—Piss on the NYPD." Another man carries a large wooden cross with that word again: REPENT.

The word makes me think of Lillian Hellman, who wrote: "Old paint on canvas, as it ages, sometimes becomes transparent. When that happens it is possible, in some pictures, to see the original lines: a tree will show through a woman's dress, a child makes way for a dog, a large boat is no longer on the open sea. That is called pentimento because the painter 'repented,' changed his mind." This is what New York is doing in the pandemic. For years, as the new paved over the old, I've searched for the city's pentimento. It was hard to see. But now New York has changed its mind. With the newest layer scraped away, the buried lines are visible again.

The city's id is shaking loose. Impulses, constrained by the order of civilization, are pushing upward. I'll say it again: We have no stores, no shoppers, no restaurant reviews or fashion trends to incite consumption and competition, no office workers rushing around, no eyes staring at iPhones, no outward signs of bourgeois acquisition and productivity. For over two months, we've been left alone. This is a profound shift. As Herbert Marcuse explained, for the modern capitalist system to dominate, "The individual is not to be left alone." Otherwise, unchecked by the pressure to perform and produce, the id's libidinal energy—the force of life—thrusts against imposed limitations until it breaks through. Right now, all around, you can feel New York's thrust, roots heaving up from under pavement.

Barbie yawps while a plague doctor pushes his "Corpse Cartte" through Times Square

Back in Times Square, I'm listening to Barbie sound her barbaric yawp when a new character appears, a seventeenth-century plague doctor dressed in a black overcoat, wide-brimmed leather hat, goggles, and a beaked leather mask. Calling, "Leeches, leeches for the plague," he strides through the empty plazas pushing a shopping cart labeled "Corpse Cartte" in which another man, looking half-dead, sits and moans. A homeless man joins in, gazing wide-eyed into the plague doctor's goggles, shouting along so the two preach together, pointing fingers to the sky, while Max Neuhaus's sound work drones its ghostly voice from the past and Barbie goes on yawping, "oh, ay, oh, ay, oh, ay." I'm yawping, too, as the few passersby also yawp, all of us unable to resist echoing back this joyful madness, this collective moment of wild togetherness. We are cracking up. Cracking open. A tattooed woman with missing teeth tells me she likes my bike and says, "They're stealing bikes now. In Hell's Kitchen. They knock you down and take your bike." Things are getting sketchy, she says. "They're smashing the windows of all the 7-Elevens and stealing cigarettes." Optimistically, I go looking for smashed 7-Elevens, but all I see are unsmashed 7-Elevens. Was the woman lying or did she give me a prophecy? I feel something brewing. It's inside me too, the barbaric yawp coalescing into a new shape, spiky and winged, so when I'm biking back to Washington Square, I feel it take hold.

Maybe it's the idea of smashed windows mixed with the sight of elite-panic plywood on the luxury stores of Fifth Avenue that makes me want to throw a brick. I am too well behaved, however, to throw bricks. I throw words instead and now the perfect word forms in my gut. *Fuck.* A solid brick of a word, transmitted to me from my mother and father, who wielded it on the streets of their cities in gang fights, this word my birthright, uttered early in defiant toddlerhood, along with *ball* and *truck*, my first words, this elemental *fuck* pressing forth, *fuck* the years of suppression as my city disappeared, homogenized and blandalized, its wild soul crushed under the boots of the normative order. *Fuck* boils inside me as I sail down Fifth Avenue, running all the red lights because there are no cars, no people, just me, standing tall on the pedals, shirt in the breeze, all muscle and speed, full of *fuck*, bubbling up until it spills. Joyfully, angrily, I bellow, "Fuck you Victoria's Secret! Fuck you Coach! Fuck you Lululemon!" What did David Wojnarowicz say in the middle of his plague? "My heart is a vacuum of horror. I want to run amok but I am too civilized." What if all the queers, the others, the strangers become uncivilized at once? What if we all formed one barbaric *fuck* and ran amok?

The Big System wants to straighten us out, turn us not only into consumers but products, material objects and personal brands. What if we got together in the expansive potential of collective queerness? *Queer* doesn't have to be limited to sexual identity. It can offer, as political scientist Cathy J. Cohen argues, a "liberating, transformative, and inclusive" political identity for "all those who stand on the outside of the dominant constructed norm of state-sanctioned white middle- and upper-class heterosexuality." In the pandemic, New York belongs to these "queers"—the ones outside the center—the Black and trans, punk and poor, the immigrant, dissident, and resistant. Left alone, without all the static, we see each other. We connect. And we remember.

"You know," Toni Morrison said, "they straightened out the Mississippi River in places, to make room for houses and liveable acreage. Occasionally the river floods these places. 'Floods' is the word they use, but in fact it is not flooding; it is remembering. Remembering where it used to be. All water has a perfect memory and is forever trying to get back to where it was . . . like water, I remember where I was before I was 'straightened out.'"

Today is the day before Memorial Day. The wake of history is re-forming, reminding us not to forget—who we are and where we've been. "In the wake," writes feminist theorist Christina Sharpe, "the past that is not past reappears, always, to rupture the present." My *fuck* is one small piece of a larger *fuck*, collective and shared, gorgeous in its sharply shimmering tails. Just days from now, the word will be made brick, and these windows along Fifth Avenue will break, the streets of the city queered, because *all that is solid melts into air*, that which destroys will in turn be destroyed, and from out of the cracks will shine a new light.

PART THREE

4.

THE PHASE OF BREAKING

The word *apocalypse* comes from the Greek αποκάλυψη (*Apokályp-sis*), "lifting of the veil," to uncover and reveal, and in this apocalyptic time, many veils will be lifted. But the end of one world and the start of another rarely come without grief and tribulation. On Memorial Day, a Minneapolis police officer kneels on the neck of George Floyd for nearly ten minutes, taking his life as he cries for his mother. The killing sparks a global uprising. In New York, protest begins on Thursday, May 28. I'm in Times Square, listening to Barbie yawp, when a Black man walks into the plaza wearing a mask with the words "I Can't Breathe" handwritten on it. He removes his shirt, a Stars & Stripes tank top splashed in blood-red paint, wraps chains around his wrists, and gets on his knees, hoisting onto his shoulders a painting of a white police officer consumed by flames. The man holds the weight, silently, on his neck for nearly ten minutes. Later, when I hear a voice shouting through the quiet East Village streets, "Justice for George Floyd," I'll wonder if it's the same man, but something much bigger has begun.

The Black Lives Matter movement (BLM) has been building since the acquittal of Trayvon Martin's killer in 2013, gaining momentum in protests against the police killings of Michael Brown in Ferguson and Eric Garner on Staten Island. The list of names keeps growing, a record of extrajudicial executions with roots sunk deep in American policing's racist history. While I have marched for many principles, including the rights of women, queers, and immigrants, I have yet to join a BLM protest. Where was I in 2014 when thousands took to the streets after a jury failed to indict the cop who strangled Garner? Like many white progressives, each time the video of another police killing of another Black person has crossed my Facebook feed, I've felt a growing anger and grief, but these emotions have not pushed me into the streets. Today is another day.

At Union Square on Saturday, the park is packed by a racially mixed crowd of mostly young people. They carry simple cardboard signs inked with Sharpie to say, "Black Lives Matter," "White Silence Is Violence," and sets of initials I don't yet recognize, FTP (Fuck the Police) and ACAB (All Cops Are Bastards). I stay at the edges with the other older folks vulnerable to the virus, maintaining social distance from what I imagine are clouds of corona. Everyone wears a mask, but it's still early in the plague and we don't know what will kill us. In the march, I ride my bike alongside, in the breeze, as we head to the Hudson and seize the West Side Highway. When I ask myself what I'm doing here, I think: I'm here to obstruct the machine—for Black people, white people, and everyone else—because white supremacy fucks it up for all of us. Because American capitalism is rooted in slavery, as neoliberalism is rooted in racism. Because the sickness that reproduces this racial capitalism is the same sickness that fuels the climate catastrophe. Because the pandemic has revealed not just more inequality, but more interconnectivity. Because it's the end of the world and I'm tired of feeling powerless.

By nightfall, after I've gone home, the march returns to Union Square where darkness shifts the mood. On my living room couch, watching CNN and Twitter, I'm gripped by the sight of protesters breaking the windows of empty police vehicles and setting them on fire. My excitement, difficult to explain, likely comes from my waywardness, as Saidiya Hartman describes waywardness, "to inhabit the world in ways inimical to those deemed proper and respectable. . . . To strike, to riot, to refuse. To love what is not loved." The flames, primordial and bright, call me rushing out to meet them.

My neighborhood has transformed, a scrim of disorder draped over it. Under the eggbeater thrum of helicopters hovering low, I pass toppled trash cans, their contents littering the streets, and graffiti so fresh it smells of wet aerosol, spelling out FUCK COPS. The air is sharp with charred rubber. I inspect a mess of wreckage in the street, a dark blob that used to be a mattress, burned black and twisted. For days I've been seeing mattresses on the sidewalks, so many expensive mattresses that look brand new, discarded by the fleeing New People, the ones who throw away good things because they'll just buy more good things. Now those same mattresses, where the New People slept and dreamed, are kindling for a righteous blaze.

At Eighth and Broadway, I meet the tail end of the rebellion. A small crowd gathers in the street to watch the scene unfold a few blocks north, where police and protesters stand off across a barrier. I'm not sure I should be here but my excitement is greater than my fear and I walk up the middle of Broadway into the fizz of people giddy with the pleasure of incendiary possibility. Everyone is wearing masks and many favor black bandannas, giving them the look of an outlaw gang. Someone says, "Light it up," to which someone else says, "Gimme some ____," a slang word I soon forget, a word that means fuel, like *slick* or *grease*, the oily sound of acceleration. The young man who says the word sets a trash can ablaze while three women flick a Bic to light another. When they kick them over, sparks fly in a pyrotechnic swarm and my heart sparks with it, fluttering in the freedom of fractured reality.

I'm at Tenth Street when a crowd of protesters breaks from the standoff. My body recoils until I realize they're not running, they're skipping, dancing and cheering as a boom box plays a song joyful and wild. The crowd is young, all genders and colors, so giddy, I catch their giddiness, high on transgression, our bodies abuzz. The euphoria swirls and blooms under the streetlights, gathering into a loud, resounding thwack, a vibration like the collision of metal and electricity. I turn to see boyish silhouettes kicking at the windows of the Wells Fargo bank. Another thwack, another, and then a thunderous *whoomp* as the windows shatter and collapse. People hoot and cheer. I gravitate to the scene, crunch of broken glass like candies under my feet.

Before I can reach the heart of the riot, a troop of bike cops rolls up from the south, sending a dark ripple through the air. This is the NYPD's militarized anti-terrorism Strategic Response Group, SRG, like *surge*, because that is what they do, aggression preceding them like a compression wave before a locomotive. In seconds, something I feel but can't see sets off a panic. Protesters stampede as cops charge and I bolt. Running for the sidewalk, I collide with a young woman—her face flashbulbs in memory, white girl in black bandanna and wire-rimmed glasses, wheat-blonde hair, reminding me of a girl I kissed in a barn at the age of eighteen—wham! She's spinning and I start to say *sorry*, but a cop is tackling her, his force propelling us both into the wrought-iron fence of Grace Church. I'm entangled with them, my body bulldozed by the cop's body, his armor of muscle fueled by a drive that feels like rage but without emotion, the blunt violence of a shark ramming prey. My ankle twists. Afraid of arrest (the last thing I want to be is a trans man in a jail cell during an airborne plague), I limp painfully aside and lean against the church as the cop cuffs the woman's wrists into plastic zip ties and more cops pile on more protesters in a scrum of bikes, bodies, red and blue flashing lights, one young man shouting, "What did I do? What did I do?" I brace, waiting to be grabbed, but I've escaped. Almost. I'm in searing pain and surrounded by cops. They form a line with their bikes and push us downtown, a voice repeating through the LRAD speaker, "This is an unlawful assembly, if you do not disperse you will be placed under arrest." I've heard trans men talk about what can happen in jail—humiliation and sexual assault—so when the LRAD gives its fifth warning, I decide it's time to go.

As I limp home through the abandoned streets, past burned mattresses and capsized trash cans, starving rats darting underfoot, I am the only human in sight. Until a couple approaches from the opposite direction. They are young, straight, white hyper-normals, not wearing masks, not paying attention, walking their popular dog, one of those ubiquitous Australian shepherds. They are chatting and laughing, taking up the width of the sidewalk, letting the dog's leash stretch all the way across. I'm limping toward them, waiting for them to make room. We're the only ones here, but they don't see me. They laugh as if they're an advertisement for fast-casual salads, the good life, everything clean, in a world where the world is not on fire. When the dog's leash hits me across the knees, the woman gasps, performing shock. Oh! I am a specter materialized from the ether. "Saaree," she says, in the empty way they all say *sorry*, not meaning it, and they walk on, through garbage and broken glass, past the still smoldering coils of mattresses, hovering above it all in their stainless, worry-free bubble, confident that nothing will ever touch them.

■ ■ ■

IN THE MORNING, I WAKE WITH A BADLY SWOLLEN ANKLE, BUT THE pain is overcome by a Christmas feeling that sends me rushing out to see what the rioters have left. I can't walk, but I can ride my bike. All the way from Union Square to SoHo, the windows of banks are smashed. I count at least twelve—TD Bank, Bank of America, Citibank, Chase. Protesters wrecked the chain stores, too, knocking a hole in the window of a Starbucks where some optimistic employee, weeks ago in another world, wrote: "Every day is a new beginning! Take a deep breath, smile, and start again!" A police car, burned and flipped on its side, slumps in front of Bloomingdale's SoHo, the sidewalk littered with shattered glass, glittery chunks in piles like crushed ice for snow cones. Looters have ransacked Adidas, Swatch, and the Journeys shoe store, where, propped under a punk-rock Doc Marten boot, lies a cardboard sign lettered with the names of George Floyd, Breonna Taylor, and Tony McDade, a Black trans man shot and killed three days ago by police in Tallahassee. At Union Square, like beached whales scorched by the sun, five police vans sit charred and blighted, covered in graffiti: PIG and OINK and ACAB. Overnight, the city has blossomed in graffiti, a splash of wild color: Black Lives Matter, George Floyd, Fuck Trump, Fuck the Police, Fuck 12 (another term for police), symbols for anarchy and socialism dappling the sides of buildings. On one wall, next to a burned wooden police barricade: "Riots speak louder than words." We have entered the phase of breaking.

NYPD Smart car, burned and flipped in front of Bloomingdale's SoHo

I've made my injury worse and decide to sit out Sunday's protests, spending the day on the couch, my ankle elevated and iced. At night, from out of the silent streets, I hear a man yelling. He is walking behind a woman hurrying down the avenue, her arms piled high with pizza boxes. She has just done something to insult the man and he shouts, "Oh, yeah, well, what are *you*? You with your . . . five . . . fucking . . . pizzas! You're just gobbledy-gobbledy-goo-goo! You, you, you, gaaargh!" The man, who resembles the actor Harold Ramis, sixtyish, dressed in sandals, actually utters *gobbledy-gobbledy-goo-goo*. Like a baby. Like a person so enraged he has lost the capacity for language.

The looting begins in earnest, shattering the luxury shops of SoHo. Early in the morning, before my Monday patients, I wrap my ankle in an ACE bandage and bike again to the wreckage. Victoria's Secret, Coach, Lululemon. Wasn't it just days ago I was shouting *fuck you* to these same chain stores? How often is a wish granted, and so quick? The plywood of Yves Saint Laurent is ripped open and graffitied with FTP, BLM, and "End Wage Slavery." Chanel is ransacked, clothing hangers scattered in the street by the body parts of mannequins, arms and legs thrown against parked cars. Crisp one-dollar bills litter the sidewalk, too small to take. There are loose shoes tossed everywhere, display samples without mates, and in a sidewalk planter I find a leather boot propped before a wall of plywood spray-painted: DIY REPARA-TIONS. People will insist the looters are not protesters, that they are criminals giving in to materialistic desire, but these political messages accompany every smash and grab. In the broken glass, a sign says "End White Supremacy." On the side of a building, it's "Burn Down Babylon." As I gaze over the carnage, a woman dressed for a jog in high-performance athleisure shakes her head and says, "Isn't it terrible?" She assumes I'll agree. "Actually," I reply, "I find it exciting." Stricken, she turns and hurries away.

"Decolonization," Frantz Fanon wrote, "is always a violent event." To feel anything positive, or even complicated, about rioting and looting is not a popular stance. When I post photos of the sacking of SoHo on Facebook, I'm surprised by the responses of friends I thought were politically aligned with me, people who've complained and protested for years against the corporatization of New York, the suffocation of chain stores and banks. Didn't we all want to see them destroyed? Apparently not. These friends are whipped into a frenzy of indignation. Don't they know the corporations can easily repair the damage? Their comments are overwrought and I wonder what unconscious mechanism is giving them such powerful charge. Do my white liberal friends privately identify with Starbucks and Citibank? Do their bodies psychically extend into the embodiments of the corporations, so when they're smashed my friends feel the violation in their own bodies?

I find relief when talking with my friend Avgi, who also feels excited by the rebellion. She's queer, an immigrant from a country where it is not unusual for protest to take the shape of property destruction, and I wonder if anti-riot anger is not just a white thing, but also a hetero-American thing, an attachment to the meritocratic myth that, with enough hard work, we can all be billionaires. Don't attack the dream.

Months from now, still processing these questions, I'll discuss the looting over coffee with my friend T., who is white and affluent, as well as thoughtful and willing to examine herself. "I'm more bourgeois than you," she'll say. "When I watched the looters from my apartment windows on Madison Avenue, I felt afraid." Does she identify with the luxury stores? "For you," she'll say, "Prada took something away. But for me, it's different. Prada gave something to me." When I ask what it gave, she'll tell me about growing up in wealth, escaping to New York, being socially conscious, doing charitable work and also wanting to hold on to her money, trying to walk the line of opposing desires. We're friends because we both mourn the lost character of our city, me from the Lower East Side and T. from the Upper, and because we can talk across the distance without bitterness. I want to hear more about Prada and what she felt when it was looted. "Prada was my safe space," she'll tell me. "My happy space. If I was down, I would go in and walk around. Not always buy. It's like Holly Golightly in *Breakfast at Tiffany's*, when she says, 'Nothing very bad could happen to you there.' So let me have my safe space in the big city. Don't come at night and smash it to bits. But perhaps that is just white privilege talking. It sounds that way when I say it out loud."

■ ■ ■

TIME KEEPS SLIPPING, THE PANDEMIC HOURS UNFURLING IN STRANGE loops, so the days get muddled. I'm losing the thread. How can it still be Monday? I've spent months seeing patients over Zoom, eight to ten hours in front of a screen. It's good enough for now, in our crisis of social distance, but so much gets lost without the body—their body and my body, together in the room. I miss the heat, the intensity of the work, which is sometimes like mutual breaking, the pleasure of eruption. Is it any wonder that each morning this week I get up early to bike to the scenes of breakage, and each afternoon, when I hear the police copters come to thrash the sky above a protest, I'm struck by a Pavlovian hunger for bodies colliding and connecting in the streets? These days, the city is a room of heat.

After last night's sacking of SoHo, East Villagers spend the afternoon battening down the hatches, covering every shop and restaurant with plywood. All day, electric screwdrivers whine, drilling the panels shut. The New People who reappeared in the warm weather vanish again, terrified of the uprising, leaving the neighborhood quieter than it was in the early weeks of quarantine. Mayor de Blasio has imposed an 11:00

p.m. curfew, the first in New York since the Second World War, and just before dusk, I go for a limping walk with my friend Christine. We're the only ones on the streets, except for a few small-business people, guarding their shops. Outside one restaurant, a man sits with a baseball bat across his knees, waiting for looters, but I can't imagine anyone stealing his chicken soup, no matter how good it is. Excited by the tang of mayhem, Christine and I venture to Broadway, where we look uptown and see a wave of people coming toward us. We think they're protesters, another march, but they aren't chanting and don't carry signs. When the crowd breaks into a run, whooping and leaping, we see they're young men, punching the air, getting psyched, and it's clear they're looters, or smashers, maybe two hundred strong. Using skateboards like cudgels, they break the windows of banks and chains, sending up thunderclaps of shattered glass. Christine and I run away, laughing like teenagers who got scared and quickly realized there's nothing to fear. We stop to watch the crowd flood down Broadway, a river sprung loose after the breaking of a dam.

Back home, I put my throbbing ankle on ice and visit Facebook to watch a live-streamed video of the lootings in Herald Square, where a lone cameraman is following crowds as they break windows and fill rolling suitcases with booty while police officers stand watching, arms folded across their chests. The looters are men and women, a few kids, mostly Black but also white. I'm surprised to see the mood is jubilant and friendly. (My friend Tank, who witnessed the scene, will later tell me she saw people sharing, asking, "What's your size," trading sneakers, trying on clothes, helping each other find a fit.) Curiosity seekers watch the spectacle and the camera pauses on a young onlooker. He is white, long and lean, with artfully monochromatic tattooed arms and Art Garfunkel hair. Dressed in black, including a black COVID mask, he sits on a cement anti-terrorism barrier, looking posed, as if he's sitting at a sidewalk café, watching the beautiful people. He looks queer, maybe trans, maybe *she* and not *he*, or else *they/them*. The cameraman sees it, too, the queerness, and asks, "Bruh, what are you, the supermodel of Thirty-Fourth Street?" The supermodel says nothing, just blinks in cool, New York detachment, and the camera moves on to capture a band of looters breaching the ramparts of Macy's department store.

At midnight, a loud series of bangs shocks me out of bed, and from my window I watch people burglarize the designer consignment shop across the street. One clambers through a hole he made in the gate and comes back with armloads of clothing, passes them through, and falls noisily into the trash cans. I don't call the police, the looters are gone in seconds, but the scene makes me shudder with fear. Why does the looting in SoHo and Midtown excite me, but this one unsettles? Is it the close proximity, stimulating my own white privilege and expectation of safety? In the morning, I talk to neighbors on the sidewalk where the shop's owners are sweeping glass. An older woman, with tattooed arms and orange hair, says she heard her fire escape rattling in the night. Was someone trying to climb in? She gives an old-school New York shrug, *whatever*, and says, "The looters were stupid. They left behind a very expensive pair of Balenciaga jeans."

On the side of Victoria's Secret at Thirty-Fourth Street, protesters have written "This Is Your Fault" and "Stop Oppression." (The store, which will not reopen, has stopped paying its rent of $937,734.17 a month and sues the landlord to rescind its lease. New York isn't worth it anymore.) The small businesses in the East Village add "Black Lives Matter" to their plywood, with Black Power fists, an obvious attempt to ward off destruction. The mayor has tightened the curfew to 8:00 p.m. and caravans of cop cars circle at dusk, playing a recording that tells us to get off the streets. On a bench in Tompkins Square Park, someone writes FUCK CURFEW and BURN IT DOWN. Tonight, protesters will trash the Starbucks at Astor Place and scrawl over the mermaid logo with a hammer and sickle.

The NYPD uses the curfew to justify excessive force, beating protesters with batons, slamming them to the pavement, and trapping them in a violent, panic-inducing tactic called kettling, where cops use their bodies to corral and attack. Police charge onto front stoops and patios, attacking people who aren't protesting, including families outside to enjoy the air. Months from now, the Department of Investigation will conclude that the NYPD response was a failure, speculating that officers were unprepared for the city's anger. But there is also something about looting, and the loosening of the city, that activates a hysterical masculine response.

Taking it to theatrical extremes, Saks Fifth Avenue has gone full macho dystopia. After triple-wrapping the building in plywood, chain-link fence, and loops of razor wire, they position a phalanx of twenty security guards along their Fifth Avenue frontage. Gripping the leashes of pit bulls and German shepherds, the men are imposing, muscled and

Saks Fifth Avenue fortress

tattooed, dressed in black with the slogan "Savage by Nature, Aggres-sive by Trade" on tight T-shirts. Each evening before curfew, I bike up to Saks to marvel at the scene and think about gender. The guards are butcher than butch, the embodiment of phallic control, steroidal emblems of patriarchy's law and order, while the rebellion belongs to the queerness of this moment. Riots, as author Vicky Osterweil points out, are "femme as fuck." Often dismissed as irrational, chaotic, and driven by desire, "they rip, tear, burn, and destroy to give birth to a new world."

In a blizzard of passion and fury, the city is all at once showered in FUCKs. In black Sharpie and red spray paint, on sidewalks, walls, and plywood, FUCK bursts forth from the collective rage. We the Left-overs, the non-normatives, the queer in every sense of the word are tired of being squeezed and controlled and told to like it. FUCK this, FUCK that, FUCK you. FUCK FUCK FUCK. That perfect brick of a word, heavy and sharp, rains down like hailstones, and every time I encounter it, it's like a cool mouthful of oxygen, so I feel, deep inside my body, the unfurling of another clenched cell.

5.

QUEER NEGATIVITY:
NOT GAY AS IN HAPPY,
BUT QUEER AS IN FUCK YOU

Why do I feel such relief in the turbulence of the disorderly city? I keep asking myself this question, wondering what makes me thrill to broken windows. Yes, the chain stores are an affront to my politics. Yes, I can tell you why they're bad for the city. But I'm a psycho-analyst. I want to know how we arrive at our destinations.

As a child I was told to smile. I didn't do it enough. Adults pinched my cheeks, trying to force it. They called me Smiley because I wasn't—*Hey, Smiley*—to which I only frowned harder. I was a defiant killjoy. Happiness can be an instrument, says queer theorist Sara Ahmed, a technology of discipline, a way to straighten people out. For how many photos did my mother grit her teeth, telling me to smile? I remember her knuckle in my back, *Stand up straight*, but I was not straight and would not go along with the program, a refusal that yielded an existential punishment that reverberates still, making it difficult to enjoy what most people enjoy. This coerced version of happiness can feel like submission to a regulatory authority. *Don't you like this doll, this dress, this lipstick*—such demands for gender conformity, statements of wrongness (*don't you* implies *you should* and *what's wrong with you?*), might accrue to other demands to conform to more general ideas of what brings joy: *Don't you like summer, sunshine, the beach, picnics, birthday cakes, clinking glasses together when you drink, restaurants, travel,* and *did I mention picnics?*

Girls who are really boys, or tomboys, or take some other shape of masculinity, don't smile enough, and this adds to the ways we are disappointingly gendered for people. We often grow up to be unintelligible—to others and ourselves. Out of joint, we are unhappy queers, a kind of *affect alien,* "the one who converts good feelings into bad" in Ahmed's words. I wonder: Do we also convert *bad* feelings into *good?* Leave it to unhappy queers to shake crumbs of joy from tribulation. Is that why I feel so good in this bad time? "To be an affect alien," says Ahmed, is to be "out of line with the public mood," and here I am in alternative Times Square, bouncing on my wheels with the wheelie bikers, the weed dealers, the weirdos, while newspapers cry, "Times Square is dead!" Yet I find its streets so full of life. To be out of line emotionally can be a form of resistance against the demand to enjoy, especially when we're told to take pleasure in a world that is not working for us. It seems to me that loving what is not loved, wherever it is found, can be a defiant way to reclaim disparaged parts of oneself.

I'm trying to make myself the problem, but why should I? I've always been the problem, the queer, gender-fucked, not-smiling-about-the-right-things problem, the surly, introverted, won't-wear-a-dress tomboy problem, the ambiguous object of obscurity, *what are you a boy or a girl* problem, walking like a truck driver, swearing like a sailor, talking back with my *smart mouth,* too smart, *you think you're so smart, I'll slap that smile right off your face* (wrong kind of smile) problem, the gone-to-college snob, feminist, wrong kind of feminist, bull dyke in combat boots problem, the trans before trans was cool, pawn of the patriarchy problem, the shirt-and-tie but wrong kind of man problem, followed by the wrong kind of trans man problem, eventually the New York complainer problem, the still-angry, too-cranky, can't-get-over-it, *quit complaining, enjoy life, smile* problem. And I'm right back where I started, even though I've spent a lot of time trying to fix myself so I could be less problematic, more socially acceptable, financially viable, more likely to survive. Didn't I successfully shed my working-class accent, my ethnic name, my queer skin, passing in public as an unremarkable—and unmarked—middle-class man? What could be more acceptable? And yet. The past that is not past stays with us, haunting the present. What if you're not the problem? What if the problem is the world? In my search for answers, I find my way to queer negativity, and this will inform everything I think about the disorderly city and my affinity for it.

When queer studies took an antisocial turn, away from the respectability politics of homonormativity (monogamy, productivity, consumerism), it embraced queer otherness with all its negative stereotypes. Antisocial doesn't mean "that lesbians and gay men are unsociable," says queer theorist Tim Dean, "but that some aspect of homosexuality threatens the social and that it might be strategic politically to exploit that threat." This means making the most of "bad" feelings, including (as listed by critical theorist Mari Ruti), "self-destruction, failure, melancholia, loneliness, abjection, despair, regret, shame, and bitterness." Permitting and expressing such affects can be a way to resist the heteronormative, capitalist injunction to smile and enjoy: *go shopping! have brunch! forget the pain of the world!* To which the negative queer replies: *fuck, no!* We won't get over it and move on. We will remember and remind. "I insist on the importance of clinging to ruined identities and to histories of injury," writes queer scholar Heather Love. "Resisting the call of gay normalization means refusing to write off the vulnerable, the least presentable, and all the dead." For those who've climbed into more privilege, as I have, it also means remembering where we come from, staying connected to the wake that churns behind us, because history isn't over, it can turn on a dime, and we outsiders have to stick together.

If there's a punk adolescent quality to all this, it's not incidental. Queers, as Love points out, are seen as backward, refusing to grow up. We're also melancholic, holding on to the past, and there's a nostalgic strain in queerness, an attachment to longing, but longing for what? Ideas of home come to mind, home as an experience of belonging, a place that never was and never can be, Judy Garland clicking her heels, *no place like home.* For those of us who are what feminist philosopher Mariana Ortega calls marginalized multiplicitous selves, occupying several conflicting social positions (race, class, sex, gender), we are constantly aware of "not-being-at-home, not-dwelling, a marked sense of not feeling at ease or having a sense of familiarity in many of the worlds" we inhabit. We are in-betweens, border dwellers, forever navigating and negotiating space, shifting from one social identity to the other—for me, it looks like: here I'm trans, there I'm cis-assumed; here I'm queer, there I'm not; sometimes showing my working-class past, ethnic-white and accented, other times bourgeois, Anglo-passing, speaking in the flat tongue of General American. Everyone has a multiplicity of selves; however, as Ortega points out, "there is a crucial difference between those whose experience is one of being mostly at ease in the world and those whose experience is marginalized, oppressed, or alienated."

The hyper-normal apparently feels at ease in most spaces, carrying an internal sense of being-at-home, but outsiders, no matter how much we sometimes blend into a norm, do not have the "privilege of always feeling as if one has a home." (This privilege, I would add, is one of the entitlements that make the hyper-normal so comfortable intruding and expanding into spaces of otherness—they don't have to read the room because every room might as well belong to them.) For queers of all kinds, the lack of home privilege can stimulate longing for a home that feels lost because it never was. Capitalism seduces qualifying gays, lesbians, and now trans people into its house, with the promised goodies of an acceptable life and a guarantee that it can replace *longing* with *belonging,* but that shift means leaving other outsiders behind. "One may enter the mainstream," says Love, "on the condition that one breaks ties with all those who cannot make it—the nonwhite and the nonmonogamous, the poor and the gender deviant, the fat, the disabled, the unemployed, the infected, and a host of unmentionable others."

I broke those ties when I started passing as a cisgender man, slipping into the mainstream, transformed from abject, unintelligible gender to acceptable, seemingly seamless gender. Doors opened. One day I was a monster and the next I walked into J.Crew and the salespeople swarmed me, asking, with smiles on their faces, "Can I help you?" This had never happened before. Now people smiled at me all over town, making small talk, telling me I was one of them. Except I wasn't. I enjoyed being stealth, took pleasure in my new privileges, but it also felt like erasure. For the trans person who passes for cis, for the gay person who embraces acceptability, we enter the mainstream breaking ties not only with the others who cannot make it but with *the parts of ourselves that cannot make it*—the weird, failed, fucked-up parts that don't get unfucked just because we're wearing J.Crew (or shopping at Whole Foods or getting married or buying property). Why even try to unfuck those parts? Embracing backwardness is something queers do well, says Love, "in celebrations of perversion, in defiant refusals to grow up, in explorations of haunting and memory, and in stubborn attachments to lost objects." The lost object of my current exploration, to which I am stubbornly attached, is queer New York, city of outsiders, the place that has come closest to feeling like home, and about its loss I have many negative feelings.

I am overly attached to my anger. I won't let go. Like everything else, this dynamic is multi-determined, but I'm curious about the gender piece. Can I understand my negativity as a transmasculine one, rooted in the gravelly soil of tomboy/butch disgruntlement, trailing a wreckage of feminine failure? (So many trans men come to therapy and talk about what it's like to flunk out of girlhood.) In *The Queer Art of Failure*, Jack Halberstam describes what might be a masculine female style of queer negativity, an antisocial archive of rage, brutal honesty, intensity, and overinvestment, affects found in "Dyke anger, anticolonial despair, racial rage, counterhegemonic violence, punk pugilism," where a "truly political negativity" promises "to fail, to make a mess, to fuck shit up." This makes sense. When a masculine female child is gender-policed to smile, be sunny and light, sugar and spice, they might cling instead to snips and snails, the jagged and gloomy stuff that everyone's always trying to take away. Transmasculine negativity, held tight like a melancholy object, can therefore function as resistance to coercive femininity with its demand for a pleasant disposition. It can function as resistance to the normal and nice. And it can find resonance in the act of breaking.

A memory comes. I'm maybe six years old, 1977-ish, in the coffee shop of a crummy five-and-dime department store with my mother and her younger sister. The vapor of fried chicken and cigarette smoke surrounds their orange Formica table, welded to two benches I still see clearly, the contoured kind, covered in brown wood-grain laminate. I'm sitting on a nearby swivel stool, whining as they tease me about buying a doll I desperately do not want. I'm whining because I'm not permitted to say no. My refusal can only come out sideways, in whimpers and moans, grumbled complaints of "I don't *want* it," never a forceful, straightforward no. The doll I do not want is Shirley Temple, sixteen inches tall, in a white dress with red polka dots, blonde hair curled into signature ringlets. She is smiling, doing the simple thing that everyone is always telling me to do because I don't do it enough and this makes everyone unhappy. I'm supposed to be lighthearted, but I'm not. Life is difficult and confusing. I'm not just required to do things I don't want to do, I'm required to enjoy them. "You'll do it and you'll *like* it." The injunction to enjoy begins early, searing my insides. Shirley Temple is my nemesis because everyone says I look like her and I resent the resemblance. At restaurants, when I order my favorite cocktail of 7-Up and grenadine with extra maraschino cherries, I defiantly call it a Mickey Mouse because fuck Shirley Temple. My mother twists my curly hair into corkscrews with a hot iron. *Sit still.* I hate this. Like I hate the dresses she puts me into. Like I hate the smile I am told to perform. I am supposed to be like Shirley Temple, but I'm not, I'm all wrong, and I hate Shirley Temple in her perfect girliness, her successful acceptance of compulsory femininity, everything at which I am failing because I cannot be what I am not. The doll, against my wishes, is purchased and placed on a shelf in my bedroom with all the other dolls I do not want but am supposed to love. When we are alone, I take Shirley by the ankles and bash her head against the floor.

What is the shape of transmasculine rage? Does it look like Franken- stein's monster, the form that trans theorist Susan Stryker gave to her trans(feminine) rage? She dressed the affect of her "transsexual mon- strosity" in the "genderfuck drag" of 1993: combat boots, Levi's, biker jacket decorated with handcuffs and stickers that said FUCK YOUR TRANSPHOBIA. (I wore the same jacket that year and had had recur- ring dreams of Frankenstein's monster, my skin crisscrossed with dark sutures, a body in transition.) Does transmasc rage differ from transfem rage—does it matter? There's something inward-turning about trans- masc anger, something seething, mostly hidden. When my patients describe it, it takes the shape of unborn, half-formed hybrid objects, toad-like creatures hiding in holes, spiders burrowed in the belly, *Alien* chest busters gestating in esophageal chambers. It's the haunted sensa- tion of phantomized flesh, something you know is there but can't see. It's picking a scab, muttering under your breath, brooding over a cigarette in some moody scene. It's spending a rainy day in a cemetery, sitting in the back seat of my first car, age seventeen, reading *The Well of Loneliness* and seeing myself in Radclyffe Hall's gloomy trans-mannish invert, that open wound of unrequited everything, trying to be good, to get along, nursing sweet bitterness. Transmasculine rage blisters and seethes. Is it ever allowed to explode?

Another memory: Sitting on my bedroom floor, taking my Fisher-Price Adventure People in one hand and a steak knife in the other. Sawing off the limbs of the brawny men I love and envy, I'm a six-year-old transsexual serial killer, that old trope, star of my own slasher flick. When the deed is done, I am horrified. Awash in guilt, I push the plastic shavings deep into the carpet fibers. How did I dispose of the body parts? I only remember the act of disarticulation—murderous rage I could not put into words.

Abandoned by the normals, pandemic New York relaxes into queer failure, an undisciplined space of beautiful ruins, those left-alone sites that "represent a perversion of desire, the decay of the commodity" (Halberstam), stepped away from the hetero-futurist, capitalist demand to grow and win. As the plague pulls us from the shiny knife blade of hypernormativity, the city sits back and slumps, getting messy with outsider rage and joy. Wherever the rejected are creating sites of refusal, the city is becoming the sort of inclusive queer scene that Michael Warner calls "the true *salons des refuses*, where the most heterogeneous people are brought into great intimacy by their common experience of being despised and rejected in a world of norms that they now recognize as false morality." Left to the Leftovers, a motley bunch historically marked as backward— including "sexual and gender deviants" along with "colonized people, the nonwhite, the disabled, the poor, and criminals" (Love)—New York overspills, and my trans rage and joy spills with it. Alone at first, it is about to find a community and a coherent shape in the shattered glass of broken windows and the bright splashes of graffiti, in the rough arms of New York Fuckin City, a lost home that is home again, where I am free to enjoy because no one is telling me it's what I have to do.

6.

THE COP IN MY HEAD

Washington Square Park becomes the heart of the uprising in
Manhattan, a place for marchers to rally before taking the
streets, and this energy revives the park's outsider soul. Originally part
of an indigenous village known as Sapokanican, this land was colonized
for Dutch farmers, granted to freed Africans who'd been enslaved, and
then turned into a potter's field for victims of yellow fever epidemics. It
became public space in the 1820s and has been a hotbed of protest and
riot since 1834. At its center, the large stone fountain has served as a
countercultural hub, attracting folk singers and poets after the Second
World War, a culture of racial mixing that parks commissioner Newbold
Morris tried to squash in 1961, claiming the music attracted an undesirable element "from the Bronx, and so on." ("You know what 'undesirable'
means, don't you?" a jazz musician said at the time. "It means 'Negro.'")
When folk singers protested, shouting about real estate and fascism, the
cops rioted, swinging clubs and dragging people from the dry fountain.
Now it's the past all over again as the freedom and waywardness of
pandemic life fills the park with musicians, artists, and protesters. All
summer, there will be no tourists and very few hyper-normals, but plenty
of panhandlers, wheelie bikers, breakdancers, Tarot card readers, and
transgender burlesque performers who show up with a portable pole to
twerk to Cardi B's "Wet-Ass Pussy," the song that will become a kind of

anthem for the year, an exuberant, femme-top *fuck you* that crackles with a sexual electricity to match the voltage in the streets. At the start of all this wild unwinding, the queer, pot-smoking, sometimes naked Jesus of Washington Square takes the fountain.

Barefoot and sunburned pink, the boy Jesus believes he's the second coming of Our Lord and Savior and that the best place for the Lord to be is on his throne, the fountainhead, a circular dais from which jets of water usually shoot, but not during lockdown. Now it is covered in flowers, a memorial for George Floyd, and the boy reclines among the blossoms. Half-nude, surrounded by dying yellow roses and bunches of lilies, piles of books, and bright wedges of fleshy watermelon, he looks like a homoerotic Romantic painting, a *vanitas* still life, here to remind us that earthly pleasure is transient and we will die. With great focus, he writes in his notebook while skateboarders swirl and, now and then, people approach to hand over bouquets of flowers, which the boy carefully places in the arrangement. I visit nearly every day.

Jesus acquires furniture, a desk and chair, at which he writes his scriptures. He hangs a sign asking, "Please bring me Injustice regarding" a lengthy list, including War, Hunger, Housing, Imprisonment, Slavery, "and all other evil Manifestations." His assemblage grows to include a large stuffed unicorn, an upholstered armchair, and followers, including the woman in the tinfoil hat, smoking weed from a pipe carved out of an apple, an erratic sort of Eve. Jesus puts up another sign, naming his fortress the Assembly Camp of the Party of Life, and a racially diverse group of lost pretty boys join the camp to get stoned and dance shirtless, showing off their bodies while beaming druggy joy into the sun. Jesus looks happy. He takes up his messianic calling and begins to preach. Young people, hanging around after a Black Lives Matter rally, stand outside the fountain to ask questions about life and the universe. Jesus talks about Jupiter and spaceships made from 3D printers, methods for harnessing the power of asteroids to protect the natural environment of our planet. A trio of New People, bully boys in backward baseball caps, snicker and roll their eyes, but they are outnumbered by the deviants and quickly move away. This is not their park anymore. It has slipped from their grip.

In the afternoons, when the park is buoyant with its new chaos, I ride my bike around the fountain, around Jesus and the flowers, enjoying the illegal pleasure of breaking a rule usually policed with ferocity. In the Before Time, I maybe dared to ride through the park twice, and both times people fiercely corrected me. But now those people have abandoned New York, or else they understand their power isn't worth much anymore, because no one yells at me. The pandemic has changed the norm. Others circle the fountain too, biking, skateboarding, roller-skating through clouds of patchouli, weed smoke, and music. The park is our bliss. But when I venture in on a weekend morning, I encounter an invisible force that, while surely felt before, has never been so clear.

The park is different in the morning. The protesters, skateboarders, artists, and tinfoil hatters have yet to arrive, Jesus is absent from his church, and the space belongs again to the orderly and normal, the almost all-white, upper-class, heterosexual couples who live nearby with their baby strollers and dogs. There aren't many of them, but there's enough to make everything feel clean and quiet, domesticated, as it used to be. Sitting among the normals, without my fellow deviants, I notice a discomfort inside me, a feeling of alienation that grows into the heavy weight of a bad mood. I feel, once again, cranky and out of place, the way I felt before the pandemic. Maybe a ride around the fountain will bring relief. I grab my handlebars but can't get on the bike. A strong internal prohibition stops me. I look around at the normals and realize: It's radiating from them.

Social control, defined by sociologists, can be formal, enforced by police and laws, or informal, enforced by everyday individuals. It can be as straightforward as correcting someone for incivility, like blocking the subway doors. We all do it to some extent, but it most commonly takes the shape of downward control, in which people with more power exercise control over people with less, like calling 911 to remove a homeless person from the sidewalk, enlisting formal enforcers to exert control on one's behalf. But not all policing is so blatant—or conscious. More insidious expressions of downward social control bleed through the urban atmosphere.

In *The Taming of New York's Washington Square*, sociologist Erich Goode describes the inconspicuous ways that normals control deviants in public space: "they may simply withdraw from the presence of persons who do something they don't like, or they may ignore an invitation to interact with them, or they may wear a facial expression of disgust, outright disapproval, or annoyance, or roll their eyes." Conscious or unconscious, contemptuous disregard is one of the most common subtle methods of downward social control. Think of the New People who close doors in our faces, bump us on the sidewalk, and don't respond when we say hello. I believe this disregard functions as micro-control, not unlike micro-aggression, an everyday mistreatment you feel but can't prove. Did that just happen? Is it me? These are questions that minoritized subjects ask all the time in the presence of the dominant. Yes, it happened. If it feels like the New People are telling us we don't exist, it might be because they don't *want* us to exist. We are wrinkles in the smooth experience of their ideal city, a master-planned environment they expect to be as frictionless and predictable as the suburbs to which they're attached. And the suburbs, from inception, are all about control, the straightening out of deviance.

You don't have to be a lunatic or criminal to get socially controlled by the New People, you just have to deviate from whatever they're conforming to; and because hyper-normals are hyper-conformists, policing and patrolling the boundaries of self and others, anxiety swarms in the presence of the slightest deviation. I suspect that anxiety, that sense of threatened boundaries, often turns into aggression. But sociology can't tell us that. To theorize what might be going on inside the hyper-normal psyche, we need psychoanalysis.

. . .

IN THE 1980S, PSYCHOANALYST CHRISTOPHER BOLLAS BEGAN TO notice a new personality type. He called it the normotic, someone with "a particular drive to be normal . . . typified by the numbing and eventual erasure of subjectivity in favor of a self that is conceived as a material object among other man-made products." When Bollas says "erasure of subjectivity," he's talking about the way consumer culture has the power to take us over, drowning out our singularities as human beings and turning us into commodities. The normotic colludes with this takeover to remain blank and shallow, "abnormally normal," an extrovert who talks mostly about mundane daily activities, sentences stuffed with meaningless words like *uh-huh*, *yeah*, and *wow*. Instead of fully experiencing life, the normotic prefers "mnemic excreta," so a photograph is better than a lived experience (hello Instagrammability). In his drive not to be human, the normotic sees himself as an object, "ideally smart and spruced up, productive and sociable," and relates to consumer products as "part of one's family." In a foreign environment, he becomes stressed, so "the simple discovery of a familiar object, such as Coca-Cola, can be greeted with an affection and celebration that other people reserve only for human beings."

In 2018, Bollas developed his theory, changing the name to *normopathy* and taking neoliberalism into account as he linked the evolution of this personality to an "identification with the machinery of globalization," a machinery that demands "global-selves, uniform beings." This process of homogenization, the "need to eradicate difference and fashion a world of indistinguishable beings," creates personalities that don't waste time with internal reflection, making them more productive in a free-market capitalist system. This extends Michel Foucault's idea about how neoliberalism expands beyond the economic into "a model of social relations and of existence itself" to create a personality that he called, in 1979, "homo economicus," the entrepreneurial self, the neoliberal subject. Intertwined with market forces, historian Philip Mirowski explains, this type "is not just an employee or student, but also simultaneously a product to be sold, a walking advertisement. . . . She is a jumble of assets to be invested, nurtured, managed, and developed; but equally an offsetting inventory of liabilities to be pruned, outsourced, shorted, hedged against, and minimized. She is both headline star and enraptured audience of her own performance." These are the New People—ideal neoliberal subjects, hyper-normal to be most marketable, walking advertisements exerting influence.

The life of a normopathic, entrepreneurial, neoliberal self is surely painful—forever competitive, never good enough, always striving for

"a world of indistinguishable beings"

improvement, terrified of vulnerability, disconnected from one's interior. It can be difficult, however, to feel for them. Bollas noticed a difference between the hyper-normal patients of the 1980s and those of the 2000s—they no longer aroused compassion in their caregivers. "Instead, in their android-like enthusiasm for their app world, imbued with an arrogant sense of privileged access, if anything we tend to find them off-putting." In addition, they "often appear indifferent to the suffering of those around them," and it is especially challenging to feel empathy for those who do not feel empathy for others. Free-market capitalism doesn't have much use for human tenderness. It isn't profitable.

Thinking about Bollas's theory and the hyper-normals of New York, I linger on their aggression as I try to understand what, exactly, they are *doing*—to the city and its people. I suspect it's tied to how the normopath relates to subjectivity. A word that's hard to define, often shifting, *subjectivity* might simply be thought of as one's interiority, the state of being a unique, conscious person who is not alienated from their own and others' humanity. This is what normopaths annihilate in themselves through the process of what Bollas calls "subjecticide." I believe normopaths also try to annihilate subjectivity when they encounter it *outside* themselves, in both people and places. "The fundamental identifying feature of this individual," Bollas explains, "is a disinclination to entertain the subjective element in life, whether it exists inside himself or in the other." He "does not think about others" or "look into the other." Furthermore, there is "violence in this person's being . . . not in his utterances, but in his way of shutting life out." That subtle violence is the element I am trying to excavate. The hyper-normal's disinclination to see the humanness of others—his not thinking, not looking, shutting out—is not just a refusal to engage. It is an act of aggression and control.

■ ■ ■

CONTROL MIGHT RADIATE FROM THE HYPER-NORMALS, BUT TO SUC-
ceed it requires a receptive body, what Foucault called the docile body
of the disciplinary society. Discipline, he explains, is a normalizing force
that imposes homogeneity, operating through the panoptic schema, a
system of surveillance in which the objects of the gaze can always be
seen, but don't know at any given moment if they're being watched.
Like the cameras in my building that may or may not be operational,
the "faceless gaze that transformed the whole social body into a field of
perception" successfully disciplines us in part because we can't be sure
if it's real. This system of micro-power gets strength from intangibility.
When a police officer shoves you, you know what's controlling you—and
what you might resist. But the quiet coercion of normativity is harder to
see—and that makes it harder to resist. Discipline is regulatory, aligned
with heteronormativity and capitalism for the purpose of increasing production, and because this system punishes deviance and rewards compliance, the winners are the productive and the reproductive. The more
they conform, the more they are rewarded—and the more, I believe, they
act as agents of the controlling system, using their power as winners to
exert downward control on deviants. Winners or losers, however, we
all participate to some extent in this system. We are all docile bodies,
because discipline also functions through internalization.

"If power is exercised too violently," Foucault explained, "there is the
risk of provoking revolts." Don't send in riot cops. Send in cameras.
Send in eyes. Power must be exercised quietly and continuously through
surveillance, so there is "no need for arms, physical violence, or material
restraints. Just an observing gaze that each individual feels weighing on
him, and ends up internalizing to the point that he is his own overseer:
everyone in this way exercises surveillance over and against himself."
This is what happens to me in Washington Square when the cop in my
head stops me from getting on my bike and riding around the fountain,
but—and this is important—it only happens when the number of nor-

mals perceptibly exceeds the number of deviants. In a crowd of deviants, I am free to ride. Because the normals *are* the cops.

As French sociologist Pierre Bourdieu said, "The very lifestyle of the holders of power contributes to the power that makes it possible, because its true conditions of possibility remain unrecognized." They don't have to *do* anything to *affect* something. Just sitting there, with their babies and haircuts, their Polo shirts and athleisure, drinking iced coffee and laughing with mouths full of good teeth, the normals regulate public space. If deviance appears, they use their quiet weapons of social control, expressions of contempt and disregard. The discipline of the regulatory gaze is subtle, yet effective enough to neutralize resistance, said Foucault, crushing "agitations, revolts, spontaneous organizations, coalitions." This is why, I suspect, the leaders of New York, since the neoliberal reorientation of the city in the 1970s, have worked to attract and cater to hyper-normals, not only because they spend money, intensify gentrification, and bring tax revenue but also because they are super-controllers who keep the deviance of the city under wraps.

During the plague, as this covert police force continues to flee Manhattan, control goes with them, and the deviant, defiant Remainders become ever more undisciplined. Since the start of lockdown, those of us who've been constrained—the Black, trans, poor, and other Others—are expanding into the open fields of the abandoned city. While we are not the same—it is important to note, as Afro-pessimist scholar Frank B. Wilderson III says, "Black suffering is of a different order than the suffering of other oppressed people"—we stand outside the center together. Without equating or collapsing one identity into another, I am interested in the places where we intersect, where we share, in this moment of divergence, a public feeling of expansiveness. It's in our bodies, in muscles growing stronger and voices louder. It's in the space we take in the left-alone city.

7.

TO BE OF USE

The Leader is shirtless, dressed in black track pants with a red stripe down the leg that matches his red-and-black fixed-gear bike, the frame decorated with a single Supreme sticker, red and white, Futura Bold. He is Black and wears a black bandanna over his face. His head is shaved clean. He's the Leader because he knows what to do and I follow, falling into a rhythm of speeding up and stopping at each intersection, placing my bike like a shield in front of oncoming traffic to protect the marchers. This is the first time I've been a bike guard. I didn't plan it. My sprained ankle still hurts too much to march, so I've been joining the protests on wheels, riding at the edges, but now there's this new role to play. No one asks me to do it. No one says a word. I just follow, rolling into it, and it feels natural. Next to me is an older butch, hair chopped into a gray mohawk and a pair of silver chrome Elvis glasses on her sunburn-pink face. She's riding a bike with three wheels and a rear basket in which a little dog sits by a sticker that says "Trump/Pence Out Now." There are other bike guards, but I am attached to the Leader and Mohawk, a duckling imprinted. Right away, we feel like a team. Or a family.

For now, I think of this activity as *bike guarding* because I don't know what else to call it and I never really will. The Internet eventually calls us bike marshals, corkers, and blocs, but I don't hear those words in the streets. Over the next year, whenever I ask a biker in the movement how they refer to themselves, and this thing, they'll shrug and say something vague, like, "We're biking in marches." I will come to understand that to name it, to set it apart, is to differentiate it, and this movement is about being one, a mass organism collectively spreading like mushroom threads below the soil.

As the bikers ride up Fifth Avenue, none of us speak. We don't need words. We watch each other's eyes, bodies, and wheels, following the Leader's quiet strength as it pulls us along. I already have a crush on him, the kind I keep getting on leaders of this movement, like a kid looking up to cool camp counselors, that kind of crush, and I feel small in a way that's comforting even though I am twice their age. Behind us, the march keeps coming, led by two young Black people, a guy in a Slushcult tee that says "Resist Lame Snacks" and a woman with a golden Afro that looks like a dandelion about to launch its seeds to the wind. We are chanting, "Whose streets? *Our* streets!" Supporters roll up in a car with bottles of water and a cardboard sign that says "Sex is good but have you ever fucked the system?" The Leader pulls us ahead, sailing up the wide, empty avenue, commandeering the city. After years of being pushed and shoved, this is triumph. At the next light and the next, we take the intersection, barricading from curb to curb with our line of bikes, links in a chain, wheel to wheel. Since the beginning of lockdown, my bike has become an extension of my body, my self, and I feel grateful to it, the way you feel grateful to a living thing that has carried you. And set you free.

As we fly through the streets, the connection between the Leader, Mohawk, and me feels so fundamental, my eyes fill with tears in a way I don't understand, except to know that I feel full and also useful. "To be of use" is the phrase that comes to mind, the title of a poem by Marge Piercy, in which she writes, "The pitcher cries for water to carry and a person for work that is real." She wrote the poem during the Vietnam War, and I read it in high school when I first began to march in protest, when that desire emerged, to be of use, to carry water. To experience my body as an object with purpose is to be unburdened of this body as I also inhabit it more completely. To be and not to be. Maybe this is what Jia Tolentino means when she says, "To deepen your understanding of race, of this country, should make you feel like the world is opening up, like you're dissolving into the immensity of history and the present rather than being more uncomfortably visible to yourself. . . . People ought to seek out the genuine pleasure of decentering themselves." In the pleasure of following, I feel myself dissolve into the march and its collective purpose. I feel the pitcher of my body fill and think this is what psychoanalyst Emmanuel Ghent meant by *surrender*, a word chosen to "convey a quality of liberation and expansion of the self." Surrender is not the defeat of submission. It is ecstatic and joyful, the experience of being in the present, the oceanic feeling of wholeness, a "sense of unity with other living beings." It is both letting go and becoming a part.

Most of the drivers are on our side, honking horns and thrusting power fists through open windows. Deliverymen in UPS trucks do it. Cab drivers do it. When bus drivers do it, there's an extra thrill because they possess authority, in city uniforms behind Plexiglas barriers, but now the boundaries are coming down. In a moment of insurrection, one bus driver has changed his LED destination sign from "Limited" to "Black Lives Matter." But not all surrender with us. At one stop, an impatient man behind the wheel of an SUV leaps the curb and guns through a gap in our line. I shout for Mohawk to watch out, she steps back, and the SUV nearly grazes her bike. We shake it off like it's nothing, but as we hurry on to the next light, we know bad things can happen.

A few blocks up, the Leader falters and flies over his handlebars, bike folding beneath him. He skids on his bare chest across a sewer grate. I swerve toward him but stop short as he leaps to his feet, the way men do, refusing help, "I'm fine, I'm fine." I know that shock of crashing, the shame that follows, and give him space, but I can't stop checking as we take off, watching him touch his road-rashed skin, elbows ripped into raw steak. I want to get him some Neosporin. I become obsessed with Neosporin. I could duck into a drugstore and get some, but he'd probably reject it. When I finally say, "Hey, want me to go back and find a medic," he says, "No, no, I'm fine." Men are too often like this, not letting themselves take the tender pleasure of being cared for, especially by another man. Once, in the middle of breakfast at an outdoor diner, I saw a cyclist get hit by a cab and rushed out to hold him, pressing my hands to his head where a stream of blood poured out with such force I heard it hit the pavement in a musical splash. He quickly brushed me off and wobbled away, but I remember how soft his hair felt and the bright shock of his red interior smearing my palms.

Police push the march along on scooters, blocking our path, diverting us from Trump Tower. We skip east, north, west again and down, organically shifting, a single organism made of many, like the murmuration of starlings, moving with a single shared will. Leaders and followers, a shiver of connection webbing us together, we are an ocean.

After his fall, the Leader is less sure of himself, holding back. The strength of his energy ebbs and I lose him when our march converges with another march above Times Square. This group carries a large American flag held upside down, "a signal of dire distress in instances of extreme danger," according to Section 176 of the U.S. Flag Code. When they join us, we cheer atop a hill, sweet victory, and when we march south again, we are twice as large. The other group's bikers join us, and I immediately dislike them. I know this is not comradely, not in the spirit of a pitcher carrying water, but these bikers are a bossy bunch. A young white man takes the lead, barking orders like a drill sergeant, while an older woman, also white, starts yelling at us because we're not blocking the streets the way she thinks we should. "No, no, no," she objects from her three-speed bike. "You've got it all wrong." I miss the Leader and his calm, quiet steadiness. I miss the feeling of love that zinged between him and Mohawk and me. Did they feel it, too?

There are so many bikers now, I am redundant, so I ease back, letting the eager, younger ones do the bulk of the work. I'm gliding through the falling golden light, the downward slope of Fifth Avenue pulling me, when the Leader reappears, looking strong and restored. Mohawk is there, too, her dog yapping from the bike basket, and it's like a family reunion, only no one says a word and I have no idea if they feel the same way about me as I do about them. How can I love these people with whom I've only spent a few hours, to whom I've barely said a word? We've never touched. We've never broken bread. And yet there is this magnetic attachment that will remain with me even after we've parted. I don't know how this variety of love works. I only know that it exists.

8.

THE RETURN OF REVANCHISM

The mayor cancels the curfew early, just in time for the Phase One Reopening of New York on June 8. Above Times Square, a giant digital screen announces WELCOME BACK NYC, and while I think *we've been here*, I know that we, the Remainders, are not the ones the screen is so eager to welcome back. I'm writing at my kitchen table when I hear a loud noise in the hallway. And I know: The Influencer has returned.

I freeze with dread as she comes stomping up the stairs, bumping a suitcase and squealing with performed excitement, a crescendo of keening that climaxes when she flings open her apartment door and screams, "I'm home!" I leap to the peephole to see the audience of her performance, her father, unmasked. He shakes his head and, in a paternal tone, says, "The city is becoming a very dangerous place." He doesn't mean the virus. He means broken windows, rebellion, rumors of rising crime. He means Blackness uncontained, as suburban whites often do when they speak about the dangers of cities.

For the next two hours, I'm in a state of anxiety as the Influencer knocks around her apartment, banging through the kitchen, tossing food in the garbage. Is she staying or going? I listen for clues. From behind her half-open door, she whines and huffs as her father insists, "The city isn't safe anymore." He wants her to go. She wants to stay. Or she wants to put on a show of wanting to stay. I wonder if she's frightened, bewildered by the violent disruption of her glossy object world. I wonder what it's like for her to go through SoHo and see her beloved chain stores smashed, covered in plywood and *fuck*s, graffitied with REDISTRIBUTE WEALTH, REDISTRIBUTE POWER. Her upscale brunch spot, site of so many avocado toasts and matcha lattes, lies ravaged. For a moment, I allow myself to imagine that she might feel what I have felt for years, ambushed and displaced.

When she goes into the hall, I follow, acting casual, like I'm heading down to check the mail. I have to know what's happening. "Hi," I chirp, performing her brand of cheerfulness. "Welcome back!" Without regarding me, eyes on the floor, she mutters, "Hey." Is she staying? No, she says, she's just here to get a few things and go home again. Relief floods through me. "You're smart. It's getting rough around here," I say, reinforcing the paternal injunction, the fantasy of unsafety, to ward her away. To this she drily replies, "So I have heard." On the street, I watch her climb into her father's alpine-white BMW and ride away. When she's out of sight, I do a little dance of joy.

Before heading back upstairs, I check the trash to see if she's thrown out anything worth salvaging. There are odds and ends, a few storage boxes from Pottery Barn, a set of good white sheets I guess she didn't want to bother washing. Nothing I want. Then I see, half-crushed under bags of rotten food, a few green spears of the houseplant I dreamed of liberating from her apartment. Just barely alive, it feels like a miracle, a sign meant for me. Carefully, I lift it out and carry it upstairs. It's a snake plant, a hardy succulent that is difficult to kill, but after three months of no water, the soil is so dry it has pulled away from the pot and the leaves are scorched from thirst. I gently break up the dirt with a fork, trim away the dead, and soak the plant in my kitchen sink, letting the soil drink and grow dark. I find a bright spot on a windowsill, place it in a beam of light, and speak softly to it—to *her* I think, bestowing a gender—telling her she's safe now, whispering, *Everything's going to be alright.*

■ ■ ■

TWO WEEKS AGO, ON THE MORNING OF MEMORIAL DAY, THE SAME day George Floyd was killed, a smaller but related incident occurred in Central Park when a white woman called 911 on a Black man, falsely accusing, "I'm gonna tell them there's an African American man threatening my life." The woman was walking her dog off leash, and the man, who was bird-watching, asked her to put it on. He was exerting the kind of social control common in cities, correcting a rule breaker in public space, but he defied the usual order, directing control from Black to white, and this was apparently intolerable to the woman. Dialing 911, she threatened his life. "To imagine herself as a rescue," Claudia Rankine will later say of the woman, "to imagine herself into a rescue narrative, is to activate a covert white female power trigger that can easily call in the violence of white men." The white woman in America enjoys—and suffers from—a long history as "a piece of high-value white property," and when she is in jeopardy, white men act as her protectors.

The Central Park birdwatching incident ended without physical violence, the man and woman left the scene before police arrived, but the story reverberates. I keep wondering why the woman snapped at that moment. She could have acted out this centuries-long drama about race, gender, and power at any time, and I wonder what role the pandemic played. By Memorial Day, after white flight, central Manhattan had become Blacker and browner, more visibly working-class and poor, already stimulating anxieties about a return to "the bad old days" of the

'70s and '80s. The woman in Central Park lives in a luxury tower, built with Trump's name on it, and works in finance. (Neighbors say she has "a sense of entitlement.") Did she hold the false memory of the Central Park Jogger attack, ghosts of 1989 returned to the present, whispering the word *wilding*? In the vernacular of hip-hop, *wilding* belongs, according to Stephen J. Mexal, to young men ironically performing "the absence of rationality." They reappropriate wildness with this word that, through journalists' misinterpretation, got woven into an idea of Central Park, "a civilized simulation of nature: a landscaped *repudiation* of wilderness." In today's replay of white flight, did these specters of distorted racial history haunt the woman with the dog, making her more anxious and angry? Under the influence of the racist imaginary that transforms Black men's bodies into threats, did she seek white revenge?

Revanchism, from the French for *revenge*, refers to public policies that seek to regain lost territory. In the city, it is a form of recolonization. Urban geographer Neil Smith modernized the term in the 1990s, using it to describe not only New York's official policy of gentrification but also an affective state, a take-back mentality that arose after the crash of 1987 when it seemed as if gentrification would reverse, failing to return the city to ruling-class whites, real-estate developers, and big business. Revanchism was—and, I argue, is once again—a territorial and violent reaction by the powerful trying to hold on to power as it slips away. The powerful cloak this defense of privileges in the rhetoric of family values and neighborhood security, Smith explains, in language laced with racism, classism, and queer-phobia. "More than anything," he writes, "the revanchist city expresses a race/class/gender terror felt by middle- and ruling-class whites. . . . It portends a vicious reaction against minorities, the working class, homeless people, the unemployed, women, gays and lesbians, immigrants." Written twenty-five years ago, this could describe New York City in 2020. After the Phase One Reopening, revanchism returns.

Long Live America

A few days after the start of Phase One, I go for a bike ride. I'm heading up Broadway the wrong way, a practice known as salmoning. It's a
controversial move, but for months we Remainders have been salmoning
with abandon, riding cooperatively, fellow cyclists (mostly delivery men,
hardly a Citi Biker in sight) making space for each other. But now, just
this week, the agents of control are clamping down. A man comes racing toward me, playing chicken. He's white and young, dressed in the
hyper-normal uniform of Polo shirt and backward baseball cap. With no
helmet and riding a Citi Bike, he's clearly an amateur, a tourist of urban
biking, and he's charging straight for me, even though I am outside the
lane, giving him plenty of room. When I move away, he follows, aiming
straight for me. Inches from my tire, he hits the brakes, wheels screeching, and screams, "Wrong way, asshole!" I tell him to fuck himself, but
I'm rattled. No one has yelled at me in three months. Something, I sense,
has shifted. Still, I write it off as an isolated incident until, the next day,
it happens again. Another young, white man on a Citi Bike yells at me,
"Wrong way, asshole!" In this uncanny repetition of the same words from

the same type, I understand: the New People are pissed. They abandoned the city and, in their absence, the streets were reclaimed by the
Blacks, the queers, the socialists, the freaks. These men, in their white
male grievance, have returned to exert the Law of the Father over the
liberated, feminine-chaotic city. On the third day, it happens again. I'm
being more careful and only go against the stream for one block. I even
take the opposite side of the street, far from the bike lane, but there's an
angry white man pedaling toward me. He's on the wrong side, but still
he shouts, "Wrong way, asshole!" This makes three identical corrections
in three days, after months of nothing. Strange coincidence? If I have
any doubt that the hyper-normals are trying to reassert their dominance,
it will be dispelled in the next day's incident.

First, I spend the day in protest. We rally at Union Square, where the
leaders tell us we're family, we keep each other safe. We look to the people
around us and say thank you. We are community. Everyone is masked.
Volunteers give out hand sanitizer, snacks, and water. I feel cared for and
connected, gifted with responsibility for others. Together we flow down
Broadway, through boarded-up SoHo, saying the names of the dead.
We're joined by a group of teenage boys on bikes, popping wheelies.
When I tell one that I like his bike, he eyes me uncertainly, a young Black
man looking at a normal-appearing white man—*the police*—but when he
sees the BLM button on my chest, he visibly relaxes. He likes my bike,
too, he says and we take off together, the bike blockers and the wheelie
boys, and for one thrilling moment I am riding with them, surrounded
and held by their exuberant crew in the wide-open street we have taken.

I never got to be a boy, throwing my body into the world to see how it
survived on nothing but muscle and fuck-it. Not even an athletic tomboy,
I was cautious, didn't climb fences or jump into swimming pools, forever
picked last for basketball. On my pink Huffy bike, "Sweet Thunder,"
the girls' consolation prize of 1979, I was too afraid to pop wheelies.

Now I have a small, black bike that conjures a body memory of the boys' black Huffy, the BMX known as "Thunder Road," the one I wanted but could not have. (I also wanted to be Fonzie when we played motorcycles, was told I had to be Pinky, and opted out of that binary, choosing the third gender, Pinky's younger sister Leather Tuscadero, played by Suzi Quatro, the tomboy cock rocker who called herself "the wild one.") Now I'm almost fifty years old, flanked by two acrobatic boys, wheels rising on both sides of me like wings. Breaking the rules of gravity, their energy lifts mine so I feel a swoop in my belly and, for a few seconds, I'm flying, too. The boy in front stands on his bike seat, raises a fist, and all of Broadway belongs to us. "Whose streets? Our streets!" This is joy and rage and love. On the plywood of a boarded-up shop, a scrawl of spray paint tells the messy, drippy truth: ALL THIS CHANGE IS MAKING ME WET.

At the end of the day, happily exhausted and buoyant with life, I head back to the East Village. All week, since the Phase One reopening began, hyper-normals have flocked to St. Mark's and Avenue A, where bars are

Boarded up on Broadway in SoHo

serving booze on the sidewalk. To step into this world, after a day of protesting, is culture shock. In the movement, everyone wears masks, but here there are none. We raise our fists as the historic symbol of social revolution, for antifascists, feminists, and Black Power, but here they raise fists to drinking songs, to the frat-party atmosphere, taking up space because it's what they've always done—and now they are taking it back. Cops stand around, sent by the governor to control this drunken mob, but they do nothing. For weeks I've watched the police brutalize people exercising the right to assemble, and now they flirt with drunk girls and laugh with drunk boys who holler *boooo* in the cops' faces because "We're thirsty!" This is their petulant protest chant. *We're thirsty! We're thirsty! We're thirsty!* No White Claw, no peace. I leave the scene in a rage and when I get to my building after 9:00 p.m., as another throng of drunk kids goes shoving past, I shout to the sky, "Fuck this!" That's when I am, once again, corrected.

"Watch your language!" he shouts. I turn to see a red-faced man walking with a woman pushing a stroller. They are blond, white, and blandly good-looking, twenty years younger than me, tall and lean, in crisp clothing and no masks. No one has ever scolded my language in New York, certainly not late at night in the East Village. This man, who I imagine hasn't been here for the past three months, who missed the ambulance sirens and the bodies in the streets, thinks he can shout at me for saying *fuck* in front of my home? All week, men like him have been correcting my behavior. What do they see—my queerness, my otherness, something they can't quite name? Does the BLM button on my chest trigger their revanchist rage? They have come back to find the city covered in *fuck*, overtaken by the minoritized subjects they revile, and they will not tolerate one more. Pumped on the empowerment of protest, I snap back, "Fuck you," and step to my door, key in hand. The man moves toward me, using his larger body to intimidate, but I am not intimidated. My body might be small, but it has survived, taking me through a plague.

It has outrun cops and held traffic. These days, it feels like a different body and it is not afraid of this man who has come to take my home, my sense of belonging, my transgender rage. He steps closer and screams, "There are *children* here!"

Let me slow down this hot moment to apply the analysis that will only come later. This man, terrified of losing power and territory, is trying to dominate me by invoking the Sacred Child, symbol of hetero-futurity, a variation on the old "what about the children" routine that's been used to suppress queers from the beginning of time. "Fuck the social order and the Child in whose name we're collectively terrorized," writes queer theorist Lee Edelman. Not a real child, the symbol of the Sacred Child is painted as innocent and pure, in need of protection. Poor children, children of color, and queer children cannot be the capital-C Child. We are not so protected. Maybe the button this man has pushed is my queer inner child, full of rage and wilderness, my trans child, tired of being policed, and maybe they are the one who, like a fury flying up from my depths, turns to the man and bellows, "I don't give a *fuck* about your children!" Dear Reader, it's not his *actual* children I don't give a fuck about. What I am pushing back against is his weaponizing of children as a way to hold on to his normative privilege, a brittle insistence that, at this moment, feels manipulative.

When I hear my voice, I am thunderous and wild, like my mother could be thunderous and wild, so the roaring *fuck* I unleash is a maternal *fuck*, tracing back through my matriarchal ancestors—Italian grandmother with her strong hands, great-aunties throwing scissors and knives, great-grandmother wielding a meat cleaver to fight off Irish gangs, great-unto great-grandmothers doing god knows what to survive the old peasant country's predations. Mitochondrial, abyssal, this *fuck* is fathoms deep, lifetimes of rage and frustration deep, guttural, from the gutter, covered in muck and motherfuck. I learned young how to wield this word, it was born into me, and it comes with claws. The man knows it, too. He freezes. I have spurned his Sacred Child, the object that carries the seed of his power into the future with a transfer of heritable wealth that ensures domination for generations. The man steps forward with clenched fists. When he tries to follow me inside, I close the door on his face and keep moving, my heart hot with lush defiance.

A QUEER LONGING
FOR RUINS AND MUD

Walking in New York on an autumn day in the early 1980s, the novelist Andrew Holleran asked his friends, "Why do gays love ruins?" They had just visited the Whitney Museum to see an artist's miniature replica of urban decay—warehouse, adult bookstore, seedy pool hall—and it reminded Holleran of the languishing West Side piers, where men met for unbridled sex. "Why do we love slums so much?" A friend answered cheekily, "One can hardly suck cock on Madison Avenue, darling." The friend went on to predict a totally renovated future, the crumbling shoreline "made pretty" by urban planners, downtown Manhattan's outlaw spaces beautified for the rich. "Ruins become decor, nostalgia for the mud," the friend continued. "We all want to escape; you escaped to the city. Would you ever have ended up in the ruins had you not been gay?" Holleran replied, "If I weren't gay, I don't think I'd be in the city at all." As their conversation concluded, they still could not answer the question, "Why do I feel a strange sense of freedom the moment I enter a decaying neighborhood?"

I keep asking myself the same question, especially now in this summer of plague, when so much of Manhattan looks like a pre-gentrified ruin, covered in graffiti, abandoned behind plywood, the sidewalks erupting with trash no one bothers to remove, streets hijacked by rats. I lean into it and stop to marvel, as if the trash and graffiti were flowers in a garden I've been allowed to enter. Why do I feel such freedom here? (Is it only relief from the tyranny of my domestic tidiness, trained into me by an Italian-American mother, those women known for their Catholic insistence on keeping all things "immaculate"? My mother's most enthusiastic compliment about my otherwise crummy apartment is always "You keep it so nice and clean!" Anything less would be *schifooz*. I might be disgusted by a sink full of dirty dishes, but I don't skeeve the dirty streets. Surely, there is more to this than just a revolt against the maternal. But is there ever?)

I first heard of "nostalgia for the mud" in the 1990s when Herbert Muschamp wrote about dirty old Times Square's transformation into a sanitized suburban shopping mall for tourists. He used the original French, *nostalgie de la boue*, defining it as "the sentimental attachment to decrepitude and sleaze" and called it "a venerable urban tradition." It's a queer tradition, too, an affect to which outsiders are inclined. Queer punk author Michelle Tea, also writing about Times Square, named it without naming it when she said, "We queers, artists, activists, intellectuals, misfits, know with the instinct of any migrating animal that we must go to the city to find ourselves, our lives, and our people," and those cities should ideally be "scruffy, scuzzy, cheap." In the dirty, spontaneous city, anything can happen. There is possibility in the ruins and queers need spaces of possibility.

Unfortunately, the expression "nostalgia for the mud" smells like slumming. I have been accused of being a "fetishist for filth" by the *New York Daily News*. It's hurled as an accusation, of course, but it is not inaccurate, and I sometimes worry about romanticizing the gutter from the safe distance of my relative privilege. Tom Wolfe might think so, though I am not nearly as privileged as the people he skewered in his 1970 essay "Radical Chic," in which he defined *nostalgie de la boue* as the "romanticizing of primitive souls" by New York aristocrats with servants and summer houses. This slumming sense of *nostalgie de la boue* goes back at least to D. H. Lawrence, who used it to describe Lady Chatterley's attraction to a working-class lover. When Sir Clifford admonishes his wife, he says, "you're not normal, you're not in your right senses. You're one of those half-insane, perverted women who must run after depravity, the *nostalgie de la boue.*" Lady Chatterley had not only gone slumming, she was also a sexually uncontrolled woman fallen from aristocracy. But slumming was not the original meaning of *nostalgie de la boue*, and in its origin I find a more generous way to think about the freedom I feel among the ruins.

First, however, *nostalgia*. Its meaning more recently reduced to sentimental longing for romanticized youth, or else enlisted in right-wing movements to restore the "greatness" of tradition, nostalgia was for centuries understood as a serious affliction. Named in 1688 by Swiss medical student Johannes Hofer, who constructed the word from the Greek *Nostos* (νόστος) for "return to the native land" and *Algos* (άλγος) for "suffering or grief," nostalgia, writes Helmut Illbruck, was "a new name for displacement, denoting not a sentimental longing but a deadly disease caught by and consuming those cut off from their homeland."

This might have been the understanding of nostalgia when French dramatist Émile Augier first coined the term *nostalgie de la boue* in his 1855 play *Le Mariage d'Olympe*, a rebuke to Alexandre Dumas's *Camille*. To Augier, Dumas's prostitute with a heart of gold was too redeemable. A defender of middle-class ideals and (in the words of one fan) a "constant enemy" of the prostitute, Augier worried that writers like Dumas were filling the young bourgeoisie with "romantic ideas of redemption through love" when, in his opinion, social-climbing courtesans were just greedy whores. In the play, men of society defend class borders, discussing the impossibility of a prostitute ever leading a life of purity. One says, "Put a duck on a lake among swans, and you'll see that he'll miss his pond and end up going back there." To which another exclaims, "*La nostalgie de la boue!*" The phrase, in the first English translation, is written as "Home-sickness for the mud." Let's be clear. The duck does not fetishize the mud. She does not look down on the mud. The mud is home for the duck and she, who will never be a swan, longs to return to that from which she has displaced herself. Of course, for any duck that tries to be a swan, it's complicated.

"Why do I feel a strange sense of freedom the moment I enter a decaying neighborhood?" The ruin is a marginal and stigmatized space, outside dominant culture. To take pleasure in ruins, wrote Henry James, "shows the note of perversity," what English writer Rose Macaulay called *Ruinenlust*, pointing to the erotic charge of the dissolute and disintegrating. And now we're back to queer negativity, the freedom in failure, the release of sexuality that stands to shatter the self, reflected in ruins both failed and fragmented, exempt from the injunction to *be productive*. The ruin is a queer body, out of bounds and out of order. For the queer who finds few mirrors in the dominant culture, to arrive in the shattered, muddy, unsettling city is to arrive, at last, in oneself.

I am, like Olympe the mud-loving duck, a class climber. I am also a gender climber, moving from less privilege (female) to more (male), from gender-nonconforming to gender-boring, from visibly queer to passably not. I've managed to shed the more obvious traces of my ethnicity and am sometimes taken for a WASP. Through this process of deracination, you might say I have gentrified myself. Displaced myself. These are gains that have made a challenging life easier, but they are also losses, and I sit uneasily with them, longing to reconnect with my origins, the queer body of ruins, the mud from which I come. It was that city, the rough and disorderly city, that first attracted me, and it is that city to which I am now returned.

NEW YORK FUCKIN CITY

When Occupy City Hall begins, I go into the mud. Literally. Led by the grassroots activist group VOCAL-NY, the occupiers claim a sliver of green at the northeast corner of City Hall Park on the night of June 23 to demand the city reduce its police budget by $1 billion and shift the money to social services. I bike down the next day to a bright, grassy hill covered with young people reclining under trees, on blankets and sleeping bags, reading Noam Chomsky's *On Anarchism* and *The Black Jacobins* by C. L. R. James. Homemade signs along the perimeter declare "Defund NYPD" and "Police: Born of Racism to Uphold Capitalism." Tables offer free sunscreen, hand sanitizer, and masks. Women hand out homemade vegan oatmeal chocolate chip cookies that taste like love, salty and sweet. I decide to spend the night.

At dusk, with a pillow, blanket, and yoga mat in a duffel bag, I find the park jammed, the crowd of occupiers spilling off the grass and onto paving stones where a band is playing funk and the air smells of weed, patchouli, and sage. I take a spot by the edge, next to a granite slab that marks a resting place for the remains of early New Yorkers buried on what became City Hall, excavated bones from eighteenth-century cemeteries for a military barracks, two prisons, an African burial ground, and a poorhouse for "disorderly persons, parents of bastard children, beg-

gars, servants running away or otherwise misbehaving themselves, tres-
passers, rogues, vagabonds." It seems like good company and I lie back
on my mat, gazing up at the gilded statue of *Civic Fame* atop the Manhattan Municipal Building. Few people know that the figure is modeled
on a real person, Audrey Munson, who posed for many statues around
town in the early 1900s. Known as the Venus of MacDougal Alley for
her bohemian sex appeal, Munson was sculpted and photographed by
well-known artists and became the first woman to appear fully nude in
American film. After her career ended in scandal, she attempted suicide
and fell into depression, committed to the St. Lawrence State Hospital for the Insane, where she spent the next sixty-five years and died,
unknown, at the age of 104, a longevity that feels like cruelty. As I recline
by the bones of ghosts, among restless freedom fighters, I think of deviant Audrey Munson, a liberated woman touching the sky before she was
taken down and caged. I bet she would join us if she could.

It's getting late as I wander through the wide-awake crowd, stepping
around bodies, sleeping bags and pillows, backpacks and pizza boxes,
where only the overnighters remain. I might be the oldest one here.
People are playing folk music on guitars like it's the Summer of Love,
including one young Black man I see all the time and think of as Bob
Dylan because he's obsessed with Bob Dylan. His name is Aaron and
he's singing "Hurricane," the story of Rubin Carter, a song for police
abolition. A hippie white girl hands out glowstick bracelets and I take a
purple one, wrap it around my wrist, and help myself to free pizza. A guy
called Officer Chris P. Bacon shows up in a police uniform and rubber
pig mask and goofs around, putting people in handcuffs. A girl says, "I'm
pro arson. I'm pro looting. I'm for all of it." The air is thick with spray
paint and Magic Marker fumes as people make art, writing cardboard
signs, including my favorite: "God is a Black trans woman from Yemen."
I get back to bed and stare up at the leaves, the night, and golden Audrey
Munson, police helicopters beating the sky into audible froth.

"This is a not a fucking picnic," a man shouts into a bullhorn, rousing us from rest and festivity. "This is an act of resistance!" In case we forget the purpose of our occupation, members of the Black-led activist collective Warriors in the Garden are here to remind us, coming through every hour in berets and camouflage pants to bang on cowbells and lead us in chants of "No justice, no peace," a slogan popularized after the 1986 killing of Michael Griffith, a young Black man beaten by a mob of white men in Howard Beach, Queens, chased into traffic, and struck by an oncoming car. "This is a no-cop zone," one Warrior shouts into her bullhorn. "Do not talk to police and, if you do, you're gonna have to deal with my Brooklyn ass." The Warriors lead protesters in a verbal bombardment against the troop of cops who have crept too close to our camp, heckling and berating them, a tactic that reminds me of mobbing, the counteroffensive survival technique employed by smaller birds, like blue jays, who harass larger, more dangerous birds, like hawks, until the hawks retreat. As a team, prey animals use mobbing to protect their community from predators. At City Hall, the tactic works and the cops retreat.

A young blond man, who I think of as Bathroom Guy, leads a final trip to the restroom. He's a queer Pied Piper, singing, "If you have to pee, if you have to poop, if you have to change your tampon, follow me!" We follow him like ducklings to a midnight McDonald's. Two of the kids in line are talking excitedly about the revolution in the earnest way that only young people can get away with. "I feel like during quarantine we were in the womb," one says, "and now we're being born." "Yeah," the other agrees, "you gotta be born to live." To which the first replies, "Deadass."

Around 2:00 in the morning I manage to fall into a light sleep that only lasts a couple of hours when I am shocked awake. Camped next to me, a guy named Lip is shouting, tripping over my legs, so I think I'm getting kicked. Everyone is scrambling and screaming. I feel a wet slash across my face and then another. We're getting pepper sprayed by cops. I grab my things in sleepy stupor, panicking, ready to run, when someone says, "It's just the sprinklers." The park's sprinkler system has activated, drenching us like stray dogs under a hose. My neighbors say it's a conspiracy, a way to get rid of us, and they might be right. They're chanting, "Fuck the Parks Department," as people build a wall of cardboard on the back fence of the park and duct-tape plastic cups over the sprinkler heads. When Lip loses his glasses, I find them in the sodden grass and hand them over as he jokes, "That's the first time cops made me wet." I'm sitting on a slope of mud, surrendering to a childlike feeling—remember when you used to plunk down in the dirt, commune with the bugs, the roots, the petrichor of rain-wet earth? Remember when you didn't care about getting dirty? I lay my head back, exhausted, feeling too old and also young. The sun is rising behind the Municipal Building, sparking golden Audrey to life. Volunteers go for coffee and I chat with my neighbors about the occupation, how it feels more promising than Occupy Wall Street. It's morning in Manhattan and we are hopeful. I pack my stuff, grab a coffee, and head home through the empty streets. My sprained ankle still hurts, but I can walk. It's getting better every day.

■ ■ ■

IN SOHO AND ALONG FIFTH AVENUE, ACROSS THE LOWER EAST SIDE and Greenwich Village, the *fuck*s are getting whitewashed from the streets. That glorious explosion of righteous anger is obliterated, covered with smarmy slogans that say "Be Nice" and "Good Vibes Only." I bristle. It's like being told to smile. On the plywood of a smashed 7-Eleven, I spot a woman chalking the word LOVE surrounded by hearts and flowers. People are so uncomfortable with anger—can't we just let it breathe? In Hell's Kitchen, someone has taken a Sharpie to cross out "Fuck You Yuppies." Another sign of revanchism?

Not once in my New York life have I bought a souvenir T-shirt on Canal Street, but now is the time. I'm the only one here, zipping my bike back and forth along what is usually a traffic-filled thoroughfare, bouncing up on the sidewalk where there are no pedestrians, searching the few lonely shops. Among sequined caps, Liberty crowns, and wind-up toy frogs swimming in buckets of water, I find the T-shirt I need: "New York Fuckin City." You can't take *fuck* away from me.

My aunt Ginny has a heartwarming story she likes to tell about my early childhood. When I was a toddler, sitting in the shopping cart she pushed through a grocery store, I noticed that a baby was crying nearby. "Baby crying," I said. My aunt responded in a sympathetic tone, "Yeah, baby crying." To which I gruffly replied, "Fuckin' kid." Throughout childhood, I continued to develop my cursing skills, following the lead of my mother, who *had a mouth on her*, the kind that delivered dazzling combinations of profanity, such as *motherfuckin motherless cunt*, and by the time I reached Catholic high school, I was a virtuoso. When Sister Rita caught me cursing up a storm, she said I had "the mouth of a fishmonger" and suggested that my mother would be embarrassed to hear it. She was right about the first part, but wrong about the second.

Studies have shown that people who curse often are more honest, genuine, and intelligent, with larger vocabularies and a more nuanced grasp of language. (I don't know if this is true, but it makes me feel better about my mouth.) They are also more resistant to pain. As Emma Byrne details in *Swearing Is Good for You*, cursing can reduce physical as well as social pain, and *fuck* provides the greatest relief. Social psychologists Michael C. Philipp and Laura Lombardo describe their study in which participants focused on a stressful memory of social exclusion. Those who swore while remembering reported less social pain than those who did not swear. *Fuck* is protective. Maybe that's why, over the next months, I will adorn myself in *fucks*, the word on T-shirts, hats, and pins, a profane armor, another feral return to my younger, muddier self, when I was a fuckin' kid and not the Sacred Child.

■ ■ ■

I DON'T SLEEP AT CITY HALL AGAIN—ONE NIGHT WRECKED MY BODY for a week—but I visit almost daily, before and after work, on lunch breaks and days off, sailing my bike through desolate SoHo and China-town, along Canal where vendors have returned in droves, Senegalese men selling knockoff handbags and playing djembe drums in the lush smoke of sidewalk barbecue. I can't wait to plunk down on City Hall's mud and be among its people. I go for free breakfast, a bagel and coffee from the food table, and then I sit, occupying a dirty plastic tarp on the northeast corner of the green space, next to a sheet painted with the words: "Shame on Bill de Blasio and All Underwriters of the Fascist Police State." Each day, the occupation tweets, "We need bodies," and once again, my body feels useful, a physical thing doing a physical thing, just being here, taking space. Sometimes, people I know walk by and join

Night on the hill, Occupy City Hall

me. Mostly, though, I am alone, quiet and mindful. The occupation has evolved to include a people's library, an arts and crafts center, a medic station, and a garden filled with mint. There are yoga and meditation sessions, teach-ins on police abolition, book discussions of *Golden Gulag*, and poetry readings. Cardboard signs proliferate, covering the trees, benches, fences—Abolish the Police, Justice for Layleen Polanco, Gentrification Is Violence—and when there's no room left for signs, graffiti blooms, spreading like colorful lichen across the paving stones, rising up the sides of subway entrances, spilling onto the sidewalk.

In nearby SoHo, an explosion of painted murals bursts onto the plywood of shattered luxury stores. There's a black panther, a Malcolm X, and a triumphant scene of looters breaking the windows of a Gucci store, guys with baseball bats, one kid popping a wheelie on his bike, led by a Black man standing atop a car, looking like Washington crossing the Delaware, strong and determined. I love the graffiti the way I love ruins, how the outlaw paint cracks open the facade of the slicked city, opening a gap through which other affects can come tumbling. There is so much life in the breaking.

Night after night, the sky bursts with the explosions of illegal fireworks. Like so much of the pandemic phenomena (white flights, protests, occupations), it's not just New York; throughout the month of June, the skies sparkle and boom over Oakland, Los Angeles, Boston, Chicago. Most of New York's fireworks are in Black neighborhoods across Brooklyn and people think it's gunfire, lighting up the Citizen app with false reports of shootings. Fireworks complaints surge by 4,000 percent, according to the *Post*, where one writer calls the pyrotechnics a "scourge" of the 1970s that will drive the "tax base" to the suburbs. While there are reasons to complain about fireworks—they're loud, they can hurt people and cause fires—the tenor of the collective complaint becomes racialized and dog-whistly, spiked with cries for "law and order."

In the mornings, the streets are littered with pyrotechnic refuse, spent Roman candles, quarter-stick blockbusters, cardboard boxes the size of twelve-packs called "cakes," wrapped in colorful packaging with pictures of wolves and eagles, names like Alpha Male, Migraine, Pulverizer. These are expensive products brought in from out of state, and some people suspect the phenomenon is a covert PSYOP campaign, a theory explained on Twitter by Son of Baldwin, the handle of author Robert Jones Jr., who writes, "this is part of a coordinated attack on Black and Brown communities by government forces; an attack meant to disorient and destabilize the #BlackLivesMatter movement." The goal, he says, is sleep deprivation and desensitization, to weaken the population for total urban warfare. It's a compelling argument. When *Vice* goes to Brooklyn to interview the people who've been blowing fireworks, they deny the PSYOP theory and talk about rage, joy, and revolution. "We want to be heard," they say. One young woman finds the fireworks beautiful, explaining, "The message is that we're gonna celebrate our independence. The real independence. The Fourth of July is something that was put on us, but it wasn't a day of freedom for everyone." This is about making a righteous noise. "You're not gonna sleep because we can't sleep. We're gonna keep you up, so you can feel what we feel."

■ ■ ■

JESUS HAS LANDED ON THE COVER OF THE *NEW YORK POST*. I FIND THIS out when I go to talk to him in Washington Square and a construction worker in an American flag mask and a hardhat covered in stickers ("Protected by 2nd Amendment") climbs into the fountain to get his autograph. Jesus, however, refuses to sign the *Post*. Our Lord and Savior is above autographs. The hardhat is disappointed but amused. He's never met anyone famous before, he says, showing me the paper's full-color photo of Jesus sitting in his pink armchair, barefoot, shirtless, and street-tanned, a dirty blanket wrapped around his waist like a sarong.

The headline: "Squat in God's Name?! 'Jesus' camps in middle of Wash. Square Park for *a month* . . . and city does nothing!" Admittedly, it is a forlorn sight, Jesus alone, abandoned by his flock, surrounded by trash, apple cores, cardboard boxes, and ruined books, his stuffed unicorn battered and muddy, the long-stemmed roses, once yellow and bright, gone dry and brown. Entropy devours everything. While the neoliberal city wants us to forget our mortality, to lose ourselves in the shiny and new, this boy has another story to tell. He's a messenger, sent on the dark wings of plague, and I want to take care of him, protect him, because I know, now that he's been exposed by the press, his day in the fountain will soon come to a violent end.

I call out, "Jesus!" I know his birth name, but what does a trans person care about birth names? I ask what he needs, and before he can answer, a man on Rollerblades shouts at me, "If you feed it, it will never go away! Don't feed it! The fountain is for everyone, not just this asshole!" Untroubled by the heckler, Jesus ambles over, walking with his self-possessed gait, his regal posture, and sits before me on the fountain's edge where he leisurely rolls a joint and tells me about God and goodness and light. When I ask how he came to be Jesus, he recalls a night in the rose garden of Brooklyn's Prospect Park, when he saw a flower "burning blue and that's not supposed to happen," so he knew a miracle was unfolding and everything inside him exploded in a rapture of joy and pain. "I came forth from the back of this mind. I was always there, but I couldn't come out." He was medicated against his will and the antipsychotics made him go "out of mind," an experience he describes as an excruciating loss of self.

In the Gospel of Matthew, in the Parable of the Sheep and the Goats, Jesus sorts human souls to his right (righteous sheep headed for Heaven) and his left (nasty goats bound for Hell). He tells those on his right, "I was hungry and you gave me food. I was thirsty and you gave me drink.

Jesus of Washington Square in his fountain

I was a stranger and you took me in. I was naked and you clothed me. I was sick and you visited me. I was in prison and you came to me." The righteous don't know what he's talking about. They have no memory of ever having done these things. Jesus explains, "As you did to one of the least of my brothers, you did to me." In my Catholic high school, dressed as the floozy Mary Magdalene type in a red feather boa, I played this scene in *Godspell* but can't remember if I played a sheep or a goat. Most of the time, the division isn't so simple.

Jesus of Washington Square is hungry so I give him food. We walk to a deli, where he orders French fries with mushrooms, a wedge of watermelon, and two packages of ramen noodles. Whatever he requests, I pay for, throwing in a marbled notebook and some pens for his scriptures. He invites me into the fountain, which he calls "the circle," but the sun is hot and I am tired. I tell him I'll be back, but when I return the next day, Jesus is gone. All of his belongings have been removed and the Parks Department has installed signs on barricades around the fountain that say NYC PARKS PERSONNEL ONLY. When I ask a park ranger what happened, she tells me Jesus exposed himself and the police took him to the psych ward for evaluation. This isn't the first time Jesus has gone naked, but now he's done it one day after the *Post* put him on their front page, broadcasting him to the world beyond the deviant little park, and he has to be controlled. Over three days, he'll be arrested three times. Forever Catholic, I think of Peter's three denials of Christ on the night of his arrest, before the rooster began to crow.

The second time Jesus of Washington Square is arrested, it's the day the upstart Queer Liberation March supersedes the traditional Heritage of Pride parade, which has become more conservative over the years, degenerating into homonormativity and rainbow capitalism, its bloated floats celebrating corporate dominance and investment banking. Last year, the two events competed side by side, but this year Pride has been canceled—you can't have a parade in a pandemic, but you can have a protest. In the heat of a blistering sun, I walk with friends from Foley Square to Washington Square in my "New York Fuckin City" T-shirt. The Queer Liberation March, dedicated in this, its second year, to Black Lives and Against Police Brutality, is a scrappy DIY procession without cops, corporations, or banks, conceived in the original, riotous, "not gay as in happy, but queer as in fuck you" spirit of Stonewall, when a bunch of street kids and Black and brown transgender folks fought the police, punching and smashing their way into a new world for all of us. Stonewall was a riot. In *The New Yorker*, Michael Schulman writes, "It's as if the COVID-19 meteor killed off a twelve-million-dollar dinosaur, and a smaller, more resourceful organism survived to fill the parade-size void." In the anarchic, righteously angry mood of the event, people wave signs that read: "Fuck Your Corporate Rainbows," "NYPD Suck My Dick," and "Eat the Rich." The march is a big, sexy gnashing of teeth and pumping of fists. As thousands of queers stream into Washington Square Park, I look to the empty fountain. Jesus should be here, a gay boy from small-town America, trying to be free in the open city. Tomorrow, he'll return, only to be arrested a third time, but not before the park erupts into riot.

As the queers dance in the street by the Washington Arch, cops rush in. In the chaos, from a distance, it's hard to say what triggers the attack. Two people were just arrested, allegedly for writing graffiti, and when the cops put them into a van, a crowd circles the vehicle, chanting "Let them go," trying to force a de-arrest. Police shove the protesters, pushing them to the ground, hitting them with batons, and pepper spraying them in the face. After a series of scuffles, the little riot burns out, the cops retreat, and the dance party resumes, a group of motley queers vogueing and twerking as a dark thunderstorm rolls in, drenches the city, and then clears, casting a double rainbow over the park. In the face of such signs and wonders, in the middle of an apocalypse, it is sometimes difficult not to imagine the hand of some divine providence saying, *I got you.*

Early the next morning, I get on my bike and return to the park to find blood-red paint splattered across the white marble of Stanford White's Roman triumphal arch. The statues of George Washington drip with gore. (Underneath, graffiti from weeks ago still reads: "Fuck12 since 1492.") Around the fountain, the graffitists have painted a mass crime scene with dozens of body outlines, each with a red splatter of gunshot at their heads and hearts. (Oddly, the same image was painted here in 1979, glimpsed in old photos, the past haunting the present.) The result is spectacular, a pointed rejoinder to police violence, and I feel the aliveness I felt after the riots of May, an internal pinball machine. Many people, including Donald Trump, feel differently—he tweets, "We are tracking down the two Anarchists who threw paint on the magnificent George Washington Statue in Manhattan," insisting they will spend ten years in prison—but this graffiti is nothing new. The arch has long provided a canvas for political slogans, especially during the 1970s and '80s, when it was spray painted and scrawled: *Down with Capitalism, Drums and Sexuality Are Subversive, Gay Is Good (Right On Baby)*. Vandalizing the arch is a New York tradition.

Later in the day, a worker in a cherry picker arrives to power-wash the red paint. At the same time, on the other side of the arch, Jesus has returned once more to the fountain and, once more, he is arrested. He lies naked on the fountainhead, facedown, holding tight to the metal grate while fifteen police officers, park rangers, and paramedics work to rip him away. When they fail to force him, they inject him with a sedative, cover him with a sheet, and strap him to a board. As they carry him to an ambulance, as he screams, "Assault! Assault!" a crowd of onlookers claps and cheers, as if the boy is not a boy, but a monster to be destroyed. The power-washer sends up silver mist. Red sluices down in rivers that stick to the shoes of the men who carry Jesus. Tomorrow, when the arch is white again, the NYPD will surround it with barricades and twelve cops to guard it day and night. The fountain, for too long, will remain empty.

. . .

AT CITY HALL, WITHIN THE SAME TWENTY-FOUR HOURS THAT THE
Washington Arch is bombed with red paint, a tsunami of graffiti floods
the facade of the Surrogate's Courthouse across from the park. *New York
in Its Infancy*, a sculpture depicting New York City as a woman dressed
in the crown of colonial rule, flanked by a Native American and a Dutch
settler, has been redecorated. The native and the settler are painted black
and the words NO JUSTICE cover New York's breast, spelled out in
safety-orange tape, like a warning. The rest of the stone facade is a riot
of ACAB and FTP, Cancel Rent, Lenape Lands, God Is Black, We
Will Win, Love, Anarchy, Oink, Pork, and We Need All Damn $6
Billion, a reference to the police budget, which is up for a vote tonight
in the city council.

Around 2:40 this morning, the *Post* will report, a teenager was taken
by the police for painting graffiti on the courthouse. At 5:00, riot cops
rushed in and started pushing and beating people with batons. In
between, there was dancing. When I wake to the news at 7:00, I get on
my bike and rush downtown, feeling a need to do something, but there
is nothing to do. The park is quiet. People are eating breakfast, reading
books, tidying their camps. The air has the hangdog feeling of aftermath.
I get a bagel and sit on my muddy slope, feeling useless. Then I see Lip,
the young man who camped beside me the night I slept in the park just
one week ago, though it feels like a lifetime. He's sitting alone on the
sidewalk and he's banged up, arm in a sling, elbow strapped to an ice
pack. He's quietly crying. I go to talk to him, reminding him of our night
with the sprinklers so he knows I'm a friend. I ask if he's okay. He's not
okay. He cries harder, telling me about the melee, the afterimage of a girl
getting trampled by cops, her leg broken, turned at a disturbing angle,
trapped under his own helpless body as cops dislocated his shoulder. The

helplessness is hard to bear. Lip keeps asking, "What happened to her? What happened to her?" He's been looking for her all morning, but she is nowhere, disappeared. Like a soldier shocked from battle, he dazedly repeats, "I couldn't do anything to help her." I reassure him, saying it isn't his fault, he did what he could, but he's carrying a heavy guilt and won't let go. "I pass for white," he says. "I've got a debt to pay." He tells me he was beaten in the legs and chest the other day because he can't stop throwing himself into the breach, because he's got a debt to pay and he's paying with his body. I ask him when will it be enough. I say it's okay to take a rest. He hangs his head and sobs, hard enough so his tears make dark stains on the concrete.

Tonight the city council will pass the budget with cuts to the police department falling short of $1 billion and without the transfer of money to social services that the occupation demanded. Mayor de Blasio will call it progress. Others will call it smoke and mirrors, a sleight of hand, "funny math." Down at City Hall, the mood shifts and the occupation begins to change shape. The original organizers step down. Others step up. What was Occupy City Hall becomes Abolition Park, a wilder, murkier zone of contention.

11.

QUEER TIME

The more time I spend riding in marches, blocking traffic, the more my bike becomes an extension of my protest, another limb of my body. I've started covering it in signs—queer political stickers and hot-pink spoke skins like the wheelie bikers have, reclaiming the dysphoric color of my misaligned childhood, mixing pink Sweet Thunder with black Thunder Road, a gender blend—as I also flag my body to make it legible to my people. For years I've been invisible, looking—not hyper-normal, but regular normal, nondescript, but now I'm covered in buttons and stickers like a teenager, like it's the '80s again, only this time I've got the trans flag and a decal on my helmet that says *Stealth*, white on red in Barbara Kruger's Futura Bold Oblique, because "stealth" is what you call a trans person who doesn't read as trans, because testosterone and respectability make my queerness invisible and I need these signs to unveil and connect me. In private moments, I wonder if this is all just some midlife crisis, a last grasp at youth before fifty, and then another part of me says: *Don't fall for it! The midlife crisis is just a heteronormative capitalist construct. Stay gold, Ponyboy!*

Pandemic time bends and lags, expanding as it falls back on itself in a churn that coughs up debris from the past and casts it forth into the present, a return of the lost that was not lost. "A thing which has not been understood inevitably reappears," said Freud; "like an unlaid ghost, it cannot rest until the mystery has been resolved and the spell broken." Instead of midlife crisis, we might think of it as midlife *recovery*, a necessary and pleasurable return to developmental tasks left unfinished in adolescence. Queers are loaded with incompletions, all the things we never got to do. As the pandemic days go slant, we slip into queer time, a strange temporality that Jack Halberstam describes as a departure from the "frames of bourgeois reproduction and family, longevity, risk/safety, and inheritance."

In the queer time of this plague, as schedules shatter and conspicuous consumption stalls, many have broken loose from what Elizabeth Freeman calls *chrononormativity*, "the use of time to organize individual human bodies toward maximum productivity." On this approved timeline, dictated by institutional forces, we know when we're supposed to have our first kiss, marriage and children, achieving adulthood buoyed by careers that move in straight lines, secured by the accumulation of wealth and property, and then retirement and death, which should not come too soon or else we have failed. For some of us, for me, the queer time of the pandemic is liberatory. Maybe it's because, from early life, queers are out of sync, running behind, not giving up toys, not kissing boys, not behaving like adults—almost every belated tomboy, dyke, and trans guy has the memory of watching their girl friends apply lipstick and move toward sex while we're still climbing trees. *Time to grow up*, our mothers insist. Should boyhood linger, it's *just a phase.* When we don't grow out of it, we become the left-behinds, stranded on the wrong side of chrononormativity's gap, a painful divide that also gives us distance from the dominant expectations. We're free to grow sideways. I had forgotten this.

• • •

ON THE FOURTH OF JULY, I JOIN A BLM RALLY IN WASHINGTON SQUARE to "Eradicate the System." These days, the radicals, skateboarders, artists, and eccentrics hang out on the sunstruck pavement around the fountain, while the normals stay on the grass, safely tucked behind fences, where they drink White Claw and work on their tans while the world burns. As the centered retreat to the margins and the marginal take the center, I feel our power growing. Now and then, the activists try to reach the picnickers—today the organizers lead us in a chant of "Fuck your picnic"—but nothing seems to penetrate their bubble. They don't know what they're missing. A white boy with a queer vibe squirts sanitizer into my hands, a gesture of care in the plague that is always with us, in the air we share and the surfaces we touch, reminding us that we are all connected. I rub the warm, astringent gel into my palms as a woman with an exuberant Afro offers me a cold bottle of water, heaven in summer heat. She's a water angel, like the snack angels and the sanitizer angels, and she's wearing a shirt decorated with hundred-dollar bills set on fire, because to hell with money when so much is freely flowing. I appreciate her. She appreciates me. At every action, I am cleansed, watered, and fed. It is elemental.

After the rally, I ride around to see the city on this day of independence. At Columbus Circle, the Revolutionary Communists, aka the Revcoms, are burning flags. At Union Square, BLM activists are burning sage. At City Hall, a white woman dressed as the Statue of Liberty is trying to convince a Black woman in a Re-Elect Trump shirt that he is not her man. When evening comes, I am back in Washington Square, which has turned into a party. There's a salsa band playing, all the musicians over sixty, one woman in silver eyeshadow drinking a tall boy of Coors as she hits a set of cowbells. People dance and spin. A guy who looks like a guy I could have known in childhood—an Italian cousin with greasy curls, sweaty baseball shirt, belly hanging out—walks by with a twelve-pack under his arm, calling, "Ice cold Bud Light one dollah!" I take one and it is cold and good. When the light begins to fall golden across the tree-tops, the fireworks start, bursts of radiance at every corner of the park, Roman candles and sparklers, bottle rockets shooting off at alarming angles, hissing into the trees and skittering at our feet. Skateboarders light up whistling fountains and, as the flares shoot and pop, the boys jump over, letting the sparks prick their bare legs, filling the air with gunpowder smoke and laughter.

■ ■ ■

ON MY DOORMAT, A LARGE, GREASY-GOLDEN RAT IS CURLED AS IF sleeping. Her dark, shining eyes are open and I can't tell if she's dead or dying, alive enough to dart into my apartment, so I close the door quick. I can't get out without stepping over the rat and I have no intention of doing that. She gives me the shivers. In twenty-six years, I've never seen a rat inside the building and this intrusion unnerves me. The exterminator will later tell me that, since the pandemic began, the desperate rats of New York have been leaving the subterranean zone to venture upward into buildings, into hallways and apartments, searching for food. This, he will say, is unusual behavior for rats.

After the building super sweeps her away, the memory of the rat clings. I feel infected. I worry about rats squeezing under the door, but this is irrational, the gap isn't big enough. For weeks, I will hesitate before opening my door, expecting to see her again. Why am I gendering this rat as female? She comes from underground, the chthonic mother-world with its earthy chaos of nature and instinct, the dark interior with its symbolic vaginality. She dwells in the urban unconscious, yet here she is, high above ground where she does not belong. She represents the city's disorder, which I appreciate but not on my doorstep. Careful what you wish for.

It's Jung who talks about chthonic mother-worlds, but I take Freud to Central Park, sit on a stone bench between Bethesda Fountain and the green-skinned lake, and read his account of the Rat Man, "Notes Upon a Case of Obsessional Neurosis." The patient recalls a method of Chinese punishment in which a pot of rats is strapped to a criminal's buttocks, forcing the rats to attempt escape by boring into the man's anus. The horrifying image stirred up the patient's anal erotism, writes Freud, and the rat symbolized money, the penis, the greedy oral aggression of children. As a child, the Rat Man had been "a nasty, dirty little wretch, who was apt to bite people when he was in a rage." Sex and aggression, the usual stuff, and the poor rat had to bear it all away. What does my rat hold for me? Right now, so much of New York feels like a return of the repressed, the chaotic, sexual, aggressive city pushing up from under. Historically, chaos has been depicted as feminine, diffuse, messy, and untamed, witchy Mother Nature with her wild storms and dark, lawless forests, feared and dominated by the order of masculinity. Is that why I call the rat "she"? Trans people tend to be haunted by our cast-off genders, the buried contours of our former bodies. Maybe the rat represents my own chaotic feminine, the part I had to subdue to exist as a man within the limits of a binary. Here she is, smashing windows and splashing graffiti, clambering up from underground to curl at my doorstep and say, "Don't forget me."

It's only a coincidence that 2020 is the year of the rat in the Chinese calendar. It's only a coincidence that when I leave Central Park with Freud's Rat Man in my bag, I bike past Scabby the Rat, the large inflatable rodent that unions park outside of buildings to protest the use of non-union workers. This Scabby is special. She's wearing a mask to protect her from COVID. In rat + mask, chaos meets order. Scabby will not be penetrated by the lawless virus. I try not to make too much of this. On Freud's couch, the Rat Man quoted one of the Apophthegms and Inter-

ludes in Nietzsche's *Beyond Good and Evil*: " 'I did this,' says my Memory.
'I cannot have done this,' says my Pride and remains inexorable. In the
end—Memory yields." However, the Rat Man insists, his memory has
not yielded. Is my rat a reminiscence, the sort hysterics suffer, a memory
that cannot be remembered and so it takes up residence in the body? I
keep feeling the rat's rattiness on my skin, the kind of itch you get when
close to filth, the sensation of crawling insects you know aren't there but
still you scratch.

• • •

I KEEP GOING TO CITY HALL, BUT IT'S NOT THE SAME. IN JUST A FEW
days, the people I knew from before are mostly gone and others have
taken their place. Large numbers of unhoused people, mostly men, have
moved in, seeking shelter under the slapdash jumble of tarps and tents
spread across the plaza. The subway entrance to City Hall Station has
been redecorated, renamed CHAZ Station for City Hall Autonomous
Zone, the sign amended, "No Pigs" and "If you see something, mind ya
business." (Confession: I can't bring myself to refer to cops as "pigs." It
makes me feel too much like a 1970s caricature of an urban guerrilla,
Patty Hearst when she was Tania in her peacoat and slouch hat, sawed-
off M1 carbine in her hands. I also have trouble with *comrade*, but I'm
trying.) The People's Library is still active, meals continue to be served,
and gardeners have set up a Free Seedlings cart with a sign that reads:
"Monoculture lawns are an act of colonial violence. You are on Lenape
Land!" But you can feel the degeneration. The new occupiers are suspi-
cious of outsiders, stopping people at ramshackle checkpoints, shouting
"no cameras!" Many of the unhoused people are unstable and don't sub-
scribe to the politics of Abolition Park, catcalling women and breaking
into fistfights. Activists move out of camp. Others arrive. Community
meetings splinter into arguments—white people are hogging the mic,
taking up too much space, or else they're too submissive, too debased—

one Black organizer shouts at another, "These white folks are not your slaves!" To which a white girl, on her knees, replies, "I'll do anything! Anything!"

Day after day, I watch the occupation lose air as it changes shape, working to accommodate the unhoused population, to provide mutual aid, health care and meals, trying to heal generations of trauma. The task is overwhelming. I volunteer as a clinical social worker at the Mental Rest Tent, but when I see what's required, and how little structural support is available, I chicken out after one day. I'm not proud of this. As a young social worker, I counseled homeless people, but it's been a long time since I've de-escalated an angry psychotic and I don't want to do it during an airborne plague. The other volunteers drop out, too, and soon the Mental Rest Tent succumbs to piles of empty pizza boxes and beer cans, a man who is probably not a clinical social worker nodding out in the therapist chair. On the ground, someone has spray-painted: RAT RULE.

The numbers of occupiers keep dwindling. The medic station departs, citing "lack of safety and consent," explaining in an Instagram post that medics "have been repeatedly assaulted physically, emotionally, and sexually." The People's Library reduces its hours, citing the "hostile and abusive enforcement of heteropatriarchal attitudes about safety and dominance, almost entirely by a small group of cismen towards others." The loose structure of the camp gets looser in a rapid unraveling. The cast-off mattresses left by the people fleeing New York travel here, washing up like detritus on a cluttered shore, and various bodies sprawl atop them. Library books lie scattered and torn, bloated with rainwater. The food donations come to a standstill. I find the Free Seedlings cart upended and smashed. When I run into Bathroom Guy, he says people are pissing and shitting behind the subway entrance because there's nowhere else to piss and shit, and he's trying to get Port-a-Potties brought in, but the cops keep stopping the Port-a-Potty delivery truck. He's trying to make it work, but the forces are against him. Just as I'm about to write off Abolition Park as a failure, one message, scrawled on the sidewalk in hot-pink spray paint, reminds me, "The Revolution Is Not Supposed to Be Pretty." An organizer named Desirae echoes this to the *Times*, saying, "It's not pretty all the time—and we're not just going to abandon it because it's not pretty right now. We're going to stay here through the ugly." I hope there's something else on the other side of ugly, but I find that Abolition Park is testing the limits of my queer love of ruins. When does good disorder tip into bad? How much mud can I tolerate?

When I meet the Joker of NYC for the first time, he's camped at the farthest end of the plaza, living under blue plastic tarps, the borders of his territory marked in spray paint with the warning, "Do not pass—Will shoot U—Jokers World." He sits on a folding chair, drinking a pint of Georgi vodka, shirtless and tattooed, in combat boots and hockey shin guards that look like dystopian armor. His mouth is a red-painted slash, like the Joker in the movies, with one eye made to look like a black eye and the other really bruised, covered in a dirty bandage. Around his neck is a spiked dog collar and a yellow plastic chain (taken from the closed subways, it's the accessory of choice for summer 2020). Joker is scary looking, but when he calls me over, I see he's warm and open. I listen as he explains his philosophy, "All Matter Matters," by which he means the earth, the rocks, the trees. "Without the trees," he says, "we couldn't breathe." Months from now, I'll be wearing his face on a shirt that says FREE THE JOKER, contributing to his legal fund, and marching beside him. We will call each other *brother* and say, "I love you." For now, I am cautiously captivated by his ruffian tenderness.

I keep going to Abolition Park, day after day, feeling less like an occupier and more like an observer, but the place still feeds me, even without food. When meals were plentiful, I loved being fed by the occupation. The food station volunteers, mostly young women (many discussions

The Joker of NYC

on the gender politics of who was doing the feeding), were bright and welcoming, offering me bagels, pizza, plates of beans and rice. Jessie Kindig, writing about her time as a volunteer, recalls, "My first favorite thing to do is to hand out bottled drinks to incoming protesters, because then I get to dance, and chant, and delight people by handing them free Gatorade." We were, on both sides of those tables, delighted. Humans are wired to equate food with love and, yes, I felt loved each time I had a meal at City Hall. It always felt like a surprising gift. I especially loved the free breakfast.

For a while in the murky 1970s, when my father was drinking heavily and not making money, we collected welfare. My family forgets this, laced as it is with class shame, but I remember the blocks of government cheese, orange bricks in cardboard boxes perfect for stashing bubblegum cards, and I remember free breakfast, the mornings I went to school in the gray of first light to sit with other embarrassed kids for bowls of Sugar Pops, staring sleepily at the single-serving container with its yellow cartoon cowboy. No one told me that our national free breakfast was inspired by the Black Panther Party's Breakfast for Children, a program attacked by the FBI and raided by police because free food threatens a system that depends on manufactured scarcity. Have I mentioned that the pandemic city is dotted with Community Fridges that we fill with food for anyone to take? The presence of such abundance, this unconditional giving, can interrupt our sense of scarcity. That alone is revolutionary.

At some point during Occupy City Hall, I made a donation of money that covered all my free meals and then some, wanting to expunge my debt, beyond the food, though that felt impossible. I've already taken from the movement more than I've given. How could I not? I'm one person and the movement is many. My friend Avgi tells me that's how it should be. "You are not taking *from* anyone," she says. "You are receiving. It's good for you, for all of us, to feel that some things are bigger than us.

Perhaps this asymmetry is what it means to be fed by a movement, taking more than one can possibly give back. And it's how relationships that really matter are built, through the incurring of debts that don't—which can't possibly—get paid off. To be preoccupied with paying it back can look like fairness, but it makes it transactional."

Whenever I start thinking it's time for the occupation to end, that it has slipped too far into disorder, I think about Stickers. Described in my notebook as "punk trans girl on skateboard in Chuck Taylors and a sweet smile, dirty elbows, tips of her hair dyed pink," she has the glow that some people have during pandemic time, a magnetic luminosity, radiance trailing her like a sparkling mist as she sails by on her board, tomboyish in skinned knees and bold attitude. She is eighteen years old, an unhoused resident of Abolition Park who told *Gothamist*, "I have never been so fucking full and felt so healthy and felt so supported. Anywhere I go outside of here I'm a fucking freak, being trans and skateboarding and wearing different clothes. I've had transphobic slurs thrown at me for being in public. But here the first thing I get asked is, 'What are your pronouns?'" When I see Stickers zipping by, beaming a joyful smile, I desperately want the dream of Abolition Park to work. Maybe, with enough time, it can become the utopia it's trying to be. But time is a gift that will not be given.

■ ■ ■

CENTRAL PARK IS GOING WILD AGAIN. LEFT ALONE, THE GRASS ALONG the Elm Mall has grown into a meadow, waist high, filled with birds and wildflowers, feathery seedheads glowing golden in the sun like wheat. On the surface of the lake, an overgrowth of duckweed has made a carpet so thick it looks like you could walk across the water. Everything has the aura of green expansion. Grass thrusts through the bricks around Bethesda Fountain and saplings break from cracks in the terrace, the sandstone furred with vegetal film, giving it a pleasantly post-apocalyptic look, the peace of a natural ruin. In the stillness, I wait for deer to come grazing. Inside the arcade, by the glazed ceiling tiles, a mob of sparrows has taken over, building nests on ledges and inside hanging lamps, littering the floor with so much yellow grass it looks purposeful, a sheet of hay on the floor of a barn, soft and shuffling underfoot. In the Before Time, the park had become, like everywhere else, so manicured and fussed over, no wild thing could ever get hold. But now the teams of mowers and trimmers have lapsed because of the plague—budget cuts, layoffs, and of course, the lack of tourists. There's a *why bother* feeling about the city. Who's here to impress? It's just us New Yorkers.

The Ramble, long a gay cruising spot, is full of used condoms, translucent alien flowers blooming in the shrubbery. Sexual activity spreads to the edges of the Lake and along the underbelly of the Bow Bridge, where tourists usually flock and brides pose for photos. Without them, other forms of life ferment. I am alone on the bridge, a rare experience that I stop to enjoy while it lasts. A couple of silver-haired men walk by, and one says, "The other day I saw two guys here, jerking each other off, while another guy watched." His companion replies, "That's just like old New York!"

The park looks the way it does in old movies, unbuttoned and lived-in, the kind of comfortable that makes you feel the opposite of how it feels in an upscale, overly controlled apartment where you're afraid to touch anything. In its sweet dishevelment, the park recalls the shabby unpretentiousness of 1970s New York movie interiors. Jane Fonda's apartment in *Klute* with its kitchen clutter and peeling bricks. The drab, dark-brown paint job of Talia Shire's Brooklyn place in *Windows*. Karen Allen's loft in *Cruising*, expansive and bright, but still half-assed, marked by grimy windowsills and crooked shades. Annie Hall's place with its bad plumbing and bugs. The office of Jill Clayburgh's psychoanalyst in *An Unmar-*

ried Woman, with crummy cushions on the floor, wrinkled rug, and dingy pillows. (The analyst was played by a real analyst, Dr. Penelope Russianoff, who, in a 1978 interview with the *Times*, called her Upper West Side penthouse "very seedy.") In these movies, I love catching the shadow of grime around a light switch. The mark of handprints at a door's edge will thrill me, a shitty sofa makes my day, and oh, the sight of paint on top of paint, the years clotted along a strip of molding! In Claudia Weill's *Girlfriends*, after frizzy-haired Susan Weinblatt loses her blonde roommate to marriage and a house in the country, she gives her apartment a sprucing up, painting over a hole in the wall without bothering to patch it first. In all these failures, I find liberation from the tyranny of domestic perfectionism, a gesture abolished from the sleek, aspirational, barely human interiors of today's cinematic urban fantasy, the one that says, "You will never achieve this slick catalog dream, but keep striving," a frosty space with nothing to remind us of our own mortality.

The sparrows in the Bethesda arcade are so numerous they make an impressive racket, loud enough to nearly drown out the music the classical guitarist plays, music he has played every day I've come since the start of lockdown. When he finishes a song, I ask about the birds. Are there really more than usual? "*Much* more birds," he says emphatically. Since the pandemic began, much more, and not just sparrows. Birds that normally stay on the water, or away in the trees, have ventured onto the terrace and into the arcade. More than once, a beautiful white shorebird has come to visit him, and he's never seen that happen in all his years of playing this spot. It's because the tourists have gone away, we agree. The absence of people permits the presence of birds. "I hope it can stay like this," the guitarist says, adding with a note of sadness that he knows it cannot. All the beautiful parts of this time will be taken from us.

■ ■ ■

EARLY THIS MORNING, WHEN THE SKY WAS DARK AND PEOPLE SLEPT in their tents, the NYPD raided Abolition Park with the precision of a military invasion. I woke to the Twitter video of riot cops advancing behind a wall of shields, shouting in unison, like a clone army, "Move back, move back, move back," as they rolled through camp, mowing down tents and tables. They grabbed a portrait of George Floyd, ripped it down, and marched over it in their boots, performing a spectral echo of his murder, the spark to this summer's blaze. People were screaming, stumbling back, shocked awake at 4:00 in the morning. "The hour when earth betrays us," the poet Wisława Szymborska calls it. "The hour of and-what-if-nothing-remains-after-us."

The timing does not feel random. Trump just threatened to send armed federal forces into New York, among other cities "run by liberal Demo- crats," if the governor and mayor didn't stop the activists. "I'm gonna do something," Trump warned, and within twenty-four hours, de Blasio made the decision to raid Abolition Park. A similar sequence happened around the vandalism of Washington Arch, and last month, too, when Trump threatened to send in the military. When he told several state governors to "dominate" the protesters, tweeting support of the Insur- rection Act, de Blasio and Cuomo announced the curfew along with a doubling of police on the streets.

I hurry downtown to find City Hall Park surrounded by barricades, reduced to a dead space, a nothing space. Everything is gone—the tables and tents, the library, furniture, art, and the people, Joker, Stick- ers, Bathroom Guy—everything that took weeks to evolve has been removed in hours, tossed into garbage trucks. Police stand guard while sanitation workers spray the ground with pressure washers loaded with sickly sweet, graffiti-removing toxins. Watery paint pours down the slope and pools at the curb, so much red, like the sloppy remains of a mass murder. That sounds melodramatic, but I am stunned, struck by the morning's violence and the sudden, total absence of life where there had been so much. You know when someone dies unexpectedly and people say, "But I just saw her and she was so alive"? Trying to make sense of the abrupt turn from something into nothing. For days, I will feel bereaved, as if grieving the death of a person I loved. The streets of the city take on a hollow look, all life drained away. Feeling lonely and lost, I keep returning to City Hall, like an elephant returning to the body of a deceased loved one, caressing it, committing it to memory, even as it disintegrates.

Many New Yorkers were profoundly disturbed by the occupation, the way they felt shaken and angered by the riots. How might we think about the intensity of their reaction? In its disorderly shape, the occupation deployed a Black, queer, feminist *fantasy* of violence that some could not bear. The graffiti spoke that fantasy, *fuck this, fuck that*, like the occupation's refusal to function the way capitalist systems do, refusing to be productive, profitable, hierarchical. Jack Halberstam, writing on the use of *imagined* violence in political protest, says it comes from what the poet June Jordan called "a place of rage," residing in a space of fantasy from which it has the potential to "challenge white powerful heterosexual masculinity and create a cultural coalition of postmodern terror," the kind that might not literally "burn it down," as protesters chant, but makes the fire of minority rage imaginable and intimidating, "because the power of fantasy is not to represent but to destabilize the real."

Most people struggle with the difference between fantasized and real violence. One's own unconscious rage can feel dangerous, just as symbols of rage can feel dangerous. When a person sees graffiti and other signs of disorder they might think of violent crime, a false conflation often exploited to fan the flames of fear in support of "law and order" policies that restrain Black, brown, and poor people. While the association is always framed as a fear of *external* violence, I suspect the sight of disorder stimulates *internal* violence—and here I use the word *violence* to mean intrapsychic conflict, the turbulence you feel when your inner boundaries are unsettled, cracked open. Disorder has no respect for boundaries. Stimulating our own internal chaos, it can lift Pandora's lid on thoughts and feelings we've kept unthought and unfelt. Why is this frightening to some and liberating to others? My thoughts go to the 1896 painting *Truth Coming Out of Her Well* by Jean-Léon Gérôme. A naked woman, enraged and howling, climbs out of a dark well holding a cat-o'-nine-tails, ready to beat the shit out of humanity for dumping her in the hole. She is a Cassandra, the scorned killjoy coming to avenge herself. She is suppressed anger breaking loose. At the sight of her, some feel distress while others feel relief. The relieved see ourselves, coming out of the dark at last.

■ ■ ■

AFTER THE RAID, ABOLITION PARK GOES MOBILE, STAGING A TWENTY-four-hour march. On the way to a guided meditation in Madison Square, Stickers is at the front of the crowd, rolling down Second Avenue on her skateboard. In the video footage, she looks relaxed, crossing Twenty-Fifth Street, when a silver minivan stops and a man in a T-shirt and cargo shorts jumps out and grabs her. She struggles, her board skittering out from underfoot, as more men pile on and tackle her to the ground. The men don't announce themselves as police and don't show any badges. No one knows what's happening until the other protesters move in to help and one of the men reveals a gun holstered to his belt. He puts his hand on it and screams, "Get back, get back, get back," stomping his feet like an angry bull. Bicycle cops rush in, ram their bikes into people's chests, and knock them to the ground as the men drag Stickers into the van and speed away. When the protesters continue to clamor in outrage, the bike cops shoot them with pepper spray.

Watching the video of the incident, minutes after it happens, I feel frightened, enraged, helpless. In Portland, Oregon, federal officers are snatching protesters off the streets and whisking them away in unmarked vans. Yesterday I saw a Black Hawk helicopter flying low, dark against the white summer sky, and wondered if Trump was doing the "something" he threatened to do. Is this what happened to Stickers, the glowing girl with the dirty elbows? She feels like family, a trans kid I want to protect, but can't. When I tell my therapist about the abduction, I break down sobbing, surprising myself with the intensity of my feeling, and he reminds me of my own vulnerability, my own trans body and the way it has felt fragile and unprotected in a world of grabbing hands.

The abduction, the tackling and shoving, the gun, the pepper spray, was all to arrest Stickers for the crime of writing graffiti. When the governor calls the arrest "disturbing" and "obnoxious," the president of the NYPD Detectives' Endowment Association replies, "What's 'obnoxious' is your unjustified criticism of those men and women who are holding this city together, and the only ones preventing its descent into lawlessness." In his statement, he deadnames Stickers, using her former male name, as he threatens, "A society that makes enemies of its police had better learn to make friends with its criminals." Stickers was caught on camera committing the crime of scribbling inside the panopticon of the Oculus—the word means "eye"—that sterile, white-on-white luxury shopping mall guarded by cops who stand outside Lacoste and L'Occitane with M16 assault rifles. Why is a trans girl with a Sharpie such a threat to law and order? And what, exactly, is being protected?

Like graffiti, trans people are disorderly. Our bodies disturb the gender binary and everything built on its presumed stability. Angela Davis recently said, "The trans community . . . has taught us how to challenge that which is totally accepted as normal." She was talking about the carceral system and the proposal to abolish it. "If it is possible to challenge the gender binary," she continued, "then we can certainly effectively resist prisons, and jails, and police." Right now, across the globe, trans people are cast as agitators and provocateurs, destroyers of the normal way of life. We have a malevolent agenda, says the opposition, and that agenda is to overturn reality itself. Of course the trans girl on her skateboard has to be deadnamed, miscast as a bad man, dragging the city into lawlessness. Trans people are a threat to normal.

12.

YOU WANTED THE 1970s,
YOU GOT THE 1970s

At the end of July, I find my way to family, the Stonewall Protest, a weekly march that rallies every Thursday evening outside the Stonewall Inn, site of the 1969 riots that launched the movement for queer rights. Organized by Black trans women, led by the activists Qween Jean and Joel Rivera,* the Stonewall Protest is dedicated to creating "a safe space for black anger, sadness, trauma, and joy." Rooted in the Black, brown, trans legacy of the Stonewall riots, in the spirit of Marsha P. Johnson and Sylvia Rivera, the protest attracts a multi-racial, multi-gender, and abundantly queer crowd. After losing Occupy, Stonewall becomes my home protest and I will ride with them as a frontline bike blocker nearly every week for the rest of 2020, through the winter, and into next year.

As summer spins into August, the city further unfurls, a flower opening wide to guzzle as much sunlight as it can before dark. The wild, joyful energy gains momentum in the heat, grooving on long bright days and breezy nights, swirling around the vortex of Washington Square. Young artists of color make pilgrimages to the Village, traveling from Harlem

---

* Rivera's first name will change to Joela over the course of this book as her gender expression shifts. Typically, I would only use a trans person's current name, but Rivera requested that I use both, and I honor that request.

and the Bronx, crossing the river from Brooklyn and Queens, to spread their drawings and paintings on the ground around the fountain. They tell me they've never done this before, it's their first time selling art, and they are eager to meet and be met by the bighearted crowd that has made the park into an alternative space for creativity. Some have traveled far, from places like Georgia and Texas, when New York was the coronavirus epicenter, because they felt compelled to come to the city, the way young artists have long been compelled, leaving home to sleep on the streets, free and queer.

One night on Christopher Street Pier 46, I meet Avery, who came from Atlanta this spring because he felt called. Slight and quick, with painted nails and a dark scruff on his chin, Avery identifies as a "multi-gendered, mixed race, multiple personality, bipolar hacker boy whose pronouns are whatever—he, she, they, or bitch." We sit and talk on the Astroturf lawn by a group of dancers practicing their ballroom moves, dipping and duckwalking with crisp expertise. Avery unpacks an assortment of objects from his bag: medical dictionary, postcards of Rockefeller Center ("because I like shiny things"), a set of measuring calipers to use as a weapon ("because knives get confiscated"), and a volumetric incentive spirometer with a ping-pong ball and a hose that Avery has to suck to measure his lung capacity. He just got out of the hospital and still wears the johnny gown and plastic bracelet. It wasn't COVID. He went to the emergency room from an orgy because a guy called Hot Pockets put him in a Russian suplex and broke his rib. He pulls up the johnny to show off his Versace underwear, black with the gold Greca border and head of Medusa, a pair he got from a rich guy, and "If I need money, I could take them off, wash them, and sell them." A man comes by with a cooler full of nutcrackers. I've been wanting to try the bootleg cocktail, rum mixed with mango, pineapple, coconut, served in plastic juice bottles with colorful caps, so I buy one, drink most of it, and give the rest to Avery. It's strong and makes the night feel sweetly tropical, as if the pier is an island and the Hudson River has transformed into a blue lagoon. Years ago, this pier was a cruising spot for outlaw gay sex, a celebrated ruin redeveloped and sanitized. In the daytime, it's taken over by gay and straight normals doing Pilates and pushing baby strollers. At night, however, the space recalls the legacy of the lost.

When the song changes, Avery pulls off his hospital johnny and joins the dancers, doing a routine that's not quite voguing, but has its own frenetic style. The dancers applaud politely before turning back to their practice, chanting, "Work this pussy, work this pussy," invoking the word that, like *cunt*, means femininity and strength in ballroom culture. Reclaimed from its femme-phobic violent uses, this is not the pussy of patriarchy, not the *grabbed* but the *grabbing*, a pussy like a fist. Spinning and dropping, the dancers spell it out with incantatory fervor, "P-U-double-S-Y," the word that has become a kind of genderqueer feminist symbol of this open and uncontainable city.

I say goodnight to Avery and ride to Washington Square where I run into Ezra, a young white man in a dirty white suit, long hair flowing out of a Panama hat as he strolls the park with a picture frame around his neck and a battered mannequin leg in his arms. He salvaged the leg from the SoHo looting, where he did a spontaneous piece of performance art, sitting in the broken glass on the sidewalk, a dollar bill taped over his mouth. When I ask about its meaning, he says it means whatever I want it to mean, and talks about how the city has felt more open since the pandemic began, how people, cut off from the things they're used to, now have the space to ask: "Who am I really?" It's all about the journey of self-unwinding.

Avery and Ezra both spent time sleeping at Abolition Park, where people built bonds that now hold them in the orbit of Washington Square. Cast out from City Hall, many have taken up residence here, camping in tents around abandoned NYU and commandeering a row of benches south of the fountain where they hang out, smoking weed and listening to music. Joker is their unofficial leader, dressed in clown makeup, a purple helmet, and an orange prison jumpsuit, arms and neck draped in lengths of chain from which a teddy bear hangs with a button pinned to its chest that says, "We're sorry our president is an idiot." There's Smokey, stoned and sweet, dressed in a lab coat with "Dr. Blunt" on the chest; Air, who gives Tarot readings while adorned in purple velvet and leafy vines; and an artist who builds a studio from cast-off furniture where women recline topless for him to smear paint into sloppy abstractions on their skin. Stickers is here, too, released from jail to ride her skateboard, marking up everything with the tag "Sad Tranny." And there's Phineas, a young, bearded artist who carries a staff and tells me, "I heard Patti Smith walked through the park and said it's just like 1968 in here. The way it used to be. This is a summer of awakening. If this summer was a Tarot card, it'd be the Page of Wands."

The performance artist Crackhead Barney appears, dressed in a hospital gown and rubber Trump mask. Her knees are scabby from crawling on

Crackhead Barney

concrete and her mask is filthy, its blonde hair gone screwy, pale pink rubber clashing with Crackhead Barney's dark skin. Playing a lunatic, she plops onto benches next to unsuspecting parkgoers and spreads her legs, exposing her underwear. If the person doesn't respond, Crackhead Barney grinds her pelvis, slowly, erotically, for maximum discomfort. If the person still doesn't respond, she takes a rubber baby doll and smashes it against the pavement until her victim runs away. Her performance is everything, a glorious and vulgar disruption, and I can't get enough of it. Months from now, I'll ask why she does what she does, and she'll say, "I'm trying to ruin contemporary culture, because it needs to be destroyed, like the Roman Empire."

In the dog days of August, naked people start appearing all over town. I hear about them on social media where grainy photos show the bare asses and blurred-out genitals of average-looking people walking around Manhattan in the nude. They wear shoes and socks, a wristwatch and a pandemic mask, but that's it. Sometimes they carry a briefcase or backpack, like they're headed to the office, like they're not naked at all. What brings this on? Is it the disinhibiting effect of plague, the absence of the hyper-normal gaze, the anonymity of the face mask? Naked people run through the streets of Defoe's *Journal of the Plague Year* in 1665, but they're all raving mad, singing and praying to the heavens, while today's naked people are businesslike and otherwise well behaved. Like a stargazer during a once-in-a-lifetime meteor shower, I am eager to witness this rare phenomenon. Every time I go out, I look for a nudist, but keep coming up empty.

■ ■ ■

"YOU WANTED THE 1970S, YOU GOT THE 1970S," A YOUNG MAN SAYS as a fight breaks out, the crowd swarming past the fountain. "You wanted old-school New York, you got old-school New York!" He's laughing behind a surgical mask, talking to his breakdancer friends. It's Saturday night in Washington Square Park, a party that the pandemic has permitted every Saturday night, where it's safe enough to breathe the outdoor air. As the celebration continues, one of the older dancers, a man my age, is overjoyed, almost in tears, exclaiming, "We're all outside because of the virus. This is how it should be. Everyone together. It hasn't been like this for twenty-five years!"

Each week, the b-boys and girls show up at dusk, traveling in a time machine from a United Colors of Benetton ad, but sweaty and stoned. With gaffers tape they secure a sheet of cardboard to the pavement and start windmilling, popping, locking, spinning on their heads. A guy named DJ Lee Rock brings an enormous, vintage Nippon boom box, working a look from hip-hop's past, so we keep saying, *What year is this?* He calls himself a 1980s enthusiast and historian, what some call a "retro," dressed in a Fila cap and Cazals, the oversized glasses favored by DMC of Run-DMC. (Also known as Gazelles, sometimes as Cazzies, the glasses were such a status symbol in the early 1980s, people with 20/20 vision wore the frames without lenses, thieves snatched them off faces, and some killed for them.) DJ Lee Rock cranks up the volume as the dancers spin, taking me back to 1984 when a group came to my little nothing town to teach us white kids how to breakdance in the school gym. I learned to spin on my back and moonwalk, but I excelled at King Tutting, moving my head from side to side like an owl. Appreciating my unbridled enthusiasm for the art, and because I surely looked ridiculous, the instructors bestowed on me the breakin' handle Daffy G. I was so excited to have a handle, I ran to the iron-on shop at the local mall and had DAFFY G spelled out in white velvet-flocked letters on a black sleeveless hoodie. I wore the hoodie to my dance classes until they were canceled after one kid broke her arm while diving into the Worm and the adults in charge decided that all this urban culture was too dangerous.

Rolling around the fountain, circling the park, the music keeps changing—here's a pair of tango dancers, here's ballet, salsa, swing, a graffiti-covered boom box playing Kriss Kross's "Jump" with its *wiggity-wiggity-wiggity-wack*. Next to the breakdancing spot, the main party is presided over by a crew of old-school DJs, Black men on the later end of middle age, come down from the Bronx, mopping their bald heads with towels as they spin funk from digital controllers and laptops. The crowd is multi-racial and multi-generational, New Yorkers old and new: punk-rock grandmas in leather and spikes, forty-something Puerto Rican couples in straw fedoras, young people in Afros and Angela Davis T-shirts, barefoot white hippie girls, brothers in durags, one albino guy in a 1984 Paradise Garage T-shirt, a brown boy in red nail polish and matching T-shirt that says "Pussy Builds Strong Bones," people grooving in wheelchairs, artists in paint-splattered overalls, women drinking cans of beer from paper bags, old men dancing with canes, a guy in an Adidas tracksuit and Jabbawockeez mask, and a shirtless, gray-bearded man in an American flag cowboy hat with a "Fuck George Bush" button pinned to the side. That's George Bush the *first*. What year is it? Women have started going braless, adding more 1970s liberation to the scene. Dance students and Broadway professionals come to party because there's nowhere else to go in the pandemic and they need to stretch their restless legs. I've stepped into the movie *Fame* and any minute now Irene Cara is going to show up in slouchy legwarmers and start boogying atop a yellow taxi, lighting up the sky like a flame.

Being in this crowd is the opposite of alienation. We look at one another. We see and are seen. Rich or poor, no one's trying to look rich, wielding consumer status to outshine the others. We come as we are. Everyone is scrappy, in T-shirts and shorts, a few splashes of street fashion (tie-dyed rainbow sweatpants, zebra-stripe high-tops, leopard-print hot pants), but no one's worrying about how they look because everyone looks like themselves. The air smells of weed and the musky spice of body odor. The pandemic has freed us from many things and one of those things is deodorant.

Saturday night in summer 2020

In this giddy New York mixture, one type is noticeably absent. Usually dominant and ubiquitous, there are no hyper-normals. Now and then, a stray group approaches, plain white kids all dressed the same, the girls with identical Michael Kors handbags, fresh sundresses and flat-ironed hair, pristine cloud-white sneakers; the boys in pressed Polo shirts and Nantucket reds—here's one actually wearing a COVID mask that says "Ohio," I'm not kidding, like he doesn't know the New York wisecrack, as in "Go back to Ohio," that flyover metonym for conformist America. They hover at a distance, gazing uneasily into the sweaty, sexy, happy crowd of New Yorkers. They are the minority now and don't know what to do with themselves. Visibly uncomfortable, they look at their phones all at once, tapping and scrolling like something more important is happening in their hands. Eventually, they give up and walk away.

Each Saturday night, I wear my New York Fuckin City shirt. It's my dance party shirt and it feels like a signature. I'm That Guy in the New

York Fuckin City Shirt. Inspired by the hippie girl at Occupy City Hall, I bring glowstick bracelets, crack them into light, and hand them out. Now I'm That Guy in the New York Fuckin City Shirt with Glowsticks. That's when I spot Jesus of Washington Square. He's free, back from the psych ward at last, dancing atop one of the decorated balustrades of the fountain, shirtless and rubbing his ass, tugging his shorts deep into the crack, putting on a show like a go-go boy. People are happy to see him. Supplicants, we approach to make our offerings. The guy before me holds up a can of beer, but Jesus turns it down. He doesn't want beer. I go next, reaching up with a luminous purple bracelet. Will Jesus take it? He gives me a benevolent smile, reaches down, and gently plucks the ring from my hand. He slips his hands into the front of his shorts and makes a show just for me, working inside the dark fabric to turn the bracelet into a glowing cock ring.

As I often do this summer, I forget to eat dinner, but a guy in a "Power to the People" T-shirt is handing out clementines and Cheez-Its, protest food, the snacks given away at marches, and maybe this party is a form of protest, too. As the breakdancers spin to James Brown's "Get Up, Get Into It, Get Involved," the air fills with the cleansing scent of citrus. Men come around selling drinks from coolers and I get a nutcracker, mango and rum. I'm almost fifty years old, in the middle of a pandemic, feeding myself Cheez-Its with bootleg booze, and it's alright. I talk to one of the guys from the DJ crew. He's maybe sixty, tall and Black, with an air of gravitas and a head shaved clean. We get into a conversation about community and rejoicing, the power of this party, and how music brings together people who would not have connected before. When he says, "Love you man," I hesitate—what is this? shouldn't love be scarce, rationed only to an intimate few?—then I remember that love, like joy, is not made to be a crumb, and I send it back, "Love you too."

In the park, there's so much beautiful *eye work*, sociologist Elijah Anderson's term for how we look at one another in the city. He noted that "whites tend not to 'hold' the eyes of a black person" in public space and "those who see themselves as more economically privileged", also withhold their gaze, pretending not to see others, *looking through*, "consigning their counterparts to a form of social oblivion." As New York became whiter and wealthier, it became more guarded—both whiteness and wealth are properties that need guarding. Now, with so many of the unseeing eyes gone away, we're looking at each other again—our eyes doing the emotional work above masks—nodding *yes, yes*, echoing back and forth this complicated thing about joy in a time of trouble, so hard to articulate yet so easily felt. In my everyday world, I don't find many people who understand this about 2020, but here in the streets, in the protests and dance parties, everyone gets it. We're gliding on another plane, where so much unfurls in the rhythm of strangers freely sharing affection in this summer of do-not-touch.

The fight—not last week's fight, but this week's fight—is between two women activists. They're arguing about abolition. Men try to hold them back, but the women won't be held. The argument escalates. One woman slams down her bullhorn and presses her chest to the other woman's chest. The air crackles with ferocity, and while it might look like someone's about to get punched, this is not violent rage, it is passionate love that quickly shifts, slipping into a dance fight, the women dropping down to twerk it out, frustration turning into laughter, hugging, and now everyone is joining the dance, including a stuffed white tiger someone won at Coney Island. The ballerinas, breakdancers, and skateboarders go on spinning, churning up more life. And then I get my wish. From the shadows behind the statue of Giuseppe Garibaldi, a naked person steps into view. She emerges fully nude, hands on hips, defiant and barefoot in the lamplight. Someone says, "Baby, baby, put on some *clothes*," but she's enjoying her nakedness and skips away, adding her delight to the larger delight. A skater boy rolls past in a Keith Haring T-shirt with a quote from 1980-whatever, because we're in the Pandemic Space-Time

Vortex and everything is changing, revisiting the past to break from its grip, the way you take a few steps back before making a forward leap. "Nothing is an end," says the shirt, "because it always can be a basis for something new and different."

■ ■ ■

THROUGHOUT THE SUMMER, THE MOVING TRUCKS NEVER STOP, always taking away, filling the streets again with cast-off mattresses. Some of the Leavers return, maybe for a weekend, and they are angry and distraught, like parents back from vacation to find the kids threw a bash and trashed the house. They worry about homeless people bringing everything down, plummeting property values, and the disappearance of the *tax base* (they don't say *white people*, but we know what they mean). Worried about losing the city that worked so well for them, they strike back. In this next phase of revanchism, they don't scream at us in bike lanes or scold us for saying "fuck," they write op-eds. Since the spring, newspapers have been declaring the death of New York, but in August, the *Post* turns up the volume, publishing a flood of New York Is Dead stories.

August 8: "NYC moms fleeing Upper West Side amid crime and chaos"! "I feel like NYC is disappearing so fast and no one's doing anything," says one. "There was no reason to leave before," says another. "Now, I'm done. I can leave tomorrow and never look back." *August 10: "The UWS is falling apart, and lefties seem too woke to care"!* A critic from the *National Review* makes a "return visit" to find Manhattan filled with homeless people and graffiti. Downtown is "morose, grim, broken" and those who stay are "masochists." *August 11: "A mad rush for the exits as New York City goes down the tubes"!* The owner of a moving company says, "People are fleeing the city in droves." *August 17: "New York City is dead forever"!* In the collective hysteria's climax, hedge-fund manager James Altucher declares New York totally and permanently dead. Maybe because it's so over the top, this piece triggers a defensive reaction. Jerry Seinfeld hits back with a *Times* op-ed calling Altucher a whimpering putz, asserting that the city will bounce back thanks to "all the real, tough New Yorkers who, unlike you, loved it and understood it, stayed and rebuilt it." The *Post* turns about and agrees with an op-ed that begins, "Drop dead, James Altucher." The man starts getting death threats on Twitter.

While the two sides think they're opposed, they want the same thing— the city as it was before the plague, clean, controlled, and profitable—a fact illustrated when a luxury developer prints Seinfeld's article on a billboard and hangs it from his Madison Avenue tower (where apartments go for $12 million and up). Many of us, however, don't want their city. We want to break from that cruel past and move forward into a more open city. There isn't much room for this opinion. When I write an op-ed about the energy and diversity on the streets, the *Times* rejects it, even though I've been the go-to guy for all your "New York Is Dead" needs. A few voices get through. In *The Atlantic*, Molly Jong-Fast writes, "If the coronavirus brings back some of the grit we've lost, I won't mind. I'm sure I'm not the only New Yorker who thinks it's about time for a reset anyway." At *The Guardian*, Arwa Mahdawi takes aim at the "worried wealthy," writing, "Build a big, beautiful wall around New York City and don't let any of the rich people who have fled to other pastures return." In their absence, the city will be reborn for misfits and minorities—"as a queer, mixed-race woman, New York is probably where I feel safest."

Trump supporters jump into this Battle for New York with a rally at City Hall. They erect a stage before a backdrop with a photoshopped image of Bill de Blasio in a Che Guevara T-shirt, holding the severed head of the Statue of Liberty, her neck dripping blood, below a banner that reads: "Don't give up the ship! Save Your Cities!" Local politicians wring their hands about socialism, shouting, "We're not going back to the 1970s and '80s! Keep America great!" They represent South Brooklyn and Staten

Island, land of my people, the Irish and Italian working class, ideological descendants of New York's nativists, the Bowery Boys, the Know Nothings, only now they're Catholics instead of anti-Catholics, unable to see the irony.

After the rally, I mingle with the lingering diehards, curious to see what they're about. Trumpers, Proud Boys, QAnons, they hold up hand-written signs outlining conspiracy theories: masks make us sick (they decrease oxygen intake and increase toxin inhalation), the virus is being exaggerated so the mayor can destroy the city and win reelection, the NYPD is running a pedophile sex-trafficking ring in cahoots with Child Protective Services. It's difficult to tell what's real. Everything's upside down and inside out. Like the Black people in MAGA gear, chanting, "Fuck Black Lives!" Like the white men who look like law-and-order types but want to abolish the police because "they get in the way of our Second Amendment rights." They scream at the cops, "Fuck you, you suck," shaking the metal barricades between them like they're ready to bust out of a cage. One hands me a flyer outlining Operation Backfire Insurrection, a plan to use former Green Berets to ambush Bill de Blasio and place him under arrest while he cries for his mother and shits his pants like a little baby. "It will be a surprise attack," the flyer reads. I don't take it seriously because no surprise attack is announced on flyers, but I am naive and don't yet understand the level of insurrection these people are capable of pulling off.

13.

MOVING OUT IN MOUNTAINS

It's the gasping, buzzing end of August, the final weekend of true summer, and the sidewalks are piled higher than ever with cast-off furniture. The exodus from New York has reached its frenzied peak. Along the streets of the East Village stand mountains of bed frames, mattresses and box springs, wardrobes, coffee tables, kitchen tables, armchairs and dining chairs, toasters, microwave ovens, pillows and potted plants, all of it looking new. These are not the well-worn furnishings of longtime New Yorkers; these belonged to the temporary people. All weekend, moving trucks and U-Haul vans fight for space on my block, jockeying back and forth, rear doors flung open as young men and women with toned, tanned bodies carry out the things they want to keep. A few white lamps, a pair of Starck ghost chairs, objects that barely exist.

I hear a sound from the abandoned apartment next door, but it's strangely subdued, not the Influencer's typical clamor. Is it her roommate, the heiress? (No, the heiress will never return. She outsources her departure as she outsourced her arrival, hiring a team of workers to pack her stuff and move it out.) I check the Influencer's Instagram and see she's posted a photo of herself in Tulum with a caption about how much she loves vacations. She's in Tulum, but she's also walking past my peephole, because she's really here, pretending not to be here, keeping a low profile. She has traveled from a high-risk state and is not quarantining the required fourteen days. She goes out for shopping and brunch, all while posting Instagram shots of herself posing in bikinis on silky blue beaches. "Another beautiful day in Tulum!" I consider reporting her to the Department of Health, but I can't snitch. She's leaving for good this time. Let her go. I watch her sell the furniture she bought last year. There goes the white desk, the white table, the white chairs. She says to the buyers, "I'll just get more later. My dad got me a furnished apartment that can be renewed every thirty days, so if the coronavirus sparks again, I can leave and go home and, like, come back to New York whenever." Easy come, easy go.

When she finally moves out, I watch her from the window, carrying her belongings to the white BMW where her father waits. The mirror comes down last, the one with "texture" that she uses for selfies. "Be careful," she tells her father as he fits it into the car. "That's the only valuable thing I own." By valuable, I understand, she does not mean expensive. The mirror hails from Ikea and sells for much less than her Gucci shoes and Yves Saint Laurent handbags. She must mean valuable in some other sense, as if it is close to her soul, the mirror a vessel for her self-image.

I take a photo of the Influencer about to drive away forever and then another of the car actually driving away. This feels shameful, but some part of me needs visual proof, something to look at later to remind myself that she is really gone, the way I took a photo of my father in his coffin, so I could look later and know: He's gone. (Child thought: He can't hurt me anymore. Adult thought: The tension is over. Psychoanalyst thought: The conflict never ends.) My father did not look back at me, but when I take the photo of the Influencer, she takes a photo of me. Sometimes the observer is also the observed, but in this case I am incidental. She is snapping a souvenir shot of the building and I happen to be at the window. Does she notice me? Years from now, when she looks back at her first apartment building, will she see me, or will I only be a blur behind the screen, a ghost of someone she never thought much about? She has already forgotten me, but I can't let go of her. Like the rat on my welcome mat, she lingers under my skin. Each time I go out, each time I return, my stomach clenches. What if she comes back?

After the Influencer leaves, my IBS flares for the first time since the pandemic began. I tell myself I am being ridiculous. What am I so afraid of? On the surface I feel relaxed and relieved, but my enteric nervous system has gone into a state of hyperarousal. I'm embarrassed that I can't psychoanalyze my way out of this. Maybe it's not knowing where the Influencer is, the way a predator possibly hiding in the tall grass can be more unsettling than a predator standing right in front of you. How do you defend yourself against the possibility of a tiger? I need to wade into the grass with a stick and slash it around, yelling, the way, when I first lived alone and entered my apartment at night, I would fling open the closet door and throw back the shower curtain, shouting "Ha!" at whatever intruder might be waiting to kill me. Is the tiger really gone? Can I relax? My stomach has not caught up with reality. This is how the relic of early trauma lives in the body, overreacting to every little thing that looks like a tiger, the color orange, the pattern of stripes, confusing nothing for Something.

On the streets, the multiplying mountains of furniture are so extreme, people in the East Village can't stop talking about them. On Facebook, they share photos and marvel, "That's a lot of furniture." We've never seen anything like this. Entire apartments are dumped as buildings empty. "Good riddance," the commenters say. "Don't let the door hit you on the way out." Each time a new mountain appears, the gleaners come to gather. Old-time East Villagers pick over the piles, selecting choice items, so everywhere you look, someone is walking along carrying a chair, a framed print, unwanted objects plucked from the heaps, wanted again. Homeless people construct homes from the mountains, rearranging the pieces into outdoor tableaux of indoor space, creating entire domestic environments on the sidewalks, complete with rugs, sofas, queen-size beds covered in luxurious duvets and feather pillows, side tables with lamps that plug into nothing, toasters with no toast.

Many of the cast-off items end up in sidewalk sales. We used to call them thieves' markets because the objects were stolen. When you got burglarized in the East Village, the police would tell you to check the thieves' markets where, if you were lucky, you could buy your own stuff back for a bargain. We shopped the markets regularly, furnishing our apartments with the stolen goods of our neighbors. Really, though, it wasn't all thievery; most of the items were gleaned from the garbage. The whole neighborhood, and much of the city, was one big flea market until, somewhere around the turn of the twenty-first century, the markets disappeared. Now they're back, only nothing is stolen.

On the corner, I stop to talk to Jay, who is selling some excellent furniture and framed art. A gleaner with a good eye, he has a flair for visual merchandising. We're talking about the sidewalk sales, how they existed and then didn't and now they exist again. Jay says, "No offense, but the, uh, people around here throw out a lot of perfectly good new stuff." By "no offense" and "the, uh, people," I figure Jay, who is Black, means white people with money. I do not take offense. But when I later put a lamp on the sidewalk because its switch broke and, while I Krazy-Glued it back together months ago, I'm worried it'll eventually break again, so why bother, and besides, the lamp is fifteen years old at least, I feel a splinter of guilt. My mother, born in poverty during the Great Depression, taught me to be thrifty, to use a thing until it perished. I patch my pants, darn my socks, and won't start a new bar of soap until the old one has turned into a flinty, transparent sliver. I find virtue in the act of holding on to an object long after it has passed into brokenness. Sometimes I feel bad for the thing, *pathetic fallacy* bad, as if a bar of soap could suffer the unfulfillment of its usefulness should it be tossed in the garbage too soon.

It's exciting to see the sidewalk markets back on the streets, blankets covered in the promise of good junk, and the sight triggers a familial pleasure. Growing up with my mother, we did some gleaning of our own, foraging the town dump and going trash picking on Saturdays, the day for the best sidewalk hauls. I can still feel the thrill of hearing her say, "Wanna go trash pickin'?" Mostly, she was a fan of yard sales. Every weekend, early in the morning, she'd scour *The Pennysaver* and go yard-saling, a verb filled with the electricity of adventure. She'd return with her haul, holding jewelry and vases up to the light, squinting at their undersides. *Can you see that mark? What does it say?* With my young eyes, I'd proudly decipher the tiny stamp of letters and numbers. *Oh, that's worth something*, she'd say, sure she'd finally found the right sort of treasure, the one that would reward the superior intelligence of her thrifty discernment. How many times have I heard my mother recount the tale of a bargain? *Do you know what this is worth? In the store it goes for twenty bucks, but I got it for nothing. The price tag is still on. They were practically giving it away.* And her favorite: *The woman didn't know what she had.* Is there anything better than a seller too ignorant to know the value of the item she's selling? *I got it for pennies.* Always the climax of the story came when my mother approached the seller, asked the price, and received the magic words, "Oh, just give me a quarter." *A quarter, the woman says. A quarter! Can you believe it? I practically stole it!* Practically stealing was the absolute best, better than real stealing because you couldn't be punished for it. You could only be rewarded.

It's Sunday night and I take a short walk, past the mountains of furniture, through the quiet neighborhood. By a fresh unpicked pile, I consider a lamp, but this is not the lamp I need. As I approach my building, I look up to see the lights are on inside the Influencer's apartment. Has she come back? No, she must have left them on by mistake. *She's not there*, I tell my quaking gut. And she isn't. But what is it about her that gets deep under my skin? She's irritating, okay, but she's a minor player in my life, so what gives? I realize it's not this particular Influencer alone that I am grappling with. It's what she represents, the way she embodies hyper-normativity so perfectly, so mechanically, as if she's been designed, cast in plastic—and I see: It's that Shirley Temple doll again, the thing that the world tried to force me to be, the consumer product of the de-subjectified self come back to haunt me. She's the return of the irrepressible. America's Little Darling.

In the morning, a garbage truck rumbles on my street as the driver tosses furniture into its hopper. In go the tables and chairs, the dressers, lamps, and beds that the New People left behind. The man pulls a lever and the packer blade grabs the waste, pulls it into the truck's belly, and crushes it, wood popping like fireworks. The man enjoys his labor. The air is sweet and cool with almost-September and it's a good day, the man's body says, moving back and forth, arms and legs light with muscle and groove. The truck's stereo is turned up loud, playing the "Theme from *Shaft*," Isaac Hayes, 1971. It's the music of another New York, one that could be returning, for better or worse. Probably both. But this moment is good, gritty New York joy, music filling the sky above my street with hi-hat sizzle and the wacka-wacka of electric guitar contorted into funk. *Who's the black private dick that's a sex machine to all the chicks? Shaft!* The man tosses another table, another chair, flips the lever, crunch and crack. *You're damn right.* It's hard to resist the symbolism, the new city thrown into the teeth of the old, chewed up and swallowed whole to the sound of the 1970s, *bow-chicka-bow-wow*, dirty old Times Square and *I'm walking here*, all the stuff that's gone and can't come back, and yet. We keep turning and turning in a widening gyre.

PART FOUR

14.

I WOULD PREFER NOT TO

The Metropolitan Museum of Art reopens with temperature checks at the door. No one's here. It's a dream come true, a Met for New Yorkers. That means no crowds fighting for photos in front of Monet's water lilies, dueling selfie sticks whipping the air, and no bored suburban teens in stagnant herds, staring into screens. The only people are the ones who really want to be here, and the space feels like an exquisite gift. "Often I am permitted to return to a meadow," wrote the poet Robert Duncan, "as if it were a given property of the mind." Today, the Met is my meadow and I am permitted to return after a long banishment—for years I stayed away because over-tourism made it unbearable. Now, as I climb the wide, empty staircase of the Great Hall, I have to fight back tears, a tangle of joy, relief, and sadness for the lost years, all the hours I could not receive the pleasure of this place.

Without crowds to fight, I can breathe and think, letting my eyes lead me through this field without aim, past the water lilies, Cezanne's apples and pears, Pollock's frenetic splatter, but there is one painting that forever compels me. In the winter of 1997, when I first saw *Jeanne d'Arc écoutant les Voix* (1879), Jules Bastien-LePage's arresting portrait of Joan of Arc receiving her calling, I wrote in my diary:

She is standing in her parents' garden, wearing the clothes of a peasant girl, bare feet smeared with mud. Behind her, the bodies of her "voices" float in the air, trimmed in gold, almost invisible. St. Michael, in his golden armor, holds out a sword for Joan to take. She can feel, but cannot see him. Gazing at a point in the distance, outside the canvas, she is hearing her voices for the first time. Until now, she has been a humble girl, milking cows and planting vegetables. As if she could know the difficult path her life will take, she reaches out for something solid, but grasps only a few tender leaves on the tree under which she stands. She looks like a girl about to collapse, to fall headfirst out of the canvas and onto the polished wood floor of the Metropolitan Museum. But she doesn't fall. She stays standing, day after day, suspended in this dazzling moment of epiphany.

I was early in my own gender transition at the time and became obsessed with the painting, going back to the Met's library to research its history, where I learned that Bastien-LePage modeled his Joan after the hysterics, the *melancolie cataleptiques*, in the clinic of the Salpêtrière, lending her that dazed, somnambulant look. Bastien-LePage was interested in hypnosis and tried to use painting to exert a hypnotic effect on the viewer. He was successful. Each time I revisited Joan, I could not take my eyes off her. I went back again and again, meditating on her wild genderqueer life, for which she was burned at the stake. Had she lived fully as male like the "holy transvestites"—St. Pelagius, who wore men's clothes and became a monk, or St. Uncumber, blessed by God with the gift of a beard—she might have been spared, but Joan's crime was a nonbinary one. Her judges must have ignored the words of Jesus when he told his disciples in the apocryphal Gospel of Thomas that you enter the kingdom "when you make male and female into a single one, so that the male will not be male nor the female be female." Joan lived that contradiction, and the world can be terribly unforgiving of contradiction.

In the silent hall, I sit on the bench in front of Joan, by a sign that tells me to maintain six feet of social distance. There is no one here to distance from. A few people walk past now and then, but not enough to trouble the view. I have yet again fallen through time, reconnecting to the person I was, a newly fashioned man who saw in this painting his own jolt of self-knowledge, that moment when, called to an unknown future, you are struck by both the joy of possibility and the pain of loss. By depicting the moment of crux, when the voices come to tell Joan she must leave behind the girl she was never meant to be, Bastien-LePage painted an accidental portrait of transgender emergence.

It is also a portrait haunted by hysteria, a malady that many trans and queer people know something about. Behind Joan's stunned, blue-eyed expression are the shadows of the hysterics at the Salpêtrière hospital for women, studied by Jean-Martin Charcot, the French neurologist who helped lead Freud to the psychic underpinnings of hysterical neurosis. The women were photographed in the throes of their madness, images published in the *Iconographie Photographique de la Salpêtrière*, a collection of grimaces, contortions, ecstasies, *attitudes passionnelles*, hysterical winks, supplications, crucifixion poses. (In Georges Didi-Huberman's *Invention of Hysteria*, he notes that the rate of cure at the Salpêtrière was low and many women died of dubious causes, such as masturbation, debauchery, joy, "bad reading habits," and nostalgia.) Charcot's most famous patient was Augustine, a teenager suffering from profound sexual trauma. She stayed at the Salpêtrière for several years, photographed, probed, provoked, and treated with hypnosis, the basis for what became psychoanalysis. Her condition improved and then relapsed. She was put in straitjackets and padded cells, from which she attempted multiple escapes. Finally, in 1880, she succeeded—by disguising herself as a man.

Bastien-LePage painted Joan in 1879. Is Augustine the ghost behind her luminous face? Augustine in composite, in delirious poses of supplication and ecstasy, getting ready to change and escape. As I sit before Joan, in the quiet of the museum, in the middle of the plague, I am hypnotized, as Bastien-LePage wanted us to be, as Augustine was hypnotized, and I drift in reverie through layers of history, the melancholies of the body, gender and loss, transgression and liberation, making contact with an expansive awareness that can never be reached in the clamor of an unconscious crowd.

• • •

IN WASHINGTON SQUARE PARK, I RUN INTO AVERY, THE BOHEMIAN traveler I met on the pier. He rolls a joint and tells me he's moved into a hotel and I'm welcome to visit him any time. I feel a pang of self-protection. Many of the people in the park have rap sheets, mostly petty larceny, drugs, possession of a weapon, which usually means a knife for protection. I carried a knife when I first came to the city, a Gerber Gator that's small but looks serious with a clip point and a serrated edge, a gift from my friend Danny, a dreadlocked Mexican poet who'd been a bodyguard for a drug dealer, so he knew about these things. He taught me how to flick it open with one hand, kick an assailant in the crotch, and then plunge the knife in the back of the neck, a more aggressive choreography than I could ever muster. I held the Gator in my jacket pocket, worrying the grip with my thumb, whenever I walked a desolate East Village street, sound of footsteps quickening behind me.

Sometimes I wonder what could happen if all this freedom takes a hard turn, the way the good-hippie sixties turned into the bad-hippie seventies. Even as the city rides along with a disturbing nationwide wave of homicides, overall crime in New York has dropped to a record low this year. I feel a tremor of uncertainty and ask myself: What is this relic of fear? Is it my whiteness, my hard-won class status, my own normativity anxiously guarding what could be lost? Sitting with Avery, I imagine smoking together, hanging out with him and his friends, and then I recall the middle-aged man who went drinking with teenagers in Central Park in 1997, when the kids decided to kill him. They slit his throat, disemboweled him, and pushed him into the Lake, rocks stuffed in his belly to make him sink. The girl killer, daughter of uptown millionaires, became known as the Baby-Faced Butcher while her boyfriend, who did most of the work, was described as an altar boy. They were fifteen years old. I remember the murder, the scene of the disembowelment staying with me—that word in news reports, over and over, *disemboweled, disemboweled*. At forty-four, the man was too old to be hanging out with teenagers. I judged him then, when I was in my twenties, much closer to fifteen than I am today, but now I understand, how the man was trying to recapture his vanished youth when the source of his rejuvenation pulled out a knife and put an end to that bad idea.

■ ■ ■

A NEW PIECE OF GRAFFITI APPEARS ON THE STREETS, THE STENCIL of a cartoon cat, grinning as he sprints in a flurry of stars above the word *libera*. The cat is Julius the Cat, a Walt Disney creation from 1922. Born before Mickey Mouse, Julius is the urtext, the primordial body. The Spanish word *libera*, the Internet informs me, is the present form of *liberar* in third-person singular. *He liberates*. It's also the feminine form of the Latin *liber*, free and unrestricted, and the Roman goddess Libera, the free one, patron of the common folk, identified with Persephone, goddess of the underworld. There's that chthonic again, death and rebirth, that which emerges from the subterranean to push forth a new crop. I don't know what Julius the Cat means for this moment, I only know he comes from the past with a message about liberation, a ghost returning to force a new flowering. Also, he looks like he's up to something criminal. Captivated by Libera Cat, I look for him everywhere, but he only appears in three spots around the East Village. I pass by regularly just to get a dose of his fizzy emotional lift.

It doesn't take long for one of the cats to get buffed, half covered in black paint and then a large tag in lemony bubble letters. There are only two Libera Cats left, and the loss sends me into a fantasy of getting him tattooed on my arm where I can preserve him forever. I haven't had a new tattoo in a long time. I got my first one the minute I turned eighteen, before tattoos were common, so having one meant you were outside the mainstream, willing to mark yourself as irregular, and it made me feel tough and proud. The idea of getting one now feels like more spiraling through queer time, backward to my earlier self. I don't get the tattoo, but I do think about ways to put Libera Cat on a T-shirt. I want to carry him with me, a giddy, hightailing symbol of my fugitivity.

· · ·

I KEEP THINKING ABOUT THE BABY-FACED BUTCHER AND GO LOOKING for the pavilion on Central Park Lake where she and her boyfriend disemboweled that man in 1997, the same year I first saw *Jeanne d'Arc écoutant les Voix*. I stop at a pavilion that probably isn't the one, at a spot called Hernshead Cove. It is occupied by a man and woman, seated more than six feet apart, engaged in conversation about the future of pandemic New York. The man is maybe sixty, with a gray beard and large plugs in his stretched earlobes, an aged punk, while the woman is a typical Upper West Sider in her seventies, the sort of lefty, Jewish, silver-haired woman you used to see at Lincoln Plaza Cinemas, taking in the latest Woody Allen film. On the subject of New York's future, they agree: Rents will go down and crime will rise.

"The New York of Charles Bronson," the man says, meaning the criminal horrors of *Death Wish*, "is coming back. But the artist kids are going to come back, too, and they're going to make something really fantastic here. Danger and risk are great when you're young. Not so great when you're old." On cue, a large rat crawls from the rocks by the shoreline and sits in a patch of shade beneath the woman's bench as she talks about leaving, how she was considering Vermont, which is both bucolic and politically progressive, but then she read that cautionary tale in the *West Side Rag* about another neighborhood woman who "did the unthinkable." She gave up her rent-stabilized apartment to move to Vermont. "Clearly," the woman said in the *Rag*, "I was losing my mind. I had COVID brain." It didn't work out. The woman became extremely bored. There were *no people* in Vermont and *nothing to do.* She got tired of all the fresh air, drying her laundry on a bucolic clothesline, and she missed Central Park—which, in my opinion, is better than any natural kind of nature because you can't get lost or mauled by a bear, and you can always leave to get a slice of pizza.

While the conversation interests me, this is not the murder pavilion, so I move along, down the path through the wisteria arbor where a barber is giving COVID-safe outdoor haircuts and, further down, a man plays Simon and Garfunkel's "Scarborough Fair" on an erhu, the slender Chinese violin. I find the right pavilion, sure it's the right one because it looks exactly like the crime-scene photo from 1997, the one where a young couple goes rowing by, sun on their faces, while a detective seals evidence into a Ziploc bag. I take a seat and try to imagine the murder, but it's difficult because the sunlight is soft with clouds and the air is temperate, the surface of the Lake dotted with turtles. An older man comes, removes his shirt and shoes, and sits in the sun on the other side of the pavilion. I open a book, *In Defense of Looting* by Vicky Osterweil, and the man asks what I'm reading because, in the plague, we talk to strangers more than before. He's white and boomer-age and I don't want to get into an argument about looting, a subject that tends to trigger people, so I say, "It's about looting," dropping the defense part, but the man surprises me when he replies, "Oh, some pro-Capitalist argument against the radical redistribution of wealth in corporate America?" He's a nonsectarian leftist, he tells me, and as I slip into my comfortable role of active listener, he tells me more.

When he says he's being tortured by a neighbor, a young tech genius from "the generation created by corporate America to be autistic sociopaths," I'm all ears. The neighbor makes strange noises that keep the man up at night. But it gets worse, he says, do I really want to hear this? I really do. I am fascinated by the New York story of being tortured by neighbors. "Nobody believes me," he says, "but I'll tell *you*." The neighbor is watching him, he says, with tiny cameras and recording devices. The neighbor sends surveillance drones, disguised as insects, through holes in the man's window screens. The neighbor is monitoring the man's heartbeat. The neighbor has top-secret electromagnetic devices that project holographic images through the walls and into the man's apartment. I ask, "What kinds of images?" The man doesn't say and I am left to imagine as, beyond the trees, the Chinese violinist, having tired of "Scarborough Fair," is playing the "Love Theme from *The Godfather*." I tell the man that his situation with the neighbor sounds like torture. "It must be driving you crazy," I say, instead of saying he is crazy, which he probably hears enough already. He says he copes as best he can. He has a rent-stabilized lease, so he can't leave. (He's not crazy like the woman who fled to Vermont.) He prays the neighbor will move away. I am personally familiar with this prayer and begin to wonder if the nonsectarian leftist is the Ghost of Christmas Yet to Come, visiting me in this haunted place to point a finger toward my own future in which I hold tight to my rent-stabilized apartment even as I am driven mad by a neighbor, convinced that the walls have become porous, the boundaries between inside and outside peppered with holes. It could happen to anyone.

"Only part of us is sane," wrote Rebecca West. "Only part of us loves pleasure and the longer day of happiness," while "The other half of us is nearly mad. It prefers the disagreeable to the agreeable, loves pain and its darker night despair. . . . Our bright natures fight in us with this yeasty darkness, and neither part is commonly quite victorious, for we are divided against ourselves and will not let either part be destroyed."

Maybe this man, this ghost of my future, is here to tell me to move to Vermont. (Or out of the East Village at least.) Before it's too late. But I am not listening. Beyond the trees, the Chinese violinist takes another lap around Scarborough Fair, and for the rest of the day, I will not be able to stop repeating, in my head, the list of herbs: parsley, sage, rosemary, and thyme.

■ ■ ■

WEEKS AFTER MY FIRST SIGHTING OF LIBERA CAT, A GROUP OF YOUNG men spread DIY clothing on the ground in front of the fountain in Washington Square. The boys are punk or skateboard or some new genre of alternative youth I'm not familiar with, their hair in locs and buzz cuts, all pink nail polish, moon boots and safety pins, multi-racial and puppy-sweet. They sit on the ground with needles and thread, sewing their exuberant street fashions, reclaimed clothing covered in patchwork and spray paint. When I roll up on my bike, I spot Libera Cat and swoon to see his giddy shape splashed across T-shirts. This is the weird magic of pandemic time, where I'll see a person or an object and then I'll see them again, and again, in one part of town and then another, because we're all connected by the same invisible strings. "Whose cat is that?" I ask, and then louder, hoping my voice doesn't pitch too far into unguarded excitement. The artist, an olive-skinned, mustached boy who goes by Sirap, greets me with a corona-safe fist bump and says my hot-pink bike spokes are "fire." I tell him I'm obsessed with his cat and he shrugs like it's nothing special. When I insist it has something extra, one of Sirap's shaggy friends agrees, calling out, "I've been trying to tell him that cat is dope!"

The boys are from Providence, Rhode Island, but New York called them this summer, so they come whenever they've got gas money, crashing on couches or sleeping on the street until they can score cheap apartments. They might succeed now that more than 500,000 people have fled the city and rents are down. I talk with Sirap's friend B., in goatee and bleached locs, the word "fugitive" scrawled across the back of his reconstructed denim jacket, and when I ask what I am always asking these days, about the freedom to take up space during the pandemic, B. says he feels safer than he ever has before—as a Black man—he feels empowered from his experiences in the BLM movement, standing up to police and seeing so many others stand up to police. "Last year I would not have done this," he says, meaning he would not have sold his art in the park. "I didn't feel safe. I didn't know what people were about." But now everyone's about this, people are open, public space is open, and it makes so much more possible.

I need Libera Cat on a shirt, so Sirap meets me on St. Mark's, in front of the block's last punk shop, carrying a bag rattling with cans of spray

Sirap and his Libera Cat stencil

paint. He pulls out the original stencil. "It's all hand cut," he says proudly, holding it up for me to admire, the cat outlined in negative space, slices of cardboard covered in layers of paint. I hand over an old sweatshirt and Sirap lays it on the dirty sidewalk, places the stencil on top, selects a can of black and a can of yellow, and starts painting, sweetening the air with aerosol. He's wearing purple Chuck Taylors, rubber toes inked with doodles, and a leather band with silver bullets around his ankle. His fingers are tattooed with Basquiat crowns. "We love Basquiat and Keith Haring and the '80s," he says, meaning his gang of artist friends. "But we don't want to recreate that time. We want to turn it around, inside out, do it different. St. Mark's is where it all happened."

He tells me about a recent night when he felt low and spent hours communing with the Keith Haring sculpture at Astor Place, *Self Portrait, 1989*, a green dancer kicking his foot high in the air. But when he went back the next day, the statue was gone. "It's really sad," Sirap says, "because it's been there since the '80s." He says this part again, "it's been there since the '80s," and I detect a kindred soul, melancholic with longing for a lost time. I do not have the heart to tell him that the statue was installed in 2015 and that its cynical purpose was to bring bohemian cachet to the developers of the despised glass tower that East Villagers have nicknamed the Death Star. I don't want to ruin Sirap's experience of a night spent in spiritual attunement with a relic from a place and time he never experienced but feels nostalgic for anyway. I change the subject, asking what *libera* means to him, and he tells me, "it's like street slang, like punk or whatever, kind of like 'yo,' to mean freedom and liberation." I'm not sure this is true, but I like it, imagining punk kids who love the '80s going around greeting each other with "Libera!" Like anti-fascists from a much earlier time, soldiers in the Abraham Lincoln Brigade gone to fight Franco in Spain, coming home with ¡*Libera!* Can't you see them, fist-bumping their way into the rewilded city, knuckles inked with crowns?

...

ALWAYS THESE DAYS LOOKING FOR *FUCK*, I GET EXCITED WHEN, RID-
ing to the Village, I see the cyclist in front of me has the word printed
on the back of her T-shirt. Below it, like a number under a name on a
team jersey, is 12. *Fuck the police.* I'm late for Stonewall, hoping to join
the march in progress, and I bet this cyclist is headed there, too. When
we pass an NYPD van she thrusts her arm in the air and gives it the
finger. (Along with *fuck*, the finger has made a comeback this summer.)
At a red light, I ask her and her partner if they know where the protesters are. They're headed for Stonewall, too, and we set off together,
bonded in our shared mission. This is what it's like now. You run into
people and recognize each other as teammates, as family, because we're
all wearing the same signs: T-shirts, buttons, stickers on bike helmets,
ragged squares of cardboard fixed to bike frames. On the street, in the
park, in the middle of protests, people come up to me and say, "I like
your button." Sometimes they touch the button, pressing it with a finger
against my chest, smiling behind their mask, and I'll get a warm feeling
of love from this moment of intimacy with a stranger, a phenomenon
born from this sympathetic summer.

At Stonewall, the march has departed and we don't know if it went north
or south. I've done this all summer, hunting the streets for marchers, following the sound of police helicopters, listening for chants and drums,
getting lost in the canyons of Manhattan. My new biker friends, a forty-
ish white couple whose names are Ann Marie and Rob, check their
phones for clues on Twitter and Instagram. "I wish they'd leave a bread-
crumb trail," Ann Marie says. She's in the FUCK 12 shirt, sparkling in
glittery blue eye shadow that matches her blue hair. Rob has longish hair,
sideburns, and aviator glasses, so he looks like Peter Fonda circa 1968 but
in a COVID mask, with a sign safety-pinned to his messenger bag that

says: "Abolish the Police." Ann Marie finds video of a crowd downtown and we jet to Tribeca, where the pulse of copters pulls us west, and when a cop car races past we follow, skirting potholes, dodging buses, until we find a group of protesters outnumbered and surrounded, backed into a corner between the 9/11 Memorial and the new World Trade Center. It's not the Stonewall group, but remnants of an Abolish ICE march that came from Foley Square to protest the hysterectomies forced on immigrant women in detention camps.

Someone calls my name. It's Derrick, the activist I've come to think of as The Mayor because he knows everyone, greeting people with an affable fist bump, cruising the crowd to see who's there and what's happening, keeping one eye on the comms and the other on the cops. A thirty-something white guy, always dressed in a black BLM T-shirt, black pants, black KN95 mask dangling off one ear while he smokes a spliff, Derrick adopted me from Washington Square, bringing me into the circle. We run into each other everywhere and as we bump fists, he says excitedly, "Twenty people were arrested!" He's wired, bouncing back and forth in his boots. I introduce him to Ann Marie and Rob, fist bumps all around, and Derrick tells us to be careful, cops are grabbing anyone who's not on the sidewalk. "This is the New York City Police Department," comes the announcement from the LRAD speaker, a warning that means things are about to get violent. "Please be advised that pedestrians are not permitted to walk in the street or roadway. Pedestrians are also prohibited from obstructing sidewalks." On the sidewalk or street, we can be placed under arrest. In other words, they want us to leave. The tension is jittery as the protesters, dressed in black bloc, goggles and balaclavas, agitate the cops, shouting and posturing. The cops circle like sharks and I keep my head on a swivel, watching my back. When a fresh battalion in helmets rolls in with a bus for taking prisoners, my biker friends decide to keep looking for the Stonewall group and I go with them.

Away from the standoff, Rob says, "I did that black bloc stuff in my twenties, summit hopping, and then with Occupy Wall Street. I'm too old for it now." I'm also too old. "I know where that scene ends up," he continues. "It's a cold night in the Tombs." Just the nickname of the Manhattan House of Detention sends a shudder through me. The Tombs, so called in the 1800s because the original building, designed in Egyptian Revival, was modeled after an ancient mausoleum. It's where Herman Melville's Bartleby the Scrivener ends up, wandering the prison yard, refusing to eat. "The Egyptian character of the masonry weighed upon me with its gloom," Melville wrote. "But a soft imprisoned turf grew under foot." Today the grass is gone, the mausoleum razed, and in its place you'll find a dull and windowless tower of grimy brown brick. Still, whenever I hear about the Tombs, I imagine something ancient, a catacomb of vaulted marble lined with human skulls. I don't want to go there. I would prefer not to. (My former psychoanalyst, the one who compared me to Raskolnikov, also liked to say I resembled Bartleby. "I would prefer not to," she'd repeat, poking my resistance. "That's your motto.")

Bartleby's slogan was revived during Occupy Wall Street, appearing on signs and T-shirts, printed on the poster for a May Day general strike, declaring, "No work. No school. No banking. No housework. No shopping." This describes the state in which many nonessential workers found themselves during the pandemic lockdown. They became Bartlebys. Many will tell me it was unemployment and federal stimulus money that allowed them to join the movement. This unplanned strike removed them from the mill of work, consumerism, and constant self-improvement, helping set the stage for liberation. Just one step away from the normative order. I don't think the uprising of 2020 could have happened without the pandemic freeing so many hands.

Catalyst for revolution

With Ann Marie and Rob, I pedal hard uptown where we hope to catch the Stonewall group, but when we reach the Village, our steam runs out. We are not young. We are tired and hungry. We will see each other again, at next week's march, and we'll become good friends. Alone, I head east to Washington Square, where I roll by Antonio, a young Mexican artist I've been chatting with in the park. He calls out, "Hey, we were just talking about you," so I stop, fist-bump Antonio and his silent, smiling friend, Anthony from the Bronx. Antonio, the talker, expounds about life, art, New York, and freedom. "Basquiat sold art here when it was raw and wild," he says, bleached hair sparking in the last light of day. The park's more open than before the pandemic, he says, there's more connection and barriers are down. Anthony, who never came to the park before, ventured in for reasons he cannot articulate. When I ask what made him come, he shrugs, *who knows*, he just came. "You know what else?" Antonio says. "Look around. No one's on their phone. Everyone's awake." He's right. I look around and don't see a single phone. The park is alive with breakdancers, dice throwers, roller skaters, Tarot readers, and New Agers who bang on gongs with soft mallets. Everyone's awake. (Have I mentioned that my olfactory sense has increased dramatically in the pandemic? I'm so open, I can smell the city's every note from top to base.) I buy one of Antonio's artworks, an audacious drawing of a Chase Bank engulfed in flames. In the foreground, a pig that has just stripped out of a cop uniform considers a pink donut covered in rainbow sprinkles. "Did you notice the donut?" Antonio asks. "Of course," I say. "How could I miss the donut? It's the best part." "That's dope," Antonio says. "No one ever notices the donut."

■ ■ ■

ON A NEW YORK UNIVERSITY BUILDING JUST OUTSIDE THE PARK, someone scrawls: "NYU Go Home" and "100 positive cases No Good." Earlier in September, students came back to town. Rambunctious, possibly contagious, they crashed our Saturday night party like poorly behaved uninvited guests. We were dancing when a kid in a Miami Red-Hawks shirt came over, putting on a show of mockery for his buddies, goofing on us and the breakdancers. Tank leaned in to tell him, "You're not cute," and the kid slunk away, but the vibe was spoiled. I've been worried about September. With out-of-town students back, I've been expecting the forces of control to start clamping down. The next day, our New York dance party, off the radar all summer, got exposed in the press, misrepresented as a virus-spreading "NYU rager." The university banned students from the party, making the park ours again, but tonight the park police, with NYPD white shirts as backup, have come to pull the plug, making a show of force for the news cameras, a tug-of-war that will continue and intensify, all the way into next summer.

While the cops stand watching, the old-school DJs pack their gear. One regular dancer, an older Black man, says to another, "They don't want us to have nothing. They want us to stay in our shitty neighborhoods, off to the side, and not come down here." His friend nods and says, "Yeah, but it's weird, because it's a mixed party, with white people, too. Why not leave us alone?" All summer we've seen what mixing can do—raising consciousness, increasing empathy, giving people ideas about unity and revolution. There can't be too much mixing here.

A DJ hands me a clementine, a bit of sweetness before he goes, and tells me *don't worry, the party will go on.* It does, but not with these men, who are old enough to know how to avoid trouble. The Abolition Park folks, on the other hand, are magnets for trouble and they take the party across the fountain, where a send-off for Joker, who has a warrant out for his arrest, turns into a raucous protest party. A keyboard player shouts, "Fuck the cops, fuck CBS News, this is about community, people, elevating ourselves in a revolutionary moment in time! You can't shut down a party for Black Lives Matter!" The DJ cranks up Saweetie's "My Type" and when the cops walk over, MC Shaman gets everyone chanting "Fuck 12" to the beat, forcing the cops to retreat, sending the crowd into a paroxysm of pleasure and power, pulling out jugs of Bacardi, getting down on hands and knees to twerk, *fuck 12, fuck 12, fuck, fuck, fuck 12.*

I'm drinking a nutcracker, talking to Joker, Justice, Smokey, and a dancer who's bemoaning the Hustle community, older dancers so protective of the hustle that they refuse to teach it to the younger generation who want to evolve it into the hustla, a forbidden mix of hustle and salsa. She shows us some taboo moves, and it's nothing like the dance I learned in gym class in 1979, the Bee Gees' "Night Fever" playing from a crackling record, conjuring my gender-crossed fantasy of being John Travolta in a Huk-A-Poo shirt unbuttoned to show off gold chains, like the one I wore with an Italian horn and hand, amulets protecting me from the *malocchio*, the evil eye. My grandmother brought that chain back from Italy, to keep me safe, and I took it off when I went to college. Another moment of deracination.

Next time I hit the park I'm marching up from Foley Square with the
Abolish ICE protest, flanked by battalions of riot cops, moving fast
through SoHo and into Washington Square, where the cops form a
barricade to stop us from leaving at LaGuardia Place. A tense standoff
begins, cops on one side, protesters on the other. A guy called Cherokee
steps into the street, strips off his shirt, and starts gyrating his hips in
front of a cop car, yelling *fuck* this and *fuck* that. The tension pops. Cops
grab Cherokee, protesters rush, and more cops swarm, sticks swinging.
Tank gets hit in the jaw with a riot shield. People are pinned to the street
and cuffed. The energy slows and goes taut, holding tight until something shifts and whips, bodies slammed, another whirl of violence that
dissolves as suddenly as it came, chaos congealing into order, and then
breaking into chaos, again, again. It goes on like this for hours.

NYU students stand around in out-of-state T-shirts, Michigan, Virginia, in pristine white sneakers, gawking and goofing, taking selfies in
front of cops putting protesters into zip ties, while activist women scream
and cry, collapsing into the arms of other women who say *it's gonna be
okay*. A few protesters confront the NYU kids, shouting, "This is not a
social media opportunity. Get in the fight or go home! You shouldn't
even be in New York right now!" One of the crying protesters goes up to
a couple eating salad and shouts, "How the *fuck* can you eat right now?
Don't you see what's happening?" But the couple can't see, won't see,
because unseeing is a talent they have practiced well. They live in the
other New York, city of salads, white sneakers, and forgetting.

The Abolish ICE protests continue for days. In Times Square, riot cops
lock down Seventh Avenue and fill correction buses with prisoners. After
a BLM press conference, I wander the Square, past weed dealers calling
zaza, zaza, Barbie sounding her barbaric yawp, the Plandemic people
shouting about how the future vaccine is going to kill us all. "We do not
consent," they say. "The Awakening will not be televised!" It feels like a

carnival, packed with people, still mostly Black and brown working-class New Yorkers, almost zero tourists. The Pandemic Space-Time Vortex is wide open and a magician falls through. His name is Ramon, from the Bronx (which he calls "the motherfuckin' B-X"). Dressed in a threadbare tuxedo with his hair in a Jheri curl, he performs tricks with lit cigarettes, pulling them hot and smoking from the tender ears of small children. Crackhead Barney comes rolling in on her bike, and when I call her name she stops and bends over to show off the message printed on the seat of her pink short-shorts: *Slippery When Wet*. We talk awhile about her performance art, public acts of derring-do, and she says her courage comes from her uterus. "I've got a demon uterus," she says. Two blocks away, I run into Derrick and his friend V., coming from another protest that "got a little spicy" with people smashing the windows of Starbucks and banks, and when the riot cops swarmed in to kettle the crowd, they ran for it. They're buzzed, flush with adrenaline, and we marvel at the way we keep running into each other, part of a shared body, a human network cruising the same circuit in empty New York. When we say goodnight, Derrick turns back and shouts, "Small city!" And it is—a city made closer, more intimate in the absence of the unseeing others.

■ ■ ■

WHEN A GRAND JURY DECIDES NOT TO CONVICT THE OFFICERS WHO killed Breonna Taylor, riot cops troop up the Bowery and the night sky fills with helicopters. I jump into the march as it streams down Second Avenue and it's like plunging into a powerful river, a surge of anger, love, and grief. *Say her name!* The woman leading the chant has a voice cut raw and jagged from hours of screaming, weeks and months of screaming, but still she calls, *Say her name!* We call back, *Breonna Taylor!* She was twenty-six years old, an ER technician at a hospital in Louisville, Kentucky, home from work. She baked cookies that night with her boyfriend before they went to bed watching *Freedom Writers*, a white savior film starring Hilary Swank. Breonna, maybe tired of that narrative, maybe just tired, drifted off to sleep. That's when police, unannounced, used a battering ram to break her front door off the hinges. Her boyfriend, believing the men were burglars, maybe Breonna's erratic ex-boyfriend, picked up his licensed handgun and legally fired a warning shot. The police opened fire, peppering Breonna's body with bullets. Within five minutes, she was dead.

The march goes down Broadway, stopping traffic, sending up the sugary fumes of fresh spray paint, Breonna's name in red, tang of patchouli wafting off the marchers, almost all of whom are young, twenty to thirty years younger than me, so they walk fast. I get on my bike, zipping down to the front to step in as a blocker. On the way, I spot an altercation between bikers and the driver of a large pickup truck. I wedge my bike in front of the truck's grille, thrust forward into the intersection, headlights beaming. The driver has one tire on the sidewalk and he wants to push through. He's young and white, a strawberry-blond laborer with big shoulders in a sleeveless T-shirt. "I'm on your side," he keeps saying, wide-eyed and pleading. "I'm on your side! Just let me through. I can drive on the sidewalk." The biker to my right calmly explains that it's not safe and he has to wait, but the biker to my left tells the guy to "sit the fuck down and move the fucking truck." This escalates the driver's anger. He shouts, "I'm getting in my truck and I'm driving. If you're in the way, then you're in the way!"

Before he gets behind the wheel to kill us, I shout, "Wait, wait, come here! It's just gonna be five minutes. Come look." I want him to see that the tail end of the march, followed by the traffic's flow, is just a block away. It's almost over. The driver shouts to me, "I gotta get to work! I'm a contractor. I gotta make money to feed my kids. I'm on your side!" I don't know exactly what happens next except that I start radiating empathy toward the man. If this sounds odd, all I can say is that it's like a switch that turns on, developed over my years of doing therapy. It feels a little supernatural, this ability to beam compassion over several feet of space, and now my beam pulls the man toward me. I soften my eyes and nod my head, dropping my hands and opening my palms. "I get it," I shout over the noise of the march, calling him *dude* or *man*, slipping into a masculine code-switch. "I get it. You gotta get to work." And I do get it. He's like men in my family, the physical laborers, the gotta make money to feed my kids men, drivers of trucks and players of the lottery, insistent and unyielding, long-suffering but still jovial men who just can't catch a break—working-class white men who were told they deserve a break because of their whiteness, but that break still hasn't come, America hasn't been made great again, and the last thing a man like that wants, right now, is to wait patiently for a Black Lives Matter march to pass.

Eyes locked on mine, the driver steps forward and touches my arm. The aggro biker to my left snaps at the driver, "Don't touch him!" I say it's okay. He can touch me. He can touch me. The driver, locked on me, shouts to the other bikers, "I'm not talking to you! I'm only talking to *this* guy," pointing at me. He says it a few times. He will only talk to me. At first, I think it can't be my whiteness that makes him single me out. All three of us bikers are white. It must be my softness, my willingness to be soft with him, because I'm not invested in whatever masculine tug-of-war the others are waging, but also because I love those men in my family, even when they get it wrong, and so it is my whiteness, too, my experience of working-class whiteness, that makes me a soft place for this man to land.

He extends a big, calloused hand, I shake it, and he pulls me into a bear hug. The Centers for Disease Control say we're not supposed to be hugging, but I put my arms around this man anyway and we hold each other for what must only be a second. It feels longer. We sink in. He smells of sweat, stress mixed with horse pasture, grassy and animal. In the close-

ness of our embrace, he says plaintively in my ear, "I'm on your side." I
tell him, "I know you are. It's okay." Pacified, he steps back to the truck.
Instead of getting behind the wheel, he pulls a joint from the visor, puts it
in his mouth, and lights up. He exhales, shoulders relaxing, and I exhale
too. He is not going to kill anyone tonight. As the end of the march
passes, the backline bike blockers shout to us, like sergeants barking to
soldiers, "Bikers! Let's move, let's move! To the front!" I race along the
sidewalk, working my way back, still feeling the man's embrace, scent
of his skin on my skin.

The march turns onto Canal, where workers hustle to board up the windows of chain stores, anticipating destruction, and well-dressed diners
luxuriate in outdoor restaurant sheds while marchers shout, "White
silence is violence," paint on the sidewalk screaming GO BACK TO
NANTUCKET. In the crowd, I see people I recognize: Luis in his
black bandanna, Pussy with her action name, *Pussy*, in gold script on her
bike helmet, shirtless Blaise, elegant Willa, and there's Stickers gliding on her skateboard, and Mazi in his durag who—first time we ever
met—spotted my trans flag pin and told me, "I support you, I love you,"
so we gleefully bump fists, and I'm moving along, enjoying this feeling
of family, when I run into Derrick, because of course I do. He hugs me
and recounts, in his excited way, how the march started in Brooklyn,
went back and forth over the Manhattan Bridge, and then pushed on,
growing and growing. "It's like the early days," he says, and it's true.
The energy is high, like it was in the spring. "With so many of us," he
says, "the cops can't touch us."

We're headed for the Williamsburg Bridge when Derrick asks, "Have
you ever taken a bridge?" I haven't. "Tonight might be the night," he says,
eyes glittering. The steel span rises before us. I am tempted, but this high
bridge gives me vertigo, and I step away. We say goodnight, see you at
Stonewall, and Derrick goes on, blending into the crowd. I stand atop a

concrete barrier at the foot of the bridge and watch the marchers climb the roadway, claiming it for themselves, for Breonna Taylor and all the names, the list that keeps on growing. A troop of motorcycle cops stands nearby and a protester with a trumpet taunts them with "The Imperial March" from *Star Wars*, Darth Vader's Theme, a Wagnerian anthem of evil, fascism, the dark side of the Force. We are the Rebel Alliance, the good guys, cheering the musician as his trumpet gleams in streetlight and the marchers stream on, banging drums and cowbells, flags billowing, and it's a beautiful sight to see angry people rising, up and up the bridge, higher and higher, taking flight.

■ ■ ■

AT THE BOTTOM OF MANHATTAN, BATTERY PARK CITY IS A PUBLIC-private real-estate development intended, and continuing to function, as a socially engineered, controlled, semi-gated community, home to Gateway Plaza, a guarded "fortress-like enclosure" that political theorist Margaret Kohn calls "the city's response to the fear of urban upheaval, ghetto riots, and suburban flight. It was an attempt to build a suburb in the city and was marketed to professionals seeking an economically homogeneous, sheltered, safe, and private environment" in the early 1980s. The diversity of New York is lacking here. Alienating and disorienting to those who prefer city spaces more organic, the development is designed to keep out the unpredictability, chaos, and color of urban living. Tonight, however, it's about to get a dose of all three.

Overlooking the harbor behind a manicured lawn sits Gigino, a white-tablecloth restaurant serving pasta dishes under a white canopy laced with strings of Edison lights. The diners are engaged in quiet conversation and Chardonnay when the Stonewall Protest arrives, blockers rolling up on our bikes, clearing a path for Qween Jean, who bursts in, monumental and proud, resplendent in a blood-red sequined gown and golden turban spiked with pheasant feathers. Behind her, the marchers come flooding through the tables, banging drums and shaking tambourines, one young woman on roller skates twirling the queer flag like a baton. The diners make faces of displeasure. They do not want to be awakened from their elegant dream.

Qween clacks her fan open and shut, a loud crack, crack, crack, and silences the space. She begins to preach. "We the people are here. Yesterday, our sister Breonna Taylor did *not* receive justice. Black people in this country do *not* receive justice. So we are here to *demand* justice. We are here to dismantle *racism*. We are here to dismantle *white supremacy*. And we are here to disrupt your dining on *fine linen cloth*. And let me tell you, we are *not* here for your entertainment." Then she says the line we'll repeat for months to come: *Fuck your dinner.* We chant with her, stomping our feet, banging our drums, delighting together in this queer negativity, this *fuck* that comes from the soul of the outsider, fuck your

Qween Jean and marchers disrupt dinner at an outdoor restaurant shed

dinner, fuck your Chardonnay, fuck your denial. *Wake up, wake up, this is your fight, too.* Like cultural theorist Fred Moten said, "The coalition emerges out of your recognition that it's fucked up for you, in the same way that we've already recognized that it's fucked up for us. I don't need your help. I just need you to recognize that this shit is killing you, too, however much more softly, you stupid motherfucker, you know?"

. . .

IT'S SEPTEMBER 26 AND I'M HEADING INTO WASHINGTON SQUARE FOR the weekly dance party and an event called "Art of the Protest," organized by a coalition of social justice groups, including Refuse Fascism and the Black Advocacy Movement. All day they made art in the park and now it's time for celebration. But when I step through the gates, people are racing past, shouting *go, go, go,* as the trees flare with red and blue light. I bolt to the fountain where hundreds of cops, riot troops backed by a deep wall of bike cops, line up with batons in their fists. This might be the biggest display of force I've seen this summer—and for what? Two organizers, young people of color, tell me about the moment the cops rushed in on bicycles and swarmed the party, flipping over tables of art supplies, confiscating the DJ's equipment. As one dancer says, "They're terrorizing joy."

The fortress of cops stands frozen still, but I can feel they're on a hair trigger for violence. Before they can pop off, Shaman gets on a bullhorn and shouts, "This is unlawful! We did nothing wrong. Everybody please get on your phones and put this on live. We're asking you to get on Instagram, Twitter, and Facebook. Get on your phones and tell the world what's happening in New York!" Phones go up in the air, glowing and filming. Instantly, the cops scatter like cockroaches in the light. As they hurry away, past the arch to Fifth Avenue, the crowd cheers their retreat and one group breaks off, marching to the Ninth Precinct to demand the return of the DJ's equipment. I stay behind and talk with the organizers, who are shaken by the brutality.

"The cops just came in and flipped our tables," they keep saying. "We didn't do anything." While we talk, the police are attacking the splinter group of protesters six blocks away on Hudson Street, tackling them into the sidewalk tables at the Cowgirl Hall of Fame restaurant, knocking them into diners, truly fucking people's dinner. They dogpile on Joker, cuff him, and take him to the Tombs for what will be a six-month stint. Back in the park, I talk with an older Black woman, a poet from Harlem, who tells me she walked all the way downtown, six long miles, just to dance at the party. "When I'm dancing," she says, "I really feel free. This is my private democracy. Dancing outside, by myself, with other people." And then the cops swarmed in. "They were like bees," she says, squeezing her eyes shut, "angry bees in black and yellow shirts." They stopped the music, destroyed the art, and shoved people to the ground. "Then they surrounded us," she says. "It was terrifying. Why did they do that? We just wanted to dance."

HAUNTOLOGY

This week's Stonewall march ends at Foley Square, where a young man in a gold chain and no shirt gives a speech atop *Triumph of the Human Spirit*, a sculpture inspired by Chi Wara, a human-antelope ancestor of West Africa, protector of the harvest. This site was once an African burial ground, and the specter of the slave patrols lingers as the young man recounts a recent night's protest that concluded with several brutal arrests. As he describes the violence, I hear a soft sound of distress and turn to see a young woman shaking, grabbing herself like she's trying to get a grip, on the verge of tears. I ask if she's having a panic attack. She is definitely having a panic attack. I ask if I can put my hand on her shoulder, she nods, and I tell her to breathe with me. She tries, but her emotions are about to spill. I tell her my name and say, "I'm a trauma therapist." Her eyes go wide, "You are?" She throws her arms around me, like I'm a rock in the rapids, holding me tight as I hold her tight and she sobs into my chest, long and hard enough to soak my T-shirt. I think about the virus but can't let go.

"I was one of the ones arrested that night," the woman says through tears. "I can still feel it in my body. The cop's hands are inside my body." I ask if she's heard of EMDR, the trauma treatment I practice. She's done it before and loves it. I put my hands on her shoulders and tap left, right, left, right, applying bilateral stimulation, while telling her she's okay, she's safe. When I say, "You're alive," she collapses again into my chest and sobs without restraint. When she's able to take a breath I ask if she has a peaceful place in mind. "Rockaway Beach," she whimpers. Holding her, I tap her shoulders as we imagine waves touching sand. I look out and around us. At the edge of the crowd, we are surrounded by people, the glow of streetlights, contained, held by our fellow marchers, a small circle within a larger circle. Have I ever held a stranger like this? There was the truck driver at the march for Breonna Taylor, but this is more entangled, warm with sweat and tears, the salted interior of one body leaking onto another. I think again of COVID, hope for the best, and don't let go.

The young woman stands up straight and wipes her eyes, pulling herself together, and then she reaches down her shirt, takes a small drawstring bag from her bra, and rummages inside with her fingers. Assuming she's going for a benzo, I ask, "Do you have something to take?" She replies, "Oh yeah, I have lots of things. I'm a witch." Instead of Xanax, she pulls out a piece of red clay baked into the shape of a heart and presses it into my hand. "It's my Mother Heart," she says, "and it's warm." I hold it, feel the warmth, give it my warmth, and hand it back to her. "I'm going home now," she says and then, gripped by guilt, asks, "That doesn't make me a bad person, right?" I tell her she's not a bad person, she's done enough for today, and it's okay to take care of herself. She throws herself into my arms one more time, thanks me, and hustles off to the subway. Her name, which I didn't quite catch, sounded something like Calliope.

After the young witch leaves, I stand alone, feeling the cool October air on the damp patch her tears made on my New York Fuckin City shirt. I need to move, to work off the disorganized energy I took from her body into mine, along with the chills of COVID anxiety I feel whenever I get too close to someone. As the chills run up my back, I jump on my toes and shake them off, hop on my bike and do a circle around the crowd, where I run into Derrick in a cloud of weed smoke. I tell him about the crying witch and he tells me about the Wide Awakes, a protest group revived from the nineteenth century to bring us joy, liberation, and hauntology, a concept from Jacques Derrida's *Specters of Marx*, Derrick explains, "Like the way we say the names of the dead, Breonna Taylor and George Floyd, conjuring ghosts." He's talking about Toni Morrison's *Beloved*, the past haunting the present, when the crowd at the fountain moans with excitement, gathers in a flurry, and runs across the street. Someone asks, "Is it a fight?" It's not. Joel Rivera is breaking through barricades to climb the high stone steps of the New York State Supreme Court Building. At the top, in her pink dashiki miniskirt, crop top, and high heels, she stands between the Corinthian columns, lifts a bucket of red paint, and pours it on herself, letting it trickle down her bare skin like blood. This is high drama and the crowd cheers. Joel picks up the pride flag and holds it aloft, her shadow falling on the building's facade like the shadow of a towering ghost.

I don't understand hauntology and it seems no one else does either. Maybe the trick is not to understand, but to feel it, because hauntology is best experienced as an atmospheric mood. In *Specters of Marx*, when Derrida repeats the phrase "time is out of joint," saying that a breach has opened and "Time is off its hinges, time is off course, beside itself, disadjusted," he could be describing 2020, the Pandemic Space-Time Vortex that sends us simultaneously backward and forward, revolving in revolution. Why is there so much 1970s feeling in the air? Why do so many people and things seem as if they've stepped out of a time machine? You can call it mass nostalgia, but cultural theorist Mark Fisher offers another way to think about it. "What is being longed for in hauntology is not a particular period," he says, "but the resumption of the *processes* of democratization and pluralism," processes cut short in the 1970s when neoliberalism took the wheel and propelled us into our capitalist dystopia. And yet *what could have been* remains as a spectral presence. Our melancholic longing for it is not nostalgia, but a refusal to accept the current situation, Fisher says, "even if the cost of that refusal is that you feel like an outcast in your own time." Refusing the present, remembering the past, fighting for the future, "Hauntology is a political gesture."

The pandemic has opened a breach and the lost future of the past (*what could have been*) spills into the present. In moments of uncanny recurrence (graffiti, socialists, music from a passing boom box), we catch glimpses through the rift, to the juncture when it all could have gone another way. Derrick calls these phenomena "hauntological reverberations." We go back to go forward (*what can be again*). If this is a chance to repair, a cosmic do-over, it might be our last chance. We will need all the ghosts and witches we can gather.

■ ■ ■

TIMES SQUARE HAS RADICALIZED—THE RED STEPS, BUILT AS A TOUR-ist attraction, have become a rallying point for protests, and *red* has taken on a socialist hue. Here, during the Wide Awakes rally, I meet a guy called El Pollo Loco, the name hand-painted on his T-shirt, along with the words "Bronx Fried" and "Boneless and Ruthless." He's maybe twenty-five, his hair in long locs, and he's sitting on a repurposed Citi Bike tricked out with Rastafarian decorations that cover the corporate bank branding. I ask him about his shirt and he tells me he rode down from the Bronx with a pack of Bike Life riders, those (mostly) young men who travel the city in mass ride-outs, popping wheelies and doing stunts. The Bike Life movement started sometime in the 1990s, maybe in Harlem, maybe Baltimore, and expanded from dirt bikes and ATVs to bicycles. During the pandemic the bikes are everywhere, colorful spokes flashing as riders call, "We outside, we outside," a rallying cry from hip-hop culture that fits this moment of taking space. El Pollo Loco, who's been riding all summer, describes the bike as a vehicle of freedom and escape from despair. He lost two family members to COVID. The bike saved him. He's losing weight, riding because "I've got to stay alive." He wears latex-dipped work gloves, the kind with red palms, so he can punch the side mirrors of cars that get too close. He is making room. "That's how I got my name," he says. "They call me Crazy Chicken."

He shows me a video on his phone, Bike Lifers wheelieing with empty forks, no front wheels, while, at the Wide Awakes protest, the Naked Cowboy is getting too close to the Vote Feminist people. Tensions are rising as the presidential election approaches. With his guitar covered in Trump 2020 stickers, the Naked Cowboy is agitating, looking for trouble in his hat and boots, tighty-whities, a tattoo of Jesus on one shoulder and Satan on the other. He's arguing with a woman holding a sign that says, "I Have a Lot to Learn About Trans Feminism." She whacks him with it and the fight goes on.

El Pollo Loco lights up a blunt. He likes being in Times Square. It didn't used to be so comfortable, but it's different now, we agree. We don't say it's Blacker and browner and more working class, but it doesn't need to be said, all you have to do is look around. "It's more chill," El Pollo Loco says. "It's like family, know what I'm saying?" I do. "Spaces acquire the 'skin' of the bodies that inhabit them," says Sara Ahmed, because "it is not just bodies that are orientated. Spaces also take shape by being orientated around some bodies, more than others."

■ ■ ■

IN HERALD SQUARE, I RUN INTO A SMALL GROUP OF TRUMP SUPPORT-ers screaming at passing motorists who scream back at them. They're wearing red MAGA hats and waving American flags. One guy is dressed in head-to-toe Trump, from his Trump hat to his Trump sneakers, including a coronavirus mask with a photo of Trump hoisting a beer: "Chill Out. Have a Corona." He has wrapped himself in Trump flags: one with Trump's head photoshopped onto Sylvester Stallone's *Rambo* body, all muscle and sinew, clutching a grenade launcher, and the other with Trump's head on George Washington, beefed up like an action hero, standing on a pile of burning rubble with a bald eagle on his arm and a rotary cannon in his hand.

I'm separated from them by a wrought-iron fence, puzzling over this Hollywood fantasy and the work it's doing—Trump as hypermasculine strongman, a killer, a savior, bulging with muscle, draped protectively around the body of this human-sized man, who might feel vulnerable in feral Manhattan, maybe more than usual now that Trump is lying in a hospital bed with COVID, hooked to infusions of steroids and supplemental oxygen. While I'm thinking about masculine hysteria and the threat of the chaotic feminine, the guy spots my T-shirt: I ⒶNY. It's meant to be a cheeky response to Trump's recent declaration that the city is an official "anarchist jurisdiction," and any true anarchist would see right through me, but this guy believes it's real. It's not *not* real, but it's also not that serious. The nuance is lost and the guy shouts, "You have an anarchy symbol on your shirt! Are you a communist?" I shake my head, deciding it's best not to attempt an explanation of the difference between anarchism and communism. He persists. "Are you a member of Antifa?" "Well," I say, "Antifa's not actually an organization with members, it's more like . . ." He cuts me off, screaming, "You're a fascist! You're pathetic! You're a parasite on America, you fucking fascist!" I don't mention that it's impossible to be both fascist and anti-fascist. His friends join in, shouting obscenities. One starts filming me, so I take out my camera and film him back. This is what we do now, everyone filming everyone, doing our part for the panopticon. I give them nothing, nodding silently until they quit, the flag man getting in a last word, "Why don't you go destroy some more cities and burn down some more buildings while you're at it, you fucking fascist!" He turns away, adjusts the Rambo-Trump cape on his shoulders, and says to his buddies, "We really told that guy off." I linger, just to prove they can't scare me, but I feel a quaking in my stomach and it's not IBS.

I've felt this sensation many times, whenever I've worked with severe borderline personality disorder, and it's usually a sign that I've come into contact with the defensive operation known as projective identification, where the projector aggressively tries to dispose of unwanted or dangerous parts of himself by pressing them into the psyche of another. Psychoanalyst Melanie Klein called these parts "harmful excrements, expelled in hatred," and the receiver, controlled by the projector, experiences the expelled excrements as if they belong to the self. Maybe I *am* a bad person, the receiver thinks. Maybe I'm the one who's a creep. In childhood, the retort "I'm rubber and you're glue" might provide protection against this psychic shit-throwing, but I didn't use that with the Trumper and it takes effort to remove the sticky ectoplasm of his projected material. As I speed downtown on my bike, it sloughs off like mud under the spray of a hose, but the job is not complete and I am left with a ghostly residue that will take time to exorcise.

■ ■ ■

"FUCK YOUR DINNER," QWEEN JEAN SHOUTS INTO HER MEGAPHONE AS the Stonewall Protest approaches an outdoor restaurant on Hudson Street, the diners taken by surprise over pricey pizzas eaten with forks and knives. We confront one restaurant after another, working our way through the Meatpacking District and up to Penn Station, where we stop traffic to "open it up," as we do each week, making a circle for vogueing and twerking at the broad intersection of Thirty-Fourth and Eighth. Qween chants, "If you got the wettest pussy, pussy, if you got the wettest," summoning dancers into the ring, and I know witchcraft when I see it. In college, I dated the high priestess of the school coven, I've seen circles cast and daemonic energy released from earthly portals, so when Qween casts a circle and chants *pussy, pussy*, I see her calling forth some fierce chthonic power, conjuring the wild vaginal, a queer symbolic chaos, unspooling primordial vibes from Sheela-na-Gig—the medieval stone figure spreading her extravagant vulva—the stuff that the masculine forces of control don't want released.

The ritual display of the vagina, an apotropaic act meant to frighten one's enemies, was named anasuromai (αvασύρομαι) by the Greek historian Herodotus when he witnessed Egyptian women lifting their skirts as they sailed down the Nile during the festival of Bubastis, city of the cat goddess, in 445 BC. Today, in our rebellious, disorderly cities, we are again in its power. I think of Naked Athena, the Portland protester who sat in the street this summer with legs open to oncoming cops, a real-life Sheela. But the act doesn't only ward off the evil eye; it can also banish grief and stimulate joy—as Baubo did for the bereaved Demeter, flashing her vulva to make the earth goddess laugh. "Open it up," Qween Jean calls, "open it up." The dancers hump and buck, lift their skirts and bend over, getting down on their bellies to ravage the asphalt with pelvic thrusts. "Kitty, kitty, kitty," Qween chants as someone takes off her top and dances bare-breasted, the crowd whooping in exultation. All around, in stopped cars and trucks, impatient drivers honk their horns, but queer pussy is being served and it will not be rushed.

We call this "holding space," and how different is it from psychoanalytic concepts of the holding environment, potential space, the container-contained? "It is in the space between inner and outer world," wrote D. W. Winnicott, "which is also the space between people—the transitional space—that intimate relationships and creativity occur." It is in the container that intense affects are shared and metabolized. When I

The Stonewall front line, holding the West Side Highway

talk to Qween about the act of "opening it up," she explains, "We're still using the ancient rituals of drumming and dance as a form of resistance. It's a moment of euphoria and jubilation," in which the word *pussy* is reclaimed, celebrated, and respected. "The ritual is also an offering to our fallen angels, those who have been killed. It moves from mourning to a celebration of life. People come into the circle with whatever rhythmic offering their body has to give."

By the time the Stonewall march arrives at Hudson Yards, it's cold and windy, the dystopian super-mall gone dark and desolate in the plague. This luxury development was scandalously built with billions in public tax dollars. Among its sky-high towers, it includes a 150-foot structure called the Vessel, a hive-shaped tourist attraction made of spiraling staircases to nowhere. When it opened, I called it the Big Shawarma for its uncanny resemblance to the urban street food, but its fate soon turned dark as sui-cidal visitors found its height ideal for their desperate swan dives.

When Joel, in leotard and Lucite heels, takes to the steps of the Vessel, she triggers an alert response from the nearby SRG troops. Into the megaphone she shouts, "This Vessel wasn't made for New Yorkers. It was made for tourists!" She speaks about the tax money that went into the structure, money that never makes it to her neighborhood in the Bronx, to public schools, parks, and affordable housing. "We paid for this," she says. "It's ours. So why can't we go inside?" A pair of security guards moves behind her. "That's some fragile masculinity right there," she says. "I don't even *want* to go inside this thing. Or do I?" The crowd moans in pleasure. "Let's go!" Joel shouts, leading the charge, and several marchers follow, pushing into the Vessel, screaming and kicking as the guards push back and Joel shouts, "Stonewall was a riot! Stonewall was a riot!" On cue, riot cops rush in from all directions, chasing after protesters running up the stairs. As NYPD troops surround the Vessel and lock it down, our trumpeter plays Darth Vader's Theme and protesters shout, "You protect property over people! Every single time the one percent needs you, here the fuck you are!"

• • •

IT'S A GLITTERING OCTOBER DAY AND CENTRAL PARK, CONTINUING to rewild, is in the midst of an unusual owl visitation, including a charismatic barred owl given the uninspired name "Barry." Symbol of wisdom and magic, prophetess from the underworld, the owl sits high in a hemlock tree above flocks of bird-watchers, blessing us with good omen in this year of change and death. In winter she will be joined by a rare snowy owl, but until then we will have to make do with the bespectacled, white-bearded white man with the American flag over his shoulder, shouting signs and portents into a bullhorn at the edge of the park's Model Boat Pond. A flotilla of toy sailboats glides the green surface as the man points accusingly at the boathouse. The vented steeple atop the building, he insists, is not a steeple. It's a chimney, he says, proof that the boathouse was once used for burning the bodies of Jews. The man is confused. Or maybe he's speaking in metaphor. He's dressed in a tweed jacket and a Greek fisherman's cap, pacing along the pond's edge, with two small dogs following, keeping watchful eyes on their wild human.

The boat pond, beloved by the upper class of the Upper East Side, is usually a peaceful place, but not today, just days before the presidential election that has everyone on edge. The man with the bullhorn goes on shouting about fascism when another white man approaches with a pair of expensive-looking binoculars around his neck. The boat pond has long been a popular spot for watching red-tailed hawks, especially Pale Male, the bird that famously nested on a neoclassical window pediment that belonged to Mary Tyler Moore. (Pale Male is "presumed deceased," according to Wikipedia, and so is Mary, though her memory lives on in the ebullience of a blue pom-pom hat tossed in the air.)

As the birder steps close to the anti-fascist, hands raised to plead and push, the anti-fascist demands, "Which side are you on? Are you an American?" The birder says, "I'm on the side of quiet," to which the anti-fascist replies, "Oh, he wants quiet! You know how you get quiet? You kill Jews. You kill loudmouths. That's what he wants!" The birder is undeterred. He asks the anti-fascist, "Can you go do your thing some other place?" The anti-fascist storms off, shouting, "His quiet is more important than Jews' lives! These people, these rich people, they want a white Manhattan, just for white people!" In his wake, two couples fall close behind, silver- and blond-haired men and women ruddy with good health, smartly dressed for the crisp fall day in quilted Eddie Bauer outerwear. They look like the affluent boomers in Cialis commercials, always ready for the right moment, triumphantly erect. As they follow the man, they mock and jeer, like mean teenagers chasing an unpopular kid from the playground. They sing and yodel, marching right behind, exultant in their power. The anti-fascist stays ahead, shuffling into the fallen leaves at the foot of Pilgrim Hill. He's not done yet.

In 2004, the co-op board of Mary Tyler Moore's building voted to destroy the nest of Pale Male and his mate Lola. They complained about the carcasses of rats and pigeons that dropped to the sidewalk. They didn't want the mess. When she found the nest gone, Moore fought back. "I am so outraged that they would do this without so much as a by your leave," she told the *Times*. "These birds just kept coming back to the edge of the building, and people kept coming back to see them. This was something we like to talk about: a kinder, gentler world, and now it's gone." Bird-loving New Yorkers were outraged. They held vigils outside the building with signs that said, "Rich Address. Bankrupt Soul." Eventually, the co-op board relented and the hawks' nest was rebuilt.

The anti-fascist turns to the crowd and shouts, "You're all fucking idiots! High-school idiots are in charge of this world. We are cowards! We bow down before money!" A woman pushing a baby stroller yells, "Booo! Go away!" The anti-fascist ignores her. The election this coming Tuesday, he says, is phony. "Biden will win," because, "It's a show. It's a movie. It's a high-school production of *Macbeth* mixed with, aah . . . aah . . ." He draws a blank. We wait. "Mixed with, aah . . . aah . . ." We wait. Finally, it comes, ". . . mixed with *The Walking Dead*!" Today is Halloween and this man lives in a haunted house, an atmosphere of zombies and ghosts. What did he do with that hauntedness before the pandemic permitted us to get on bullhorns and rattle chains? Like so many, he has come unbound, but this wildness cannot last. Not in patrician Central Park, among the magnates of Manhattan. Atop the hill, another portent: *The Pilgrim* statue stands guard with his musket above bas-reliefs of the *Mayflower*, the Bible, and symbols of Commerce—colonization, God, money. Cast in bronze and granite, anchored in centuries of power, these ideas are so solid, how will they ever melt into air?

ONE WEEK IN NOVEMBER

It's the Sunday before the election and the mood is gray, the hours fallen back from daylight savings, as the city becomes muffled yet again, hunkering down for whatever's next. In Times Square, there is almost no one. Echoing through the emptiness, a white man in a red cap stands on a concrete anti-terrorism block and shouts, "USA! USA!" I keep my distance.

The chain stores are getting sealed behind plywood. Everywhere, again, the piney smell of sawdust spun from circular saws under a sky troubled by helicopters. It's lockdown quiet as the skittish have abandoned the city once more. I feel the absence of their pushy energy, so I know they're gone, my hunch confirmed when the *Post* reports: "Fearful New Yorkers plan to flee city on Election Day." One young man "who lives in a luxury building on the Upper West Side" has gone "to his family's 60-acre farm . . . to avoid a repeat of the unrest that freaked him out this summer." He says, "the protests were overwhelming." A woman hides at her family's house on Fire Island, sheltering with terrified friends because "protesters will try and burn down Trump Tower." Another, who fled to her parents' house over the summer "when the BLM protests got bad," is avoiding further discomfort by running to Tulum. (Several people who go to Tulum this month will create a super-spreader event, bringing countless cases of COVID back to New York.) The *Post* says the ultrarich are hiring armed guards, ex-Marine snipers and off-duty police officers with submachine guns. "The NYPD is advising buildings to get the extra security," says the paper's source. "They've never done this before."

November 3: Election Day. In the hushed and watchful city, the stores are boarded up, plywood for miles. Police stand guard on every corner of Times Square, streets barricaded to permit only a trickle of pedestrians. Activists from Rise and Resist stand in silent vigil, holding a banner that says, "Trump Lies People Die," and a few Trump supporters hang around, including the infamous transgender woman who splashed paint on the Black Lives Matter mural outside Trump Tower while baring her breasts and shouting, "Shame on Bill Bellagio," pronouncing the mayor's name like the hotel casino in Vegas, home to the famous dancing fountains. "Bill Bellagio," she insisted, "is killing transgenders and Black Americans!" Today, however, she's quiet. Everyone is quiet. There will be no riots tonight—and no decision. The votes will take days to count, so many mailed in due to fears of COVID.

November 4. We still don't know who our next president will be, but the count is leaning toward Biden. Protesters are marching down from Forty-Second Street and, after my workday, I join them in Washington Square. A few friends meet up with me and when the march swings by, we jump in, needing to blow off steam. As we go pouring through stopped traffic on Eighth Street, drivers honk their horns in solidarity, thrusting power fists from open windows. Even the driver of a double-decker tourist bus is honking and smiling. Inside, the few tourists huddle nervously as marchers shout a salty "Welcome to New York!" Meaning: *This* is the real city.

We don't get far before the police rush in. At Sixth Avenue, cops in riot gear block our way uptown, forming a line of helmets and nightsticks. SRG troops roll in on bicycles, dressed in black armor, pushing up behind, shouting, "Make a hole, make a hole!" I turn to see a Black man on a bicycle pedaling through the bike cops when words are exchanged and one cop shouts, "Get him!" They charge the man, tackling him to the ground, and the bike cops swing into position, forming a wall around the arrest. Separated from my friends, I jump on my bike to catch up at Seventh Avenue where the air smells of burning, synthetic and plasticky. It's a Biden/Harris flag, because anarchy, and it starts a trash fire, bags of garbage sparking into flames. The cops block our way south, so we go back to Eighth Street and Fifth Avenue, where they stop us again. SRG forces rush from behind, locking our group into a kettle, linking their bikes and closing them like a gate. Just before it swings shut, I grab my friends and jump out. I do not want to be in a kettle.

Inside the trap, protesters lock arms and chant, "I don't see no riot here, why are you in riot gear?" The armored SRG troops press, closing the kettle tighter. "Move *in*, move *in*, move *in*," they shout in a deep monotone, like robo-cops, and each time, on the word *in*, they press forward with their bikes, like a trash compactor, squeezing the protesters. The energy inside the kettle pitches upward into a shrieking boil. Behind us, more riot cops pour from police vans, twenty at a time. They break into the kettle to snatch protesters, picking them off the edges with clubs swinging. People scream as bodies hit the ground. Fellow protesters pull them back, away from police, and push them to safety in the crowd. Another scuffle. Another cluster of hard arrests. A swirl, and then stillness, another swirl. After forty-five minutes, on someone's order, the kettle softens and opens. Just like that. People drift back toward the park where a standoff takes shape and turns into something like a party.

Officer Chris P. Bacon, a.k.a. Piggy, shows up, strutting up and down the line of cops in his beer belly and rubber pig mask, Black Power fist painted on the back of his blue uniform. Subway DJ wanders over with his extra-large rolling speaker, and someone asks, "You got any riot songs?" Subway DJ shrugs. He doesn't know any riot songs. A guy in a Spider-Man T-shirt answers the call with a handheld speaker playing N.W.A's "Fuck tha Police" on repeat. Someone plays Darth Vader's Theme, eliciting a cheer. Then it's the Hokey-Pokey and the Macarena. A guy dressed in a black top hat and suit covered in glittering stars carries Trump's head on a broomstick, blood pouring from his eyes, from his *wherever*, and the guy simulates fellatio with the rubber mouth. Finished, he collapses to the ground, moaning, "I'm so tired of all this shit. I'm so tired of this crazy government. I'm so tired. I can't deal with this crazy government anymore!"

November 5. When I arrive at Stonewall, it's not the usual Thursday night march. Christopher Street is packed with unfamiliar protesters, their energy adding a different spice to the mix. The press, who never showed up before, has come in a hungry mob. It's Election Week, we still don't know the winner, and Stonewall is the biggest game in town. Television news anchors stand at ring lights, fixing their hair, while packs of aggressive photographers vie for shots. It looks like every cop in the NYPD is here, lined up by the hundreds in riot gear, and seven helicopters hover, our queer little march suddenly center stage. A guy comes by holding a pile of pizza boxes and a sign that says, "Free pizza unless you a cop." I grab a slice and shove it down as the bikers assemble at the front where our leaders share the plan. When the march begins, they'll send four bikers to block Seventh Avenue as a test. "If we get grabbed by the cops," says Blaise, "that means they won't let us march tonight." He tells us to keep the front line tight, close to the marchers. "If you're wearing a helmet," Willa adds, "leave it unbuckled. The cops'll grab you by the helmet and hurt your neck." I weigh what's more likely, having my helmet fly off in a fall or getting choked by a cop. I unbuckle the helmet.

When it's time to go, the four test bikers take the avenue, and when they're not arrested, Willa gives the go-ahead and we roll down West Fourth. Holding the line in these conditions isn't easy. We're supposed to ride in a single line, front tires even, but the press photographers keep shoving through and the newcomer protesters don't know how this march operates, weaving in and out, fucking up our momentum. The bikers I don't recognize are jamming too close, pedals and handlebars smashing mine, and the bike cops are flanking so tight, it's hard to move. Sweat trickles down my spine though the night is cool. Finally, we break out of the narrow Village streets, duck through a set of barricades and dodge the cops, taking over wide-open Broadway, where we can breathe, but not for long. A violent scuffle erupts. The cops surround a protester, batons flashing in streetlight, and the press photographers surge forward, shoving through. It's the bikers' job to keep the marchers calm. "Stay where you are," we yell, hands in the air. "Stay where you are!" Behind us, Qween Jean leads a chant of "You can't stop the revolution" as we stand still, straddling our bikes, watching helplessly as the police beat our comrades.

Joela Rivera, with a new name declaring the start of her social transition as a woman, materializes in a long wig and silver ball gown, white opera gloves trimmed in ostrich feather. Standing tall in her signature Lucite heels, she shouts at a pack of SRG cops through a bullhorn, demanding to know the reason for another protester's arrest. Someone's hand reaches out with a phone to film the scene and a cop pushes it back, prompting someone else's hand to smack the cop's bike helmet. Triggered, the cops plow into the crowd, knocking Joela backward and tackling her to the ground. Moments later, she is standing barefoot and handcuffed in the street, shouting, "Where are my shoes? Bitch! Where are my fucking shoes?" Her gown sparks in streetlight, dark wig whipping the air, as she's taken away, shouting, "Stonewall was a riot! Stonewall was a riot!"

Sweating, heart pounding, arms cramped from death-gripping my handlebars, I am getting irritable. When the next reporter steps in front of me, making me trip in my pedals, I run over his foot. I don't mean to, but he's in the way, like they're all in the way. A minute later, the same guy gets in front of me again, so when I run over his foot this time, it's not accidental. He barks, "Hey, hey," like he's tougher than me, but he's not tougher than me. I'm frontline. I shove my shoulder into his chest, tell him to "get the fuck outta the way," and push on. The aggression of the night is leaking into me and I consider stopping, going home, but the crowd is chanting, "NYPD eat my ass! From the back and to the front!" How can I stop? At the next arrest, after the surge of SRG, I pull onto the sidewalk beside a couple of bikers. They look shell-shocked. I must have the same look on my face. We talk about the stress—the cops, the photographers, the narrow streets. One says, "My cortisol levels are through the roof." I tell them to shake, it's important to shake it off, and I demonstrate, shaking out my arms and jumping up and down, moving the tension, whooping and shouting to unwind my body's tight coil. I tell them I'm a trauma therapist and this really works, but I don't have time to go into the theory behind Somatic Experiencing, how the antelope avoids post-traumatic stress by shaking after it escapes the grip of a lion, and the bikers only look at me like I'm crazy.

When the turning, twisting march ends in Union Square the cops stay close, guarding the southern border of the park. Crackhead Barney is here. She's tired from marching and not up for performing, holding her worn-out Trump mask in her hand. "What are you going to do when Trump is gone?" I ask. "This is your whole career." "I'll figure something out," she says. "Maybe I'll keep him going. Play Trump the loser." Leh-Boy rolls up, the smiling Liberian guy who rides his bike around protests with a basketball balanced on his head, and the mood turns festive. Piggy starts clowning with the riot cops, photographers snap pictures, and a small group gathers to goof on the police. They take it for awhile, but then the atmosphere shifts. The SRG cops who've been waiting across Fourteenth Street, assembled on the sidewalk in front of Whole Foods, snap to attention as the LRAD comes out to inform us that we must get out of the roadway and onto the sidewalk. I'm already on the sidewalk, sitting on a concrete block, resting my lower back. Nobody moves. The announcement escalates. Now it says we'll all be arrested if we're not on the sidewalk. I am on the sidewalk. I am tired. I don't move.

The SRG cops race toward us in a line, pushing their bikes out like weapons, chanting, "Move *back*, move *back*, move *back*." Their formation looks like something out of science fiction, a long bulldozer blade made of many parts, sleek and oily dark, clicky insects, the exoskeletal segments of a hive. It's meant to be terrifying but I'm fascinated, watching this machine hurry toward me across Fourteenth Street. It's in slow motion. I still don't move. When the line reaches me, a cop presses his face close to mine and says in a drill sergeant's voice, "You need to *move*." His young face, wide-eyed inside its helmet, reminds me of a soft mollusk tucked inside a shell, as emotionless and blank as a quahog. Slowly, with an

Piggy in a line of riot cops, Union Square

underwater feeling I recognize as post-traumatic weirdness, I get to my feet, but there's a second line of SRG behind me. I'm trapped. My bike wheel taps a cop, a giant, and he grabs my arm hard. Before he can do anything, the first cop says, "Let this guy out." The giant yields, places both hands on my shoulders, lifts, and shoves me away so I feel small, as light as a paper doll. Later, I'll find an Instagram video of this scene, and in the strange experience of watching myself, I look as small as I felt, as breakable as a child.

Once again, I am not arrested. I am never arrested. Other white people are arrested, but not me, and I wonder if it's because I'm older, softer, smaller. Maybe the police sense compliance in me (my former psychoanalyst used to tell me I was too compliant), or maybe I'm just good at getting out of the way. I'll never know.

The cops keep pushing into the park, "Move *back*, move *back*, move *back*," and I hurry up the steps of the plaza, thinking they won't come that far, but they keep coming and I duck out of their kettle before it shuts. There are hundreds of cops, several layers thick, in circles surrounding circles, all shaking their bikes, warriors shaking shields in an earthquake of rage as they enclose protesters and journalists, trapping them under the statue of George Washington on his horse. More cops reach into the kettle and, one by one, yank people out in zip ties. Then it all slows down. In the strained stillness, from deep inside the simmering pot, our trumpeter begins to play, Sam Cooke, "A Change Is Gonna Come."

November 6. In Times Square, people wander in a daze, watching the news ticker for election results, but there's still no word. Jesus of Washington Square is here, dressed in his Beavis and Butthead "Breakin the Law" shirt, a pair of kitten ears, and short-shorts that he hikes deep into his butt crack, like a thong, so he can bend over in the middle of the pedestrian plaza to perform a sultry dance both slow and vigorous.

At dusk, men show up with blue parrots and yellow anacondas, placing them on people's shoulders to pose for photos. Ramon the magician is pulling lit cigarettes from children's ears, the city's best bucket drummer is drumming, weed dealers are dealing, breakdancers are breaking, and Silk, the greased-up muscle man in the killer clown mask, is doing push-ups in the doorway of H&M flanked by a pair of battery-operated spinning princess dolls.

I ride down to Union Square and revisit the concrete block where the giant cop grabbed me last night. I can still feel him inside me, a prickling sensation under my skin, and I want to stay with it, to think more about this experience, how a cop has the power to press inside another body and take up lodging. After months, weeks, if I reach for it, I can feel the hands of all the cops who've grabbed me this year. They are small assaults, almost nothing, yet it is exactly their smallness that reveals the extent of their power. If such a light jab can persist under the skin, what happens to a hard thrust? What happens to a hundred hard thrusts, repeated over time? How do they bind to the body?

As I'm wondering about this, the Legendary Cyphers crew starts their weekly cypher, a communal circle of hip-hop artists rapping freestyle. I listen to a guy holding a white duck on his arm while he rhymes "fatal collision" with "anal position," and when Ulu the nutcracker man arrives, he gives me a warm hello fist bump (all the nutcracker men know me by now), and I buy a SunnyD and rum, chatting with him and a guy called Crazy Joe who sees my BLM button, so right away he's got us talking about the carceral state, white supremacy, and Joe's body, his hip replacements and the limitations of Medicaid and Medicare. He's mopping his head with a tea towel he keeps slung over a shoulder, saying, "I'm only thirty-five years old," meaning he feels worn out, meaning living in a society saturated by police brutality wears a Black man out and makes him older than he ought to be. *Weathering* is the word. This is how public health researchers describe the cumulative impact of everyday social and economic stressors on a Black body. Racism erodes health like the ocean consumes shore, wave after wave.

I feel the trace of last night's cop in my body and know this is only a small fraction of what men like Joe endure, but it's enough to dislodge something in my head. I've been getting this new thought, the kind that can only be known through the body, so it's more like a jolt than a thought, like the electric shock of nerves reconnecting after a wound. It's the kind of body-thought that comes in through a gap that opens for one second and gives you the slightest taste of what it's like to be treated as an enemy of the state. Sometimes, these days, I catch myself wondering: Will the cops still protect me after all this protest? In my white experience, I hold on to the idea that they will protect me, but this other thought has taken shape, so whenever I pass a cop on the street I bristle, tensing for a blow. You prepare for what you know. Every white person should feel the jolt of a cop's hands on their body. If only for a moment. If only to knock something loose and open a gap through which a new thought can materialize.

November 7. It's Saturday morning and still the election has not been called. Last night, hoping to hear from the state of Georgia, someone outside my building sat in their car, windows rolled down, and blasted Ray Charles's "Georgia on My Mind" followed by Gladys Knight's "Midnight Train to Georgia," but the music could not persuade the Peach State to deliver. It's 10:25 a.m., an unseasonably warm, sunny day, and I'm finishing my coffee when a human sound rises from the streets. It's a cry, a breaking howl, and I don't need to hear the cheers that follow to know: Trump has lost. I throw open a window to people clapping and hugging on the sidewalk, neighbors leaning from windows, banging pots and pans, whooping and ululating. Down below, the beer deliveryman jumps from his truck and asks the bodega man, "Is it Biden? Is it Biden?" Yes, yes. A car pulls over and the driver asks the crowd what happened. "It's Pennsylvania," a woman says. "They called Pennsylvania. Biden won." As news spreads, the applause gets louder, the crowds grow larger, everyone crying and hugging, dancing in the street, popping champagne. I'm standing in the kitchen, putting my coffee cup in the sink, when I feel an internal click and my body bends over, face in hands, sobbing with relief, four years of tension cracking like ice in sudden sunlight.

I get on my bike and race to Washington Square, packed with revelers, through the Village, and up Eighth Avenue. It's noon, an hour and a half has passed since the news broke, but the crowds are still cheering on every corner, banging pots, making a joyful noise that goes on and on, whooping to me as I whoop on my bike, all the way to Times Square where thousands have taken the street, waving flags and carrying signs: *Hallelujah, You're Fired, God Delivered Us From Evil*. I'm vibrating and can't sit still, so I ride on, up to Columbus Circle, packed with socialists, communists, queers, one man dressed in a rubber Trump mask and orange prison jumpsuit. The traffic can't move and people climb onto the roofs of their cars to dance. On the way up to Harlem, on a grassy bank of Central Park, a woman dressed in a long dashiki waves and smiles behind cut-out letters that spell, in Pan-African red, black, and green, the word: BREATHE.

Everywhere, I hear "FDT (Fuck Donald Trump)," the protest anthem by rappers YG and Nipsey Hussle, roaring from car windows, front-stoop boom boxes, the open doors of barbershops, so when I lose the beat on one corner, I pick it up on another, rolling with it back down to Times Square where the crowd has intensified, night has fallen, and the carnival is raging, everyone in the street—drummers, keyboard players, acrobats, breakdancers spinning on their hands to Frank Sinatra's "New York, New York," a guy in a rubber Biden mask riding an inflatable dinosaur. A topless woman walks by with bipartisan breasts, one painted red and the other blue. A man pulls a large, velvety black snake from a duffel bag and uncoils it onto the street, skin glistening in electronic light, as a group of motorcyclists dressed as pink bunny rabbits comes riding by. A couple of gay men grab each other and kiss, reenacting the Eisenstaedt photo from V-J Day because this, too, feels like the end of a long and painful war.

When the Bike Life riders roll up, popping wheelies, I seize my chance and jump into their ride-out, racing downtown, blowing red lights, high on the buzz of the pack as they whirl, dodging traffic and "catching blocks." In this flock of giggling, whooping young men, I am lifted, heart fizzing, and I'm not going to cry, I'm not, but I can't stop gasping because the giddiness is gripping, everyone joyful with shared elation. Is this what it's like to be a boy among boys? One turns to me, beaming an open smile, and nods as if to say *yes, you are here, I see you*. He calls "We outside," inviting me to respond. The words don't feel like mine, but he says them again, urging me to answer, and how can I not? "We outside," I shout, sending back the call. Delighted, he stands on the pedals and

Bike Life, Times Square

throws the call to another, an echo that skips from rider to rider, including one gutsy girl, wheel up high, streetlights sparking off gold hoops in her ears, ponytail airborne. The wheelie, I have to say, is magic. When it comes from behind, you feel it before you see it, a whirling flutter shifting the air around your skin. You can hear it, too, purring like a hummingbird, and then it's there at your cheek, so close it feels like a kiss about to land, and *brrrrrrr*, there it goes, rocketing by, and I am not going to cry, I'm not, but this is flying—I mean, for days, whenever I think of this night, my eyes will burn with salt.

17.

GOOD OLD BAD OLD NEW YORK

After the election, we go into a freeze as winter descends and we hold our breath, through darker days, waiting for Trump to leave the White House. Waiting for his last act of violent refusal. Still, the feral city keeps echoing with hauntological reverberations.

In the subdued buzz of pandemic Christmas shoppers, Thirty-Fourth Street surges to life, the sidewalk across from Macy's blossoming into an unofficial flea market, dozens of vendors selling knockoff handbags, boxes of rubber gloves, jugs of hand sanitizer, windup toy dogs, jars of shea butter, Tarot card readings. The ambience has the warm glow of familiarity. I spent my early life among the charismatic hustlers of flea markets. My father was one of them, first a vendor—selling Bill Rodgers Gore-Tex tracksuits, dragging me from flea to flea, glad-handing and schmoozing, sizing up the competition—and later the manager of an indoor marketplace in a rough part of a rough town famous for producing boxers like Rocky Marciano and Marvelous Marvin Hagler. At fourteen, I had my first job at that flea, a jack-of-all-trades position that included selling tickets in a dusty booth, frying Italian sausages at the snack bar, and sweeping thousands of cigarette butts into a dustpan while I wandered the aisles, chatting with odd characters, flirting with men who had no business flirting back, and dodging advances from amorous security guards. The neighborhood had a high crime rate, the flea attracted people with idle hands, and occasionally a fight broke out, ending with someone stabbed and taken away on a stretcher. The violence didn't scare anyone off, it was part of flea life, spice added to otherwise desolate days of sausage grease and cigarette butts.

On Thirty-Fourth Street, I talk with a heavyset Black man in a Yankees cap, presiding over a table loaded with pocketknives, pepper spray, and stun guns. He attracts customers by holding up a taser and making it crackle with captivating electricity. This is the table of Good Old Bad Old New York. The man sells loosies, too, one Newport for a dollar, and when I tell him I remember how they used to cost a quarter and you could buy them from a gumball jar at the corner bodega, he gets nostalgic, takes a few hits off his asthma inhaler, and recalls the 1980s in Ozone Park, Queens, loosies for a nickel, going to see a girl in Bensonhurst, a sweet memory that quickly turns with the racist killing of Yusef Hawkins and the violence of subway vigilante Bernie Goetz. The salesman's associate walks up and dumps a plastic bag of drugstore stuff onto the table, battered boxes of Allegra, Mucinex, Nexium, and the salesman doesn't miss a beat, calling "One dollah, one dollah, one dollah," as customers flock, grabbing the cheap pills, and the salesman tries to push his stun guns, zapping as he calls, "Tasers, tasers, tasers! You want a taser, baby girl?" The woman walking by says to her friend, "I don't need to go to 125th Street anymore—I can do all my shopping right here." It's Harlem come to Herald Square.

In between the tables and blankets of wares, a team of hustlers step through the Pandemic Space-Time Vortex to bring back the shell game and three-card monte. I haven't seen this in years. Behind pedestals of stacked cardboard boxes, the dealers flip cards and move shells, which are not shells but plastic bottle caps, hiding the red pea, revealing it again, flashing that elusive object of desire. As the ropers pull in players to scam, the shills place their phony bets and win, whipping up excitement, fists full of twenties and hundreds. The players make their bets, convinced they can beat this game that's been tricking the gullible since ancient Greece. The dealers let them have a few, encouraging bolder bets, and now the players lose, as the game preordains, and they walk away with heads shaking, wallets lighter. When cops approach, the lookouts call, "Charlie walkin' down," using a word that might come from "Mister Charlie," a century-old expression that *The New Partridge Dictionary of Slang and Unconventional English* calls "a gesture of resistance . . . used as a stereotypical representation of white authority over black people." When the dealers hear "Charlie," they kick apart their cardboard tables, reducing them to innocent sidewalk trash, and dissolve into the crowd. The excitement collapses and the air goes still, waiting for the cops to stroll past, and when the coast is clear, the games resume, dealers calling, "Round and round she goes," magician hands spinning the cards, the shells, the red pea that is never where you need it to be.

Shell game, Herald Square

One of the dealers chats me up. He's not working at the moment and doesn't treat me like a mark. "I haven't seen these games in years," I say, not hiding my delight. "People still fall for it," the dealer says. "It's because of their greed. That's all. They can't help their greed. They think they can make easy money, but there's no such thing." He's been dealing for thirty years, traveling from New York to Miami and Vegas, and he likes football games best, working outside stadiums where people are in a gambling mood, money burning holes in their pockets. He prefers the shells to the cards because "you get more moves, you can do more with them," like palming the pea, so it never shows until he wants it to. I wonder if the reappearance of the game is due to the pandemic's loosening of social control and ask the man what brought it back. "It's gotten easier," he says, "since the city decriminalized misdemeanors, so now all you get is a DAT," a desk appearance ticket, "and there's no more plainclothes officers coming around either." The decriminalization bill passed in 2017, an effort to undo harsh penalties for minor transgressions like loitering, turnstile-jumping, and public urination, the "quality of life" offenses that Giuliani targeted in the 1990s, unleashing police brutality and imprisonment on mostly Black and brown New Yorkers. More recently, in June 2020, the NYPD disbanded their plainclothes anti-crime unit, a remnant of stop-and-frisk, another racist policing strategy greatly expanded by Giuliani and Bloomberg. The more people I talk to, the more I understand that the city was already moving in a looser direction over the past couple of years. In white Manhattan, however, it was barely visible. It took the pandemic to bring it to the center.

The dealer says, "nice talking to you," gives me a pound with his fist, and jumps into the game, running his patter, "round and round she goes," and a guy comes by in an 8-ball jacket, calling, "Loosies, loosies! Goin' back to the '80s, baby!" Attracted by the crowd, he pulls a pack of Newports from his pocket and sells to the gamblers. Lately, it's loosies everywhere.

A box truck sits parked at the curb, driver's-side window cracked open a few inches for men to walk up, push dollars through, and come away with handfuls of Newports. No one hassles them in this hustle of necessity, and I can't help thinking of Eric Garner, stopped by police for allegedly selling loose cigarettes on Staten Island in 2014, a Black man choked to death while he gasped the words, "I can't breathe," repeating the phrase eleven times, pressing it into collective memory.

■ ■ ■

IN TIMES SQUARE, I VISIT MY NEW FRIEND MR. NINJA, A HOMELESS man who sells loosies and plays pranks, planting a rubber rat on the sidewalk to make people jump. I appreciate the rat as recurring theme, reverberation from the underground. While Mr. Ninja tells me about his scheme to motorize the rat, Crackhead Barney comes through, doing her "N——a Claus" routine. Dressed in a bikini, Santa hat, coat, and beard, holding a cardboard sign that says, "A N——a Claus Need Crack," she chases after the few tourists, shouting, "White Santa is dead!" Down at Washington Square, Buddy the Rat is running around in his rat costume while Spider-Cuz, dressed in a Spider-Man suit with Timberlands and fitted Yankees cap, is waving a bottle of Hennessy and putting up wanted posters with Batman's face and the words: "Have you seen this glizzy? Please call 1-800-FUCK-BATMAN." The city has become, again, full of characters, and one night, on a corner of St. Mark's and Second, I meet Sissy Pussy Cunt.

Seated on a milk crate by a pile of garbage bags, she is white, middle-aged, somewhere on the transgender spectrum, dressed in a tight pink sweater and skirt with matching bows in her hair. At her feet sits a cardboard sign handwritten with the words: Sissy Dance $1. When I ask what a sissy dance is about, she tells me she's a sissy and she dances. I tell her I'm trans, so she knows I'm family, but she doesn't seem to care. I give her two dollars instead of one, because a sissy dance deserves more than asking price, and she gets to her feet and tells me to take out my camera. She wants to be filmed and shared. To be seen. When I ask her name, she says in a southern drawl, "Sissy Pussy Cunt," a name that declares *I am* the symbolic Vaginal, object of desire, all in pink on St. Mark's Place, yet another conjuring of the chaotic femme, and I feel that I am again in the presence of the chthonic, risen up from underground, another Sheela, Baubo lifting her skirt to banish grief. As she dances, Sissy Pussy Cunt summons nocturnal magic, running her hands along the length of her body, moaning, "Ooh, I'm a pussy, I'm a big sissy, ooh, yeah, I'm a pussy, that's what I am, I am the biggest pussy there is, yeah, ooh, I'm such a cunt, I'm a sissy pussy cunt, yeah." She lifts her skirt—*anasuromai!*—and shows her panties, mincing on her toes as the traffic rushes past along the avenue and the hyper-normals stand apart, waiting for the light to change, unable or unwilling to see this spectral vision in pink.

Another ghost reappears. In the freedom of lockdown, with the NYPD's Vandal Squad holding back, teams of graffiti writers are redecorating the trains 1980s-style. They bomb twenty-four cars, covering them in colorful designs featuring rabbits, flames, mushrooms, and a naked, weed-smoking Betty Boop. The pictures spark my heart. As a kid, twelve years old, I loved to see the painted trains whenever they appeared in music videos on MTV, beamed into my small-town life, and I became obsessed with getting a glimpse of them in real life. The few times each year when my mother drove us down I-95 to visit my brother, a U.S. Marine stationed at the base in Philadelphia, I would wait anxiously to cross into New York, holding my camera to the window to catch the fleeting blaze of wildstyle color from the Cross Bronx Expressway, a sooty brown passage that both thrilled and frightened me, its margins littered with the carcasses of dead cars stripped by scavengers who we believed would set upon us in seconds if we ever had the misfortune of a flat tire. My photos came out blurry, but they stood as evidence that those glorious trains and I had shared the same atmosphere. In Philly I took photos of walls splashed in bubble letters and drippy tags, as I do today, still loving what I have always loved. What could graffiti have meant to me then? Maybe I already recognized queerness in urban disorder, finding myself in a place and time when I could not otherwise be found, and I looked to those hieroglyphics to detect messages about outsider life, a messy mirror reflecting from the bricks. Walking with my family through the Philly streets, I spotted a small piece of graffiti that featured two girls' names inside a heart, combined by a plus sign and the words "true love always." I did not take its picture, which would have been too dangerous, but I did write it down in my diary—*lesbians!*—noting that such strange and wondrous signs could only be discovered in a city.

. . .

EVERY THURSDAY NIGHT, THROUGH COLD AND SNOW, I BUNDLE UP IN layers and bike with Stonewall, holding traffic while we chant "fuck your dinner" to outdoor diners sitting comfortably under heat lamps. We say the names—Nina Pop, Tony McDade, Brayla Stone—performing hauntology to *disrupt and disclose*, tactics of civil disobedience identified by political theorist Erin Pineda for "arresting the attention of white citizens by temporarily denying them comfort and upsetting their expectations for consumer pleasure." A few of our comrades sit down at the tables and sociably engage diners in difficult conversations, using confrontation and education to compel them to know what they don't want to know, to see what they refuse to see. Some diners are appreciative and welcoming. Others sneer, roll their eyes, and shout, "I give money to nonprofits!" Sometimes, riot cops rush in to form fortresses around the diners (because consumer pleasure must be protected). Restaurant owners are getting testy. In the cold, business is down and the last thing they want is a crew of protesters enlightening their customers about racist and transphobic violence over plates of charred octopus and escargot.

At one French bistro, the owner grabs a protester by the arm. "This is *my* restaurant," he screams, ripping off his COVID mask, spitting with rage, "You people are so fucking stupid!" In her silver ball gown, Joela intervenes, urging us to move along before the conflict can turn into a fistfight. As we march off, the restaurateur shouts, "We're dying here! *We are dying!*" He means his business is struggling, and while that is reason for distress, the word feels wrong in the presence of ghosts, a disavowal of the actual dead.

Post-election, after Trump's defeat, there is a different anger in the air, and when we march from Times Square to the United Nations, supporting immigrant detainees on hunger strike in ICE custody, that anger comes for us. At the UN, the rally evaporates, people start to disperse, and I go, too, just missing the driver who plows into our group with her BMW. On the videos, bicycles crunch and bodies fly like bags of dry leaves. Ambulances come to take the injured. Miraculously, no one is killed. The fifty-two-year-old white woman driving the car is charged with reckless endangerment and released with a desk appearance ticket, same DAT you get for selling loosies. According to news reports, she told police she was stopped at the light when protesters surrounded her car and started banging on it, grabbing the door handles to get in. She said she feared for her life, "images from news reports of drivers being pulled from their cars and beaten flashed before her eyes," and she stepped on the gas to escape what she claims was an angry mob. The claim is common and needs some unpacking.

First, the image of a protest mob surrounding cars, banging and grabbing door handles, is false. From my experiences of bike blocking, I know that when a driver is stopped at a light, we stand in front of the car with our bikes, several feet away, and hold up our hands, two fingers to say "two minutes." If the driver is agitated, one biker will approach the window to talk with them, calmly explaining it'll be quick, de-escalating

them if their agitation rises. I've done this many times and it almost
always calms the driver down. The only time I've seen bikers or marchers
bang their hands on a car is if it starts to accelerate and we're trying to
stop it from hurting people. I've never seen anyone grab door handles.
There is no mob. Still, drivers who hit the gas will repeatedly make the
same claim, "I was afraid for my life." Are they lying or is this something
more complex?

I keep thinking about the image this woman had in her mind of drivers
getting pulled from their cars and beaten—white drivers, she doesn't
say, Black mobs. What is this image and where did it come from? I
imagine she is remembering, as I do, the attack on Reginald Denny, the
white driver pulled from his truck and beaten by a group of Black men
during the 1992 LA riots after the acquittal of the police officers who
beat Rodney King. In the full reel of shaky news copter footage, there
are three drivers pulled from vehicles and beaten, but it's only Denny
who is remembered. In all three incidents, other Black people come to
the aid of the drivers, but that, too, is forgotten. What I remember, and
what the driver who plowed into the protesters likely remembers, is an
image of rioters opening the door of Denny's truck and pulling him out.
This memory is vivid, I can clearly see Denny fall to the ground from
the truck, but I can't find it on the news copter video. My mind filled in
the blank. By the time the camera pans to the scene, Denny is already
on the ground, surrounded by his assailants, one of whom lifts a heavy
object and heaves it onto Denny's head. In almost all reports, the object
is called a cinder block, and in my memory I see a cinder block, but in
reality it looks nothing like a cinder block. It looks like a white plaster
pedestal, the kind that holds up birdbaths you can buy at outdoor stores
that sell concrete lawn ornaments.

These mis-rememberings do not diminish the brutality of the attack on
Denny: He was dragged from his truck, struck hard enough to severely

fracture his skull, traumatized for life. But they might open a space in which to think about the way collective memory congeals around distorted images that repeat for the purpose of undoing. While Black people might remember the King beating vividly, with strong emotion, what happens in the white imagination to that memory? Is it less vivid, replaced by images from the beating of Denny? As Mike Davis noted, "The narcotic-like repetition of the footage of the Denny beating on television . . . erased most of the white guilt over the King beating." This repetition and erasure might make it easier, nearly three decades later, for some people to hit the gas and plow into activists for Black lives while telling themselves that they fear for their own life, because what remains emotionally charged in memory is not the police and their nightsticks raining blows on a Black body, but something else: a door pulled open, a white body dragged out, a mob of Black hands lifting cinder blocks. That is the scene that reaches back through generations of American whiteness and confirms the fantasy of the beast-like "super-predator" Black male, the scene that erases not just white guilt but the memory of lynching—and today's extrajudicial executions—with the attendant rationalization: "He must have done something to deserve it."

There have been over a hundred incidents of people driving into protesters this year in the United States, and throughout we hear the refrain *I feared for my life*. Sociologist Martel Pipkins calls the phrase "the most salient single narrative" in police killings of unarmed Black people. As a master narrative, a cultural product that repeats, it is a discursive strategy meant to "reinforce racialized fear, avoid blame, and invoke empathy" for the police officer. In 2020, the phrase *I feared for my life* has taken on a viral quality, jumping from police to drivers who run down protesters, juiced by fantasies of demon Black men, a perception that generalizes to other protesters by association, because this violence has always been about the maintenance of white supremacy. Weeks from now, Republican politicians from several states will propose legislation to grant immunity to drivers who hit protesters. The bills will pass in Iowa, Florida, and Oklahoma, essentially making it legal to kill a person with your car because you don't like their politics.

. . .

IT'S CHRISTMAS AND I'M RIDING THROUGH UNION SQUARE WHEN A guy in a red tracksuit, long braids, and a Louis Vuitton mask flags me down like it's urgent, saying, "Bro, bro, what's up with the pink?" He means the pink spoke skins and stickers on my bike. I ask, "How do you feel about pink?" and he says, "I like it as a color, but it's not very masculine. It's 2020. You need everything to be masculine to be safe!" He walks away and, as I ride off, I wonder: Safe from what?

I continue to Times Square, which is lively but not crowded, and after a pandemic Christmas dinner of dirty-water dog with sauerkraut and relish, I talk with Rev, short for Reverend, "because I'm preachy," also known as Hater Hobo because he carries a cardboard sign that says: "Fuck You! Pay me! I Need $&¢ 4 Drugz, Hoez, And Weaponz Mother Fuckerz!!!!!!" Underneath, he has drawn various images, including: an axe, a marijuana leaf, a black cat, a stick of dynamite, an anarchy symbol, a gun, a bomb, and a naked woman. Rev is a white man, a weathered forty years old, with a scruffy goatee and missing front tooth. He's in duck-cloth coveralls and a red knit cap, like a lumberjack or a stevedore, only Rev doesn't work. Mostly, Rev drinks from a bottle of Nikolai vodka and shoots the shit with whoever's willing. I am willing.

When he spots my BLM button, he talks about his dedication to the revolution, tugs down the collar of his T-shirt to show the Guy Fawkes mask tattooed on his deltoid, and tells me that COVID's nothing to be afraid of. "You know what you need to be scared of? Mosquitoes. Second-most deadly animal on the planet. Mosquitoes can give you AIDS." I redirect the conversation to Times Square and he agrees it's become wilder and freer during the pandemic. The cops leave people alone, he explains, they hate Bill de Blasio, so they're all on strike. "You should be here at night," he says, "when the vampires come out. We're out here drinking, dancing, smoking weed, doing Molly." Recently, he says, he was walking around with a rapier sword, "my weapon of choice," and decided to see what would happen if he poked some cops. He walked up to a group of six cops and poked each one in the chest. "They didn't do nothing. They just stood there and let me poke them for a good while before they took my sword away and sent me to the mental hospital." Rev likes to test the limits, which, during the pandemic, lie somewhere beyond a white man poking six cops in the chest with a rapier sword. While we're talking, a group of children who can't be more than twelve years old walk by and hand Rev an expertly rolled spliff. He thanks them and sticks it in his mouth. With cool confidence, one of the boys reaches up with a Bic to give him a light—and then gives me a wink. These kids aren't raggedy urchins. They're in brand-new puffer jackets and Nike sneakers, white and Black kids who look suburban rich, but edgy, like artful dodgers from old Times Square, only much better groomed. I'm struck by their self-possessed adult attitude, but it doesn't faze Rev, who never looks in the mouth of a gift horse bearing substances.

A man who calls himself Hot Chocolate Santa walks over. He's Black, muscular, and shirtless, in red Santa pants and hat, white beard and wire-rim glasses. On a chain around his neck, a large hip-hop pendant reads "Ho Ho Ho." He looks at my bike and says, "I love the pink." I tell him what the guy in Union Square said about pink not being mas-culine and Hot Chocolate Santa disagrees, reassuring me, "Real men wear pink."

■ ■ ■

FROM A SPEAKER, CARDI B DEMANDS, "BRING A BUCKET AND A MOP for this wet-ass pussy," as the protest crew outside Stonewall dances in the cold on New Year's Eve, drinking mango-pineapple nutcrackers and posing in holiday finery. Miss Simone, who runs the drag show in Christopher Park, is reading palms for a dollar. In her leopard-print jacket and red-glitter lipstick, she calls me Sweetie and tells me I'm a very creative person who's going to "make it big" one day. Derrick is here, Rob, and Ann Marie in her FUCK 12 shirt, the one that connected me to them on a night that feels like years ago. Qween is in a crown and silver sequins and Joela is a phoenix rising from ashes with fiery wings. As we go marching through the Village, there is no one on the streets but our family. The outdoor restaurant sheds are empty, abandoned, and the sidewalks are silent. We're blocking the intersection of Fourteenth and Fourth, dancers twerking and voguing, when midnight strikes and we cheer and embrace, before marching north again, taking the Park Avenue viaduct, around Grand Central, and into the carnival-ride tunnel that cuts through the Helmsley Building, where we stop in the echoing dark to dance and cheer in the sweetness of this night together.

After the march, I ride down the middle of empty Fifth Avenue at 2:00 in the morning, cut over to Times Square, barricaded to revelers because of the plague, and sneak inside so I'm gliding through the swirl of confetti swept by the clean-up crew's leaf blowers under the glittering ball dropped onto 2021. Everyone wants 2020 to end, except me. Everyone wants to go back to normal, move on and forget, but I'm not ready. I keep riding, through the cold, forsaken streets, music resounding from my speaker, same song on repeat: Lou Reed's "Walk on the Wild Side."

PART FIVE

18.

BACK TO NORMAL

Washington Square goes still under a rind of frozen snow and Times Square is tranquilized into a quiet broken only by the calls of weed dealers, men so bold they walk the plazas with gallon-sized baggies of bud, inviting passersby to pull down their masks and inhale *kush, diesel, purple haze.* COVID rises into a punishing second wave after the holiday gatherings and my newest neighbors party through it, packing their apartment with unmasked kids for White Claw and karaoke, as if indoor singing is not one of the most dangerous things you can do in an airborne plague. When I knock on their door, they turn the volume down, apologize, offer to bake me cookies and banana bread, but then the singing and stomping goes on. As for the baked goods, they never materialize.

On a chilly night downtown, I get the vaccine. In a cubicle of plastic sheeting, I roll up my sleeve, take the jab, and thank the nurse for helping save the world. She protests, but her eyes go dewy as she feels the truth of it, the possibility of a future, saying she looks forward to one day telling her grandchildren about this time in her young, hopeful life. Outside, in the cold and dark, I look up at the Municipal Building to see golden Audrey Munson, the bohemian angel who watched over me when I stayed at the occupation of City Hall. I take her presence as benediction and give her a salute, my arm sore from the shot, a hot swarm of antibodies working to keep me alive.

All through winter I bike with Stonewall, tires slipping in snow, bones aching in cold, but I can't complain because the trans femmes do it in strapless gowns and heels, and I need to be here, in the anger and joy, among my people. We call it *church*. We call it *family*. The group is smaller, only the diehards, and we're proud of this, the way diehards are proud of their toughness. The city belongs to us because we're taking it and, besides, no one else wants it. They have left the streets for dead. One bright and glassy afternoon I take my first bridge, that rite of passage. Tire-to-tire, my comrades and I stop cars from entering the Brooklyn Bridge, holding traffic until the marchers safely pass and the backline leader yells "Blockers clear," sending me pedaling hard up the incline, racing to the front where there is nothing before me but the rolled-out ribbon of asphalt, vibrating strings, blue sky, seagulls. My friends ask, "How does it feel? Your first bridge!" It feels powerful, I say, like my body is unbreakable, made of steel and flight.

■ ■ ■

THE APARTMENT BELOW MINE HAS BEEN SITTING EMPTY SINCE THE landlord bought out the rent-controlled tenant, a woman who fought until she ran out of lawyer money, and now the gut renovation has begun. All day, workers pound my floor, shaking up dust and making the building quake so hard I hear its bones crack. One of my old-school neighbors thinks it's about to fall down in a heap. They're cutting into the wooden beams, he says, which are only inches thick and already sag. This in addition to the fact that they removed a layer of brick from the facade to embed a billboard in our tenement's flank to generate ad revenue, extracting as much as possible from this battered body, this pimped-out derelict of brick and mortar, listing like a scuttled ship. I shudder, imag-

ining the floor beneath me giving way as I sleep, my bed sliding out the
window with me inside. I can't stay here.

To avoid the noise of demolition, I put on real pants and shoes and walk
thirty minutes to see my patients over Zoom in the quiet of my abandoned office. It's been nearly a year since I've been here. My windowsill
is dusted with soot and dried-out flies, along with fallen bits of insulation
I jammed in the window frame last winter, so the bitter wind sends a
chill down my spine. It feels strange to be here, like going back to your
childhood bedroom after you've left to become a different person. I feel
too large for this place—and then too small.

On my lunch hour I walk to a sandwich shop, a fast-casual chain because
there is nothing left but fast-casual chains, and on the otherwise empty
sidewalk I'm assailed by a group of hyper-normals, whip-thin and razor-
sharp, taking up the width of the sidewalk, not seeing me because I don't
exist for them. It's been so long since I've encountered this everyday
human bulldozer, my defenses have slowed, and when I shift, I'm too
late. My body braces as they run into me, laughing, slamming me backward. How can they not see me when I'm the only one here? My body
remembers when these assaults happened every day, before the pandemic
chased these people away, and I have the panicked thought: Are they
back? At the crosswalk, I look for more, but the streets are quiet. It was
just a random pack, stragglers from the rapture. Still, my blood stays
hot and bristled.

I want to break out of my tight clothing and shoes, like one of those
cavemen who gets thawed out of prehistoric ice in a 1980s movie, and
when he puts on a suit and tries to act civilized, he goes crazy from all
the fucked-up modernity—or something like that (see also *Greystoke* and
Cast Away, the bourgeois white male fantasy of a natural prelapsarian
self)—so when the light changes, I bolt across the avenue and could keep

on running but the bike lane stops me short. This is my bike lane, the
trail that has carried me, racing and free, only now I'm a gravity-bound
pedestrian. As the bikes whiz by, I glimpse a parallel universe through ·
the vortex, but I'm on the other side, in exile from the feral city. I don't
want to be here. I want my work, my life, but in the other New York, a
comfy spot where I can be one of those psychoanalysts of the twentieth
century, a shaggy, thoughtful mind in the tidewrack of time, surrounded
by books and paper piles, threadbare rug, ticking clock, the freedom to
be imperfect before we all had to become entrepreneurial selves. What
will happen to the feral part of me when the vaccine takes us back to
normal? What will happen to this world? I step across the bike lane, get
my stupid fast-casual sandwich, and eat it with a bellyful of uncertainty
and dread.

· · ·

IN WASHINGTON SQUARE, ON THE FIRST FINE DAY IN EARLY MARCH,
almost-spring breaks open like a piñata and everything bright and bril-
liant spills out, so I'm rolling around on my bike, fist-bumping and hugging folks I haven't seen in what feels like years. There's Joker, freed
from jail, delighted by my "Free the Joker" shirt. There's Stickers on
her skateboard, in a purple miniskirt and battered Vans, hair whipping
as she tears around the fountain. There's Antonio the artist, Aaron the
guitar-playing Bob Dylan fan, and here come a crowd of wheelie riders,
bike spokes flashing like confetti. Without water, the fountain bursts
into life, filled with skateboards, guitars, and boom boxes, a scene so gorgeous, so multi-racial, multi-gendered, multi-queer, it's like a drug-trip
vision of a utopia we've yet to achieve, but here it is. And in the center,
in the swirl of rebirth, Jesus of Washington Square reclaims his throne.
Sitting lotus-style in a floral sarong and his "Breakin the Law" T-shirt,
peacefully sucking weed from a pipe he's carved from a tree branch as
long as an alpine horn, he looks like a slapdash bodhisattva grooving on

his mountaintop. When he gets up to dance, people dance with him to the rhythm of a goth girl's bass guitar. I talk to her friend, a girl smoking from a bong, about my hopes for the year and she reassures me, "Kids my age are gonna keep the 2020 energy going." I want to believe her, but 2020 is over and we no longer have New York all to ourselves.

More Leavers, encouraged by the vaccine, have started trickling back from their suburban hideouts and country retreats. They are terrified by emancipated Washington Square, a place so remade it acquires the nickname "Wash," though it is anything but clean. At dusk, when the nocturnal festivity begins, when Queen Breesha dances shirtless in leather pants and spiked heels, when the music is Cardi B and Megan Thee Stallion, Pop Smoke growling his sinister beat, "Welcome to the Party," and the atmosphere grows swampy-lush with weed, the hyper-normals run for their lives. Fresh from the plains, still smelling of clean air and new clothing, they clutch their bags of Sweetgreen salad and scurry through the queer darkling space of funk and fug, eyes straight ahead, never slowing down to see. The park has so much subjectivity,

In the new Wash

so much humanity and aliveness, they cannot look. It must be painful, reminding them of parts of themselves they had to kill off. On the few occasions they do stop, secure in the safety of a gang, they try to turn us into objects. Screeching girls jump into the dance circle, not pausing to read the energy, taking space in awkward convulsions as they gracelessly hump Queen Breesha's leg while their male counterparts stand watching with arms crossed, goading them on and sneering like the whole thing's a joke until, just as abruptly, they all hurry away, beelining for the exit. In these hit-and-runs, it's clear—they want something *from* this world and have no idea how to be part *of* it.

At night I circle the fountain on foot, music gushing from the speaker clipped to my belt loop, adding to the river of groove as I delight in the swirl of skateboards, roller skates, bicycles, and dancers, taking pleasure in being part of the park's anarchic choreography. Our bodies are so graceful together, so agile, no one hits anyone. How is it that on a wide, empty sidewalk, a hyper-normal will slam into me, but in this crowd there's no collision? We are awake and attuned. What looks like chaos is a complex system, the organic order of human nature when it is not alienated from itself and others. We see and are seen, our rhythms in sync, and it is transcendent to be a body with these bodies, in this musical space where we agree, without words, to hold one another. So when the breakneck skater boy rushes toward me, I know he'll swerve, and he does, with a precision that reveals the swerve as a gesture of recognition. In this circle, I never flinch. I float and glide.

■ ■ ■

WHEN YOU WANDER OUT ON A TIDAL PLAIN, ACROSS THE WATERSHED of mudflats, to commune with the forms of life gathered in pools revealed only by the receded waters, it is easy to forget that the tide always returns. Soon the sea is trickling back, faster than you thought, snaking across the mud in rivulets, gathering and swelling in channels, swirling over the pools. Your islands of sand shrink fast and disappear, leaving you knee-deep in waters that cover the mud and all it contains. The month of March is like this, the city opened by business imperatives, by a collective social clock that says *enough, it's been a year already, we're going back to normal*. That phrase, *back to normal*, I'm sick of hearing it. Normal is the last thing I want to go back to.

When people say they are desperate to *go back to normal*, I understand they mean back to their usual lives, to restaurants and theaters, work and school, friends and family. It is not, on that level, objectionable, but is it also an attachment to the status quo? "We will not go back to normal," says author Sonya Renee Taylor. "Normal never was."

Last year, uncertain about the city, the hyper-normals came and went in odd patterns, but by the middle of March, exactly one year from the start of lockdown, the trickle becomes a flood. They are decidedly back. It's the moving trucks I notice first, coming in instead of out. Empty apartments refill, walls freshly painted, lights bright again in windows at night, housewarming parties so loud I hear their conversations from across the street, young men in backward caps talking to young women with ironed hair, shouting, "She was, like, yeah, I work at J.P. Morgan so I can totally expense our drinks!" Back to our boring dystopia. On the sidewalks, instead of mountains of furniture, there are stacks of empty cardboard boxes from Pottery Barn, West Elm, Crate & Barrel—new beds, tables, and chairs to replace the ones tossed out a year ago. Easy come, easy go, easy come again.

The streets become remarkably whiter, more white people in white clothing, white sneakers so freshly white they hurt to look at, soles so spotless they must never touch the ground, floating on immaculate clouds of another reality. The New People bring back an obliterating sameness that

cuts into our difference, a scythe in the wildflower meadow that blossomed in their absence. Dressed in identical clothes, carrying packs of
White Claw—the boozy seltzer described by the *Times* as "aggressively
bland" and "unextraordinary"—they go striding through the streets like
they still own the place. It chafes me. Working to understand why the
2020 departure of the hyper-normals made her so angry, artist Molly
Crabapple writes, "They dined, consumed, and profited" through the
good years as they "dulled the city to their generic, Connecticut tastes,
driving out so many of us in the process. When a bad year came, they
felt no responsibility. Why would they? They only had ties to each other."
Now they pick up where they left off, as if the city was not transformed
during their flight.

The past year of pandemic has provided a profound social experiment.
What happens when the city suddenly empties of hyper-normals and
then, just as suddenly, refills? The experience takes the shape of an ABA
experimental design: A, the baseline period (New York pre-lockdown),
followed by B, the experimental phase in which an intervention is applied
(lockdown), and then A again, the reversal phase, when the intervention
is withdrawn (New York reopens) and behavior returns, more or less, to
baseline. The pandemic is, of course, not a perfect analogy—the variables
are not controlled or possible to manipulate—but for those of us who
remained and held space in the streets, it comes close enough. What
can we observe from this unintended experiment? For the past year, as
New York deviated, a cluster of behaviors vanished. Now those behaviors return in a surge that is startling to behold, so absolutely unlike the
past twelve months.

As if their collective neural net has agreed, people are all at once walking
again with heads bowed to iPhones, unconscious and unseeing. They're
taking selfies again, stopping short on sidewalks to fake-smile into
screens. They're riding Citi Bikes in unskilled packs, staring at phones,

taking selfies as they wobble. Everywhere I look, young white men carry golf clubs, posing with 9 irons in hand, slicing the air as they wait for Ubers. The noise of the neighborhood intensifies as the New People go screaming through the streets, reclaiming space with their dominant laughter. They're in a hurry again, looking busy and rushing around like there's somewhere important to go when there's nowhere to go, except maybe brunch. They are brunching once more with ferocity, and also shopping, emitting the aggressive energy of acquisition, armloads of bags knocking into people. Of course, the bumping is back. I can't get one block from my apartment without them hitting me on otherwise empty sidewalks. In my building, once again, Amazon packages pile in the hall, new products arriving every day for the market-rate people. Finally, there is the ubiquitous phenomenon of people dressed in shirts and hats printed with the names of places not New York—Virginia, South Carolina, Michigan, Newport, Southampton. Souvenirs from the 2020 exodus? Like everything else on this list, they appeared en masse in the mid-aughts, vanished in the plague, and now rematerialize in numbers impossible not to notice. You might say a shirt is just a shirt, but is it? My "New York Fuckin City" shirt is not just a shirt; it's a stance, just as "Michigan" is a stance, an emotional position that places the wearer outside New York, maybe in opposition to urban life, declaring the pride of American elsewhere. In the past, we transplants were too embarrassed to wear hometown gear in the city. We wanted to be New Yorkers.

I am also an accidental subject in this experiment and, with the return of the hyper-normals, I again feel alienated and displaced. My anger comes back. Not the righteous, joyful anger I've enjoyed all year, this is archaic anger, sparking an inflammatory brush fire that spreads through my body, reviving my sciatic nerve pain, my neck pain, my IBS. (I find the New People so distressing that just writing about them, in this moment, makes my sigmoid colon shudder.) In its symphony of hysteria, my nervous system manifests a new symptom, a migraine that blooms inside my optic nerve with scintillating scotoma, blurry snakes that shiver in my vision for fifteen frightening minutes.

Next comes a cluster of thoughts that feel like not-me, thoughts from outside. The constellation first manifests in a sense of scarcity. For the past year, I felt largely satisfied with my life. My apartment, in all its shabbiness, felt cozy. I was comfortable in my body and didn't think about buying "nice" clothes or losing weight. I felt neither deprived nor competitive. But now, as normal returns, my thoughts shift to shopping, exercise, productivity, and I know: I'm back in the grip of internalized capitalism. A social disease, capitalism travels virally from host to host, and while many of us are carriers, the hyper-normals, those successful neoliberal subjects, are super-spreaders, shedding massive doses, exhaling capitalism's viral particles in invisible plumes the rest of us can't avoid breathing. Most don't intend to infect others, but many do. Isn't that what "influencing" is about? Isn't that why they turn themselves into advertisements, to stimulate lack? Sometimes I feel envy for what I don't want. Sometimes I can't tell the difference between what I want and what I've been told to want. My desire has been colonized.

The stickers on my bike start to look childish. I become self-conscious about my Black Lives Matter buttons. My trans flag pin feels unsafe. Outside of protest, people aren't wearing these signs anymore and I consider removing them, going back to invisibility, back to normal. This thought, like the others, troubles me and I work to resist it.

One other thing. For the past year, remember, no one bothered to replace the advertisements posted around town. With their preferred audience gone, they expired and disintegrated, creating that old New York layering effect, a collage of resignation. Nothing to buy. Nothing to want. Now fresh ads blitz the streets. They tell us what we're missing and how we're failing as they cover up the graffiti and political street art. Their message of lack gets under the skin. I start looking at real estate, dreaming of ownership. The acquisition of property can soothe the feeling of scarcity, but it also brings the possibility of loss through theft, writes Comrade Josephine, and "as long as there is theft, people will want to protect what they have, protect who they are, protect themselves from having something that they might afterwards lose. The manifestation of that desire is the police." And the police, as I've said, have eyes everywhere.

■ ■ ■

AT THE END OF THIS WEEK'S STONEWALL MARCH, I'M SITTING ON the steps of St. Patrick's Cathedral with Derrick, Rob, Ann Marie, and comrades who introduce themselves by their action names, Jupiter and Shadow. The speeches are done and folks are hanging out, listening to music, enjoying the night. We get to talking about the symbolic violence that moves through normativity, deployed through subtle movements, a certain walk, a flick of the eyes, a smirk. "Sometimes," I say, "I feel crazy, like I'm the only who sees it." But they see it, too. We are all Cassandras, and what is more joyful to a Cassandra than being in the presence of fellow killjoys? "To kill joy," Sara Ahmed says, "is to open a life, to make room for life, to make room for possibility, for chance." To kill joy is to resist the normative injunction to smile and accept it.

A couple walks by—white, straight, moneyed, unmasked—and as the man steers the woman along, she glances at our queer, colorful group, one corner of her mouth lifting into The Smirk. It's only a split second, yet she has deployed a weapon we recognize at once. Rob and I look at each other and shout, in unison, "There it is! Did you see it?" The Smirk is a splinter biting skin, one of those invisible filaments you feel but can't quite see, a fiber of glass. The Smirk is contempt, the hallmark micro-expression of hyper-normativity. It is a *doing* and we are the *done to*. While I'd like to say I'm impervious to it, my skin is not so thick.

Alone, I might be de-subjectified by The Smirk, but I am not alone. With my people, I am feral and immune, protected by the container we create, a space in which our bodies expand in exquisite queer negativity. The song shifts to "Wet-Ass Pussy," anthem of our open city, and we're dancing on the cathedral steps, blasphemous and bold, untroubled by whoever might be watching. Rob says, "Those people are probably afraid of us and what we represent—the destruction of their carefully constructed world." Everyone who's outside the center knows what it is to be feared this way—so feared we will have to be stopped.

19.

KILLING THE VIBE

Last April, author Arundhati Roy suggested that the pandemic, like plagues of the past, could be "a portal, a gateway between one world and the next," offering us a chance to imagine a new world, "to rethink the doomsday machine" of capitalism with its greed, violence, and polluted skies. "Nothing," Roy concluded, "could be worse than a return to normality." In the midst of despair, there was hope. One year later, the portal is closing. The skies refill with pollutants, animals retreat to the forests, and the feral city is again being tamed. Like my homeopath friend warned me: "the acute eventually recedes and the chronic always returns."

As the Washington Square fountain has again become the unruly center of interracial, cross-class connection, the Parks Department turns on the water, chasing us out. It's a month early, too cold, and it's obvious the water is a technology of discipline. On a chilly April day, with the fountain flattened into a picture postcard, a few tourists and normals sit shivering on the ledge, surrounded by shopping bags and baby strollers, staring at phones, taking selfies, ignoring the fresh graffiti that says FUCK THE SYSTEM. I vent to my friend Antonio. He says, "When they put on the water they killed the vibe. It's a whole different vibe now. They changed it for the tourists and the rich people. Last year, it was just

New Yorkers here." He tells me the park rangers have started intimidating people and, for the first time, he got a ticket for selling art. He feels less comfortable, less connected, and he's thinking about packing up and finding another park. "I've been wandering around," he says, "looking for a place that's raw."

In 2020, when the city leaders tried to subdue public space, the counterculture was too powerful, undistracted by bread and circuses. Now the rebellious energy is draining away. Trump is out of the White House, taking the urgency of liberal anxiety with him, the vaccine brings relief, and protest is no longer the only activity. As people settle back into dining, shopping, and socializing, many are eager to slide into the cloud of forgetting. We are becoming civilized again—and civilization, said Herbert Marcuse, "has to defend itself against the specter of a world which could be free."

In Central Park, the shorebirds that ventured inland recede to the water; the sparrows disappear from Bethesda Terrace, all their nests swept away; and maintenance crews keep the grass along the Elm Mall trimmed tight. With the golden meadow gone, we'll never know how many wild things went with it.

In Times Square, the plazas are getting whitewashed as tourists return. Private security guards from the Times Square Alliance Business Improvement District show up to harass homeless people, including Mr. Ninja, my mild-mannered friend with the rubber rat. They tell him he can't have a cardboard sign and can't use their street furniture to sell his loosies and blunt wraps. Counterterrorism cops start pushing out the unhoused, menacing Mr. Ninja with the threat, "We'll call an ambulance on you." When he makes a joke vaccine from a large industrial syringe and a barbecue skewer, offering passersby a special "jumbo vax," someone goes to the cops and claims that Mr. Ninja is stabbing people. He is not stabbing people. The cops take his skewer and bend it into a pretzel.

On Thirty-Fourth Street, all the vendors have disappeared. The man who sold stun guns, Mucinex, and loosies is gone. The Peruvians with their sweaters and alpaca dolls are gone. Even the hot dog carts are gone. The whole block is swept clean, dead and empty, as if the people never existed. I talk to the cops on guard duty and one tells me, "They're not allowed to be here anymore." I'm sure the same thing has happened to Canal Street and I race down to find the sidewalk cleared, from Church to Broadway, all the vendors disappeared, the only evidence of their existence a wooden sign that reads "Welcome to Little Senegal." Last summer I watched this place grow from a few blankets of knockoff handbags into a community of immigrants grilling chicken, playing djembe drums, and gathering around winter campfires. The first time I heard their drums I was riding back from Abolition Park, captivated by music echoing through silent streets, the only life in that deserted place. I lingered at a distance, not wanting to intrude on the men's space, until one waved me over, saying, "I see you, I see you" (those words) and I moved in to appreciate the music, the singing and dancing in the aroma of barbecue. Now cops stand guard, making sure Little Senegal stays disappeared. When I ask what happened, the cop echoes the same words I heard on Thirty-Fourth, "Those people aren't allowed to be here anymore. It's a new initiative."

In the Village, padlocks appear on the gates of Christopher Park, closing it early on Thursdays before the Stonewall Protest arrives. The park has been a space of queer expression, with queens dancing for a mixed-race, cross-class crowd of gay and trans folks drinking, smoking, mingling. But now, with the street flowing again with normals and tourists, the U.S. Park Police arrive in bulletproof vests, guns at their hips. When the guy next to me lights a blunt, a cop walks over and threatens federal charges. Weed was just legalized in New York, but the park is part of the Stonewall National Monument. A trans woman in short-shorts and spit curls tells the guy, "clip it, clip it." He pinches the cherry off the blunt and walks out. No music, no dancing. The park's jubilant atmosphere deflates as Miss Simone and the other performers sit slouching in their sequins and grumble.

In 2020, I saw many people bringing food and stopping to talk to homeless folks. I don't see that anymore. Now I see police taking our most vulnerable neighbors away, their possessions dumped into garbage trucks, while they scream, "Please don't make me go!" The city is sweeping people off the streets of white Manhattan so the normals feel comfortable. (The *Times* will later confirm: As the city "strives to lure back tourists and office workers, it has undertaken an aggressive campaign to push unhoused people off the streets of Manhattan.") The returning New People are calling the cops, too, worried about property values, but it isn't just them. When I watch six cops take another woman, the man who called 911 tells me he did it because "people pay a lot of money to live here." He's a roving superintendent who does jobs at multiple buildings. Maybe he's worried about his income. Maybe it's internalized capitalism. "I have to protect my tenants," he insists. I detect guilt in his voice and for the next several days he'll go on a bender, wailing drunk on the sidewalk until 2:00 a.m., blasting the same awful song on a speaker, over and over, "We Are the World." Sometimes, the feral city isn't playing my tune.

On my next visit to Christopher Park, I find a young white woman dressed in athleisure and pristine white sneakers, iPhone in hand, holding the leash of a French bulldog while she talks outside to three male police officers in buzz cuts and wraparound sunglasses. "I don't get too close," the woman says, "because I'm scared." She's describing the guy who brings the music so the queens can dance. The cops know him, he's alright, *harmless*. "But," the woman insists, "he's got an open container and there's a law about that, right? And he plays music and that's illegal, isn't it? I mean, I don't *blame* him, but he's breaking the law, so, you know." The cops nod, but they're not giving her what she wants. "I'm *scared*," she insists, weaponizing her white female fear to enlist formal control. "I don't want to be one of those people who call 911, but I'm *scared*." When she repeats "I'm *scared*" for the fifth time, one cop says, "That's why we're here," admitting the truth of his existence. I go inside the park and sit with the queens and other queers, talking about how the cops have been intimidating people, standing guard, walking in and out, giving everyone the eye. "They didn't do that last year," I say, and one guy replies, "That was a different year. The mayor wants the city to go back to normal and *we*," he says, opening his arms to embrace the people of the park, "are *not* normal."

When George Floyd's killer cop is found guilty, there's a collective sigh of relief and something else that feels like an ending, a withdrawal of energy. Nothing burns and nothing breaks. The Cassandras and revolutionaries fret: The emergency isn't over.

The governor declares New York will reopen May 19, accelerating plans to remove pandemic restrictions in time for summer, and the mayor announces, "This is going to be the summer of New York City," describing a program to funnel $30 million into a tourism campaign called NYC Reawakens. "We're all going to get to enjoy the city again!" We've *been* enjoying it, I think, but the Leftovers don't count. Now I understand: This is the new initiative. The aggressive campaign, I later learn, has a name: the Business District Recovery Initiative (BDRI). Instituted by the mayor and run by the NYPD, it launched on April 18 under pressure from real-estate developers. Nearly a hundred police officers have been deployed into Manhattan south of Fifty-Ninth Street to remove street vendors, panhandlers, squeegee men, and homeless encampments, as well as people with mental health issues—who seem to be decompensating under the stress. The BDRI, according to its commanding officer, was created to deal with "quality of life concerns . . . compounded with the reopening of New York City." It is for the "people trying to get back to some normalcy." Naming the revanchist nature of the campaign, one news outlet calls it "the retaking of Manhattan." This is why the cops removed the Black and Latinx vendors, why they're disappearing the homeless people, harassing the artists, and intimidating the queers. It's why, when Washington Square Park closes at midnight, riot cops show up with hats and bats to intimidate people, chasing them through the trees, lights splashing red on cherry blossoms. This is not a reawakening. It's the city being put back to sleep.

■ ■ ■

IN WASH, SUBWAY DJ TAKES OUT HIS PHONE AND SHOWS ME AN EMAIL sent to "the NYU Community" from the departments of Student Affairs and Campus Safety. Under the subject line "Caution About Washington Square Park," it advises students to avoid the park due to "increasing rowdiness" and "devolving circumstances." They ask students to hang out in other spots around the neighborhood, but when they do choose Washington Square, "If things turn ugly, leave the park quickly." Subway DJ and I laugh at the email. "This is the lovey-est, huggy-est park right now," I say. Subway DJ agrees. Last night he witnessed something incredible. When the police tried to shut down the park, the people revolted, gathering from all corners to stand their ground, disparate groups coalescing into one body. "It turned into a spontaneous protest march," he says. "We went through the streets, all together, and now the cops keep their distance." The people learned these tactics last summer, during the uprising, and I am struck by the way sustained protest can create a powerful shift, generalizing outward into a collective resistance that takes the shape of *no*.

I see this *no* while riding my bike along Fourteenth Street where a small pack of Bike Life kids are wheelieing through the intersection, led by a guy who goes by Big Apple E. A driver honks and presses toward them, making the boys nervous, but Big Apple E pulls up his bike, the way a rider pulls up a horse, points at the driver, and shouts, "No, no, no! This is New York. We don't do that anymore."

I see this *no* in Christopher Park when the queens stand up to police, refusing to turn off the dance music, and Miss Simone gets on the mic to throw some shade. "This is a gay park," she says. "We're not here to entertain straight families. You're running gay people, transgenders, and queens out of their own park. We're not here to take care of you and your fucking kids. If you don't like it, get the fuck out. Enough is enough. Go to Tulum, honey. Goodbye."

I see this *no* in a wheatpaste poster by street artist SacSix, a classic Grecian blue New York coffee cup printed with the words: "Welcome Back. Now Get Out."

I see this *no* in Alphabet City, the eastern edge of the East Village, where Latinx men are tired of New People walking carelessly through their games of dice and dominoes, not bothering to nod in acknowledgment. When oblivious white boys push through with golf bags, the men shout, "Get the fuck out!" (Among other, more visceral provocations.)

I see this *no* in myself when I walk by a wall that, for the past year, has been covered in political street art. Now it's covered in ads for Chanel and something called Bourgeoisie Bold. A new thought occurs. I grab the corner of a poster and tug. It comes down in a satisfying shred and

I go on peeling, one after another, revealing graffiti, making my own collage of rip and slash. Later, I notice ads are getting shredded all over town. Other people are sharing the same new thought, giving in to the resistant impulse. *No.* We won't go back.

Wheatpaste poster by SacSix, East Houston Street

REBELLION IN WASHINGTON SQUARE

The cops don't keep their distance for long. A powerful group of "fed-up" neighbors start flexing their muscles. In a letter to elected officials, they list all the things in the park they're fed up about, including: amplified music, graffiti, drug use, bicycles, and general messiness. "We are fed up," they say, "with the negative impact this has on our neighborhood safety, property values, and quality of life." They cite an increase in violent crime, but the stats don't support the claim. "In the first quarter of 2021," *Gothamist* reports, "major felonies in city parks reached their lowest level in at least six years." *Perception* of crime, however, is another story.

Disorder makes people *feel* unsafe. This psychological quirk is exploited by broken-windows policing, the form of order maintenance instituted by Rudy Giuliani and his police commissioner, Bill Bratton, in the 1990s to make New York *feel* safe for real-estate investors, mainstream consumers, tourists, and upper-class whites. Although crime was already falling, in a nationwide trend, broken windows took the credit. As urban historian Themis Chronopoulos explains, the theory succeeded by collapsing the difference between social disorder and serious crime. In this logic, one broken window leads to murder because signs of disorder supposedly produce violence. When George Kelling and James Wilson introduced the theory, they wrote, "The unchecked panhandler is, in effect, the first broken window," so the panhandler must be removed. Giuliani's crackdown on what he called "quality of life" offenses included the criminalization of homelessness, along with graffiti, boom boxes, and political protest. The theory has since been discredited, but it lives on, embedded with bias. As Chronopoulos notes, ideas about disorder are based on "perceptions of activities of low-income and racialized populations." Whenever we hear *disorder*, it is being defined according to white middle-class standards of respectability. In the Village today, when the fed-up neighbors say "quality of life," they are speaking Giuliani and, whether they know it or not, they are asking for broken-windows policing.

I can't deny that I feel an extra edginess when I walk at night down a quiet street. I am more alert, my old New York instincts buzzing. The newspapers keep insisting we're having a major crime wave, fanning flames of fear as we approach a mayoral primary that pits left-leaning liberals against an ex-cop and a Guardian Angel. NYPD statistics, however, tell a different, more complicated story. New York's overall violent crime rate remains 81.9 percent lower than its peak in 1990. Is this a return to the bad old days? Sometimes, it's difficult to tell what's true and what is radiating from a collective anxiety.

The presence of young Black men also makes some people think of violent crime. Sociologists Lincoln Quillian and Devah Pager have shown that whites tend to *perceive* neighborhoods as dangerous when young Black men are present and they will insist the crime rate is high when it's not. As more young Black men enjoy Washington Square, the mostly white residents increasingly insist that violent crime is rampant—and much of their angst revolves around noise. This spring, *The City* will report, locals will call 311 to make almost 200 complaints about the park, the majority about noise. (Last summer, with all our dance parties, protests, and fireworks, there were only twelve noise complaints—maybe because those residents weren't here?) I live in a neighborhood of nonstop party noise and it is excruciating, so I sympathize, but are the fed-up neighbors' complaints really just about noise? Or are affluent whites returning to city life from out-of-town retreats to enlist the police in retaking public space from the Black New Yorkers who've expanded into it? "Space," as Claudia Rankine says, "is one of the understood privileges of whiteness." It is not given up easily.

Pressured by the fed-up neighbors, at the end of May, on the anniversary of the George Floyd uprising, park police and the NYPD force drug users from the corner of the park where they've been quietly getting high for years. They launch a sting to ticket bicyclists. They install hostile architecture, using concrete planters to stop skateboarders. They erect a large digital billboard by the arch, spelling out the rules in light-up let- ters: *No Skating, Bicycle Riding. No Alcohol. No Sound Devices*. When the mayor institutes a 10:00 p.m. weekend curfew on the park, two hours earlier than usual, the people push back.

Boom box, Washington Square Park

On Saturday night, June 5, in the sultriness of an unseasonable heat wave, the park feels like a bar at closing time, after the lights have come on and the jukebox cord is yanked from the wall. The air has gone flat. Dozens of cops stand guard, constraining the park in preparation for the curfew. Music, above all, is forbidden. It feels like we're in *Footloose*, in the grip of a zealot who has banned dancing and "obscene rock and roll music, with its gospel of easy sexuality and relaxed morality." Whenever someone rolls in with a boom box, no matter how quiet, the cops order them to turn it off. A local police captain will later claim, "Music was driving violence in Washington Square," revealing the broken-windows mindset behind the crackdown. The forces of oppression have always feared percussive music and its ancient power of communication. In early colonial America, enslaved Africans were forbidden to play drums, the instrument most associated with insurrection after their use in the Stono slave rebellion of 1739. The drum loosens boundaries and brings people together, creating a connective tissue. In the park, without the beat we are atomized, in closed groups or wandering alone, as I am, disconnected. When music played, we made eye contact, danced with each other, said *hey, I like your drip, your style, I like your bike, what are you about?* But in this muted dead zone, we can't connect. This is by design— I don't mean a singular authority pulling strings, but something more dispersed, a "design" distributed along different systems and authorities acting in concert. For America's elites, race and class mixing has always been a threat. Music doesn't drive violence. It drives empathy, connection, and awakening.

Under police protection, the hyper-normals are no longer clutching their salads for dear life and running scared. They are sinking in, sitting down to bowls of lettuce, drinking White Claws (illegally), and posing for photos with arms around the cops, thanking them for their service. "A repressive order," wrote Herbert Marcuse, "enforces the equation between normal, socially useful, and good." When normals feel comfortable, they expand, and once they expand, they'll take over for the cops, controlling this space without the need for armed forces. This is their social usefulness. See how they glare at me? Their eyes flicker over my signs—my political buttons, my body that radiates otherness on a sub-frequency of gender that isn't visible but sensed. See how the corners of their mouths lift with contempt? As they walk toward me they do not swerve. They slam into me and keep going. I tense. Who's uncomfortable now? Without music, without attunement, the rhythm of Wash has gone to shit. It's all static.

I want to leave but I'm waiting for ten o'clock, to witness the closing as I did last night when the police walked through in riot helmets, calling, "Let's go, let's go," and the obedient normals got up at once and streamed out in a river of khaki and white, so uniform, so swift, it was almost comical, while the Black, brown, queer, and otherwise resistant among us lingered, dragging our feet before the flashing lights of law and order. I woke today in a foul mood and put a note on Instagram: "Be there to bear witness to the state suppression of our collective space." I tagged a number of organizers, folks I know from the movement, and Relly wrote back, "I'll be there tonight." Now I'm looking for him. He's hard to miss, tall and skinny as a drainpipe, with long locs, always in a T-shirt that says UNFUCK THE WORLD. But he isn't here. No one is here. I'm about to give up when I hear the drums.

Advancing down Fifth Avenue, Relly and the marchers stream through the arch with Nah in front, shouting into a microphone, "This is our fuckin' park! As long as we don't leave, they cannot kick us the fuck out!" A Stonewall regular, Nah is a two-spirited queer Black leader in the movement, tall and broad, hair in golden springs atop their head like a crown. Pulling a wheeled speaker, Nah circles the fountain, calling, "Public service announcement! Y'all listening? The cops are gonna try to come in this park and tell us to get the fuck out, but this is our motherfuckin' park. As long as we don't motherfuckin' leave this motherfuckin' park, they ain't kicking nobody out, y'all understand?" The crowd cheers, someone calls, "We outside," and the chant is taken up, "We outside, we outside!" A woman in hoop earrings, hair in a fluffy topknot, takes the mic to add, "The only fuckin' reason they want us out is 'cause there's mad Black and brown bodies out here. Don't let the motherfuckin' pigs throw all the Black and brown bodies out of here! It's our New York, we live here too, and we got every right to be in public spaces."

At 9:30, cops in riot gear mass along the sidewalk beyond the arch. Protesters squeak rubber piggies, calling *oink, oink, oink*, and Bike Life riders spin wheelies in the street. I'm not alone anymore. Justice is here with the Cop Watch team, Ranger Rick is on his bike, Tank came with her camera, and Derrick is hustling in from Brooklyn. An activist in a Yankees cap, teeth gleaming in gold grillz, recognizes me from marches and says, "I see you" (those words again), "you been here," and puts his arms around me. I am with my people—seen and met, part of the fabric of power.

Ten minutes before 10:00, the white civilians hustle out while Black and brown people join the resistance. These folks have come from places like Harlem and the Bronx to party, not protest, but they're all activists now. This is how the movement grows, like mycelium—one of author adrienne maree brown's emergent strategies for justice—the underground system of interconnection. Together we chant, "Whose park? *Our* park! Whose city? *Our* city!" This fight is about public space and what happens when those who are constrained (by racism, transphobia, etc.) expand into it, an exhalation that unsettles people with privilege, who believe every space is theirs, not only to occupy but to sink into with total comfort. When minoritized subjects dare to get comfortable, the state steps in with violence. But this crackdown is about noise and rowdiness, right? How can it be, really, when the East Village is right now mobbed by young, affluent white people, screaming, drunk, vomiting, fighting, swarming into bars where they shove security guards, smash glassware, and steal bottles of booze, but no cops arrive on that scene? How can it be, really, when the outdoor restaurant sheds blast music every night from loudspeakers, but no cops shut them down? Restraining the park is about something else—race, class, and the reproduction of capitalism. Using Foucault's concept of *illegalisms*, we can see that both populations ignore the same rules, but only one is criminalized. The "bourgeois illegalism" of loud music is productive, attracting diners to spend money and enhance New York's competitive image. The music in the park, however, is a "lower-class or popular illegalism," anti-productive, for pleasure and connection. It is a wrench in the works.

At 10:03, the police turn on the LRAD speaker, telling us that if we do not disperse, we will be arrested for unlawful assembly. We respond with a chant of "Hell, no, we won't go!" I hear a tambourine shake, a glass bottle break, and then a scream as the cops shove through the barricades and push toward the fountain. I jog backward in the thunder of drums. Rubber tires squeal and more people scream as the cops surge, wielding their bikes as weapons, chanting, "Move *back*! Move *back*!" Everyone runs, splintering into a frightening panic, and I dart onto the grass as cops crack the air with pepper spray and the slash of batons slamming down on bodies.

We fall back to Thompson Street, pull the barricades shut behind us, and spill off the sidewalk. Worried that another panic might send people running into traffic, I ask my bike comrades to block the street while I direct the cars south and away. As cops rattle the barricades, the stand-off turns into a party and I'm again amazed by the strange back-and-forth of riots, the way they shift from violence to joy, unable to contain their jubilation. Someone turns on a party speaker, flashing purple lights across the asphalt, and here comes the beat. Sheck Wes's "Mo Bamba" plays, a rap anthem with deep vocals droning like a yogi's chanted *om*, as a young man tells a camera, "We gonna stand up for something. It's the end of the pandemic, you give us the freedom to do shit, and now you're baitin' and switchin', because you get right here, kicking us out of the park, doing crazy shit, locking people up. Hey, Mayor de Blasio, in the most respectful way, suck my dick. Respectfully."

Our crowd gives up the park but not the protest, regrouping into a march down Thompson, chanting *whose streets* through the restaurant sheds full of diners. The cops follow. Derrick appears and we hug hello. He's sweaty and excited, walking down the middle of the street, shouting up to windows, "Come outside! We outside!" We're blocks away when the dam bursts behind us. The cops charge, sending people running and screaming, tripping over curbs and piles of trash. A woman is trampled. I duck between a parked car and a restaurant shed, cops streaming past on both sides. People follow me and the cops follow them, blue helmets flashing. I bolt and turn into the shed, grabbing a seat at a table. As cops troop by, I wait to be grabbed, but they're running after another protester, tackling him to the sidewalk. I film the arrest, but it's too quick, everything evaporates except the drumming of my heart, and I walk on through raucous throngs of diners, music blaring from restaurant speakers so loud it shakes the tenement buildings. Tell me again why *that* music is not forbidden? A bike cop shoves me in the back, barking "Outta the way!" He strides past and then stops when a young white woman, in gold jewelry and silk cocktail dress, touches his arm. She's asking for directions, smiling with comfort and familiarity. It's a strange moment, out of joint, happening in another reality. Imagine a woman stepping into a hot stampede to touch a snorting bull, secure in the knowledge that he won't turn his horns on her.

. . .

THE NEXT DAY, SOCIAL MEDIA LIGHTS UP WITH THE POLICE RIOT, and politicians running for mayor slam the cops as abusers and terrorists. It feels like a win. For a little while, the police release their grip and the park opens wider. People looking for trouble and fun hear the news and flock to Wash. Throughout June, the scene gets wilder and louder in what feels like a big *fuck you* to the "fed-up" neighbors. They've kicked a hornet's nest.

MC Shaman starts the We Outside Crew, throwing boisterous dance parties, and if the "Karens and Kevins" on Fifth Avenue don't like it, he tells the *Post*, they should move. Aziz, an older boxer rumored to have trained with Mike Tyson, hosts a fight club, putting young men in gloves to pummel each other inside a ring of ecstatic spectators. Comrades start WSP Mutual Aid, giving out free food, clothing, "good vibes," and fentanyl test strips. Over Henny Colada nutcrackers and slices of pizza, we watch the fights, the dancing, the buzz of unbridled life as the sky above the fountain breaks into rogue fireworks, bright and billowy chrysanthemums, comets, and brocades lacing the night, so loud and low they feel close enough to burn.

After another skirmish, in front of the Washington Square Arch

When the NYPD holds a public meeting in a local church, helicopters whip the sky, anti-terrorism troops stand guard, and angry Villagers line up around the block for a chance to complain about the park. The cops keep the protesters out. We hold our own meeting in the street, talking about race and public space while, inside, a police chief promises the Villagers, "We're going to do whatever it takes to make sure *you* feel comfortable." The Manhattan parks commissioner announces his plan to control the park: Open more lawns to picnickers. This, he says, will "flood the zone with *good* people—*normal* people," and their presence will drive out deviance. With that, he sums up my entire thesis.

Not only do the lawns open to normals, the druggie corner is seeded with coloring books and crayons, attracting flocks of children, their bodies deployed as deterrents. Hundreds of cops guard the park, more than ever, stationed around the fountain and every entrance in groups of six and eight. They enclose the arch in barricades and set up a command center with a surveillance tower holding a cluster of facial-recognition cameras and a loudspeaker that barks, at no one and everyone, "You are trespassing. Please leave the area. This area is under surveillance and you have been recorded." When I bike through, I think it's talking to me. The loudspeaker has a male voice with a Brooklyn accent. Is he watching? Am I in trouble? Again the panopticon. Under his eye.

Beating people with nightsticks backfired, but the steady pressure of cops and cameras subdues the park with little resistance. Has the commissioner been reading Foucault? "If power is exercised too violently, there is the risk of provoking revolts." Send in the observing gaze instead. Make the oppression barely visible. Quietly, with racial bias that may or may not be unconscious, the police target Black people for intimidation. I watch eight cops roll up on two Black women and kick them out for selling drinks. "When I'm playing with white guys," a white musician says, "the cops leave us alone, but if I'm playing with Black guys, they rush right over and shut us down." In a thunderstorm, I'm sheltering behind the statue of Garibaldi, where two cops sit in a squad car, guarding the area from skateboarders. When a couple of young Black men stand nearby to get out of the rain, the cops jump out and step toward them, chests puffed with aggression. The men walk away, into the storm, and the cops get back in their car. Moments later, a pair of young white men stand in the same spot and the cops do nothing.

The block is hot. People stay away from Wash and the energy fizzles as, day by day, Black and brown folks, artists, musicians, skateboarders, and panhandlers leave (or get arrested), while white normals and tourists fill the park. I talk with Aaron, the young Black guitar player who loves Bob Dylan and other "old white people music." He recalls what it was like before 2020, when he'd bring friends into Wash. "You'd see tourists taking pictures, and rich white people, and you'd be like, why would I want to be here? My Black friends would see all the white people and say fuck this shit." But the pandemic changed that. Black and white mixed in the wash of Wash, along with many others. "Coming from the hood," Aaron says, "I hate to say it, but people are gonna be homophobic. It was really cool to see gay, trans, and queer people mixing with people from the hood, all coming together, and there were no real acts of homophobia or racism. Black people who've never really engaged with white people? It was really cool to see that culture mix. That's what the park should be." Now, with the intense police presence and the demographic shift, Aaron misses the park of 2020. "I don't want to be here anymore," he says. "I can't breathe."

I willfully ride my bike inside the vanquished park, day after day. When I blast "Wet-Ass Pussy" from my speaker, no one dances along. One guy gripes, "What happened to headphones, buddy?" Christian missionaries from Ohio, dressed in Mission Trip 2021 T-shirts, stare at me in stupefaction, wide-eyed and open-mouthed. Sometimes, my music is the only music. Sometimes, the *fuck* on my shirt is the only *fuck*. I feel

compelled to assert this disobedience, no matter how small, as if circling
the fountain could keep the portal open. The normals pose for pictures
at the arch and give me dirty looks, radiating covert control. When I
sit down, they ask me to turn off my music. I get up and glide again
around the empty plaza, where a woman shouts, "No bike riding in the
park!" I've been waiting for this. No one has said it to me in over a year
and I take it as confirmation of what I know: The cops emboldened the
normals and now the normals are acting as cops. They're reinstating the
pre-pandemic norms.

Norms are difficult to resist. We are a social species, susceptible to each
other's thought viruses, the memes that travel from mind to mind. I am not
immune. Already, my eye work is suffering. Because the New People won't
see me, I try not to see them—only when I turn my gaze away are they less
likely to bump into me. To avoid their physical violence, I must behave like
them. I must appear to be absent, going blank like a human pretending to
be a pod person so he can move safely through a crowd of body snatchers.
It's painful to not-see and I resent it. This practice of absence soon generalizes, so I begin to recede from contact with all strangers, and I know:
This is the process of re-alienation. What comes next is difficult to face.
One Saturday, feeling alone on a bench in Wash, I'm scanning the park
for my people when a man approaches. He's Black, smiling, holding up a
sign. Maybe asking for money, maybe not. Without a thought, I turn away.
Dismissed, socially controlled, the man walks on. I quickly catch myself
and feel grief. A week ago, I would have been open to contact. But now, in
the contagious atmosphere of discipline and control, I've collapsed into my
own normativity—my class, my whiteness, my property—with its urge to
insulate and protect. It comes as no surprise. All of us who are racialized
as white are implicated in white privilege, and we who pass for normal are
both colonized and colonizing. We are all, potentially, the police. This is
how you kill a city. This is how you stop a revolution, not with riot cops,
but with the most banal of evils.

BETWEEN THE WAVES

Summer lapses into despair. The sun turns blood red in smoke drifting from wildfires on the climate-uncontrolled West Coast; the world's richest man flies a penis-shaped rocket into space (and regrettably returns); and the Delta variant starts cutting through the vast unvaccinated. When I ride with Stonewall, the air has gone out of our tires. Internal conflict has depleted our ranks. The end is near. Groups of normals jeer as we pass, chucking bottles at our heads, and traffic is jammed, the drivers more aggressive than ever. The city has no room for us. When a Black man asks, "Hey, boss, what's this for?" and I tell him it's Black Lives Matter, he shakes his head and says, with a sigh of annoyance, "That's *still* going on?" It seems everyone wants to get back to normal, to forget the past that is not past. In a tragedy that feels symbolic of this world extinguishing its wilder life, Barry, the barred owl that has enchanted Central Park since October, is struck while flying low, killed by a truck on cleanup duty with the Central Park Conservancy, the private group of wealthy elites and corporations that maintain the order and cleanliness of our un-public park. A necropsy will show that Barry might also have been impaired, weakened by rat poison. Nothing gold can stay.

All year I've watched the wall of the tenement across my street get tagged with graffiti, buffed by the landlord, and then tagged again, the defiant

subject overwhelming the normative order. This delighted me. Now the
wall sits untouched. There's not much new graffiti anywhere. Sometimes,
I'll find a remnant of 2020, a scribbled FUCK or BLM on a light pole,
half covered with ads, forgotten. I feel like a 2020 remnant, too, in my
slogan buttons and T-shirts, a leftover of a leftover, turned into a relic
overnight. Alone, I wander and search. Times Square no longer calls
me. Its plazas have been reprivatized by advertainment installations for
car companies and video games. The tourist clamor blots out Neuhaus's
sound work and Barbie's yawp. I can't hear them anymore. Washington
Square Park is reprogrammed with corporate-sponsored performances
that push out the unauthorized and spontaneous. All across town, the
boom boxes have disappeared, their river of groove run dry. No naked
people walk the streets. Where did everyone go?

As normal New York reopens, the other city closes. Years ago, I thought
my city had died. Now I know it split in two, a pair of parallel New
Yorks running on separate streams. The dominant stream stifled the
substream, dividing me from it. Now and then, I might drop through
the repression barrier into the succulent city that coursed below, but the
dominant always yanked me back, an alarm clock waking me from a
dream I could not hold. You're not supposed to see the people of substream. Like in China Mieville's *The City and the City*, you're supposed
to unsee them, the way the New People unsee me. They take up so much
space. In the fog of their crowd, I can't find my city.

The floodwaters keep rising. Incoming renters wage unprecedented
bidding wars, paying 20 percent over asking price, making New York
the most expensive market in America. In my building, when the most
recent batch of new neighbors moves out, my landlord converts their
apartments to more profitable short-term rentals. Leased by the room
("dynamic pricing" ranges from $1,700 to $2,050 for each cramped cell),
they are essentially SROs for kids with money, managed by a "prop-tech"

startup that populates the units with unconnected roommates, supplies them with limitless toilet paper, and controls their sex lives (overnight guests are restricted and must pre-register with the company). During the conversions, workers assemble furniture, mount flat-screen TVs, and install combination locks on the apartment doors to enable a constant flow of transients who will never become neighbors. I watch the workers through my peephole, their T-shirts declaring "Rentals Redefined," and I think: This is what alienation looks like. At least there will be no more open houses. They do it all through an app.

At Mutual Aid, giving out slices of pizza in a scruffy corner of Wash, Derrick and I talk about this difficult moment, as action declines and state repression increases. We don't know what the future holds, but we know there will never be another year like the last, a brief and also endless time that felt like a transition between one world and another. Will it get better or worse? Will the next coronavirus variant wipe us out? Will we descend into a culture of rampant violence? For now, I don't know what to do with the profound grief I feel—for receiving joy and having it taken away, for watching my city come back to life only to vanish all over again. Derrick quotes a Twitter thread from the Workers Defense Alliance in Minneapolis: "This is not about any single struggle; we live in a time when one wave subsides and another is already rushing forward." Between the waves, though, it's hard to stay hopeful.

A young trans woman comrade joins us, talking about how the plague year opened a space for emergence. "My egg cracked," she says, "and I awakened" to both radical politics and radical gender. I've heard this from several trans folks, in the movement and in my therapy practice. During lockdown, many people, away from workplaces and social spaces, away from normal life with its constant, controlling gaze, discovered other ways of being. Even the normies. Here and there, a few are breaking out, trading white clothes for black, straight hair for curls, a pair of combat boots, a new point of view. Maybe there is a sliver of hope. Through the portal of the pandemic, so much deviance unleashed. Maybe portals aren't meant to stay open. Maybe they are temporal rifts that spill and then shut, leaving ripples in their wake. What influence will these wilder lives have on our future? We cannot know. In the negative space, I find room for possibility.

Back in my apartment, in the late-night quiet, I water the plant, the one I took from the trash where the Influencer dumped it a year ago. When I rescued it, there were only a few spears of leaf, pale and dying, but now the plant is thriving, sending up shoot after shoot, bright green and glossed with life. It looked dead, but it wasn't, the way New York looked dead but was only suppressed, repressed, made unconscious to its wilder elements. As I wait between the waves, I console myself with this thought: The defiant soul of the city doesn't die. It stays alive, right below the surface, pressing up against the boot heels, crouched like the life inside an egg, the force that drives the flower, forever reaching for its next breath.

Headed for the next ride-out

ACKNOWLEDGMENTS

I am deeply grateful to my agent, Doug Stewart, for his gracious intelligence and tireless championship of this book that started out messy in the midst of a pandemic; and to my editor, Tom Mayer, for his insightful feedback and astute guidance, as well as the gift of extra time that I needed to live out the story while writing it. Thanks, too, to their colleagues, Maria Bell, Nneoma Amadi-obi, and Ellis Breunig, for their enthusiastic support and thoughtful comments.

A special note of gratitude to Marco Roth, who first saw something in a handful of my cranky Facebook posts and helped turn them into an essay for *n+1*, improbably setting this book in motion, and for his essential assistance in shaping it up.

To my generous readers and dear friends: Heartfelt thanks to Avgi Saketopoulou for crucial input and encouragement at the eleventh hour, Rob Freeman for helping me think through tough questions, and Ann Pellegrini for guiding me to Foucault and Bollas—and a decent subtitle. Thank you to James Hannaham for making sure my sensitivity was on point. And to Stacie Joy for her expertise in helping to bring out the best in my photographs.

To Rebecca Levi, my partner in crime, endless gratitude for her endless patience and loving support, for reading first and last drafts (out loud), and for biking beside me through the apocalypse.

Lastly, deep appreciation to all the activists, artists, comrades, friends, and other Others who appear in these pages, named or unnamed, and who came outside in 2020 to make New York a more vibrant, essential, and feral place to be. Whose streets? Our streets.

NOTES

On quotations: Activists whom I profile have given permission for me to quote them and describe their actions. They either reviewed and approved the material or gave blanket approval without review.

On word choice: I sometimes describe myself as a "transsexual." My use of this contested term is not a separatist gesture, nor is it against transgender politics. It is how I identified when I first came out in the late 1980s and early 1990s, when it was the only available word, and I remain attached to it. While I also identify as "trans" and "transgender," I sometimes prefer "transsexual" as a reclaiming, like "queer," appreciating its outlaw sense of wrongness and the jolt of *sex*. To be inclusive, when I write more generally, I use "trans" or "transgender." Regarding "homeless," the word is currently in flux, sometimes substituted with "unhoused," "houseless," or "displaced." I feel that "homeless" remains, for now, the most widely recognizable term and so I use it here, along with "unhoused," with the understanding that the language is evolving.

On capitalization: After much thought, I have chosen to capitalize "Black" and not "white" when referring to race. This is generally the current standard; however, it is a contested usage in flux. Some argue that capitalizing "white" follows the lead of white supremacists, while others make the case that not capitalizing "white" upholds the power of whiteness by keeping it invisible. Black scholars are currently debating the issue. Nell Irvin Painter has said, "White should be capitalized in order to unmask Whiteness as an American racial identity as historically important as Blackness." Jenn M. Jackson has disagreed, writing, "Not capitalizing the 'w' in white is a systemic disruption which decenters whiteness," it is "decolonizing work." The conversation is continuing.

PART ONE

CHAPTER 1: THE BEFORE TIME (SOMEWHERE IN 2019)

Laurie Layton Schapira, from *Cassandra Complex* (Inner City Books, 1988).

Dominant laughter: See Christopher Oveis et al., "Laughter Conveys Status," *Journal of Experimental Social Psychology* 65 (2016).

Ontological expansiveness: Shannon Sullivan writes about this in "The Racialization of Space" and "White World-Traveling," in which she also refers to ontological constraint. The quote here is from her chapter "Ontological Expansiveness" in Gail Weiss et al., *50 Concepts for a Critical Phenomenology* (Northwestern University Press, 2019).

Kyle Chayka, from "Welcome to Airspace," in *The Verge*, https://www.the verge.com/2016/8/3/12325104/airbnb-aesthetic-global-minimalism-startup -gentrification.

Being close to what you don't have can make you angry: In a study about airplane travel and inequality, researchers discovered that when coach passengers have to pass through first class to get to their seats in back, they are twice as likely to succumb to outbursts of "air rage." See Katherine DeCelles and Michael Norton, "Physical and Situational Inequality on Airplanes Predicts Air Rage," *Proceedings of the National Academy of Sciences of the United States of America*, May 17, 2016.

For a feminist critique of haul videos, see Sarah Banet-Weiser and Inna Arzumanova, "Creative Authorship: Self-Actualizing Individuals and the Self-Brand," in Cynthia Chris and David Gerstner, eds., *Media Authorship* (Routledge, 2013). An analysis of the ways hauler culture articulates authorship "through post-feminist consumption and its attendant normative femininity, both of which are functions of a neoliberal cultural ethics of individualism, and entrepreneurial visibility."

Erving Goffman, from *Behavior in Public Places* (Free Press, 1963).

Dodie Bellamy, from "In the Shadow of Twitter Towers," *When the Sick Rule the World* (Semiotext(e), 2015).

Mattilda Bernstein Sycamore, from *The Freezer Door* (MIT Press, 2020).

On Influencers and gentrification: Digital geographer Agnieszka Leszczynski finds that Influencers "can prime particular spaces for gentrification" and "amplify gentrification that is already occurring." MIT researcher Sun Xudong finds that Influencers "have an economically significant impact" on retail rent in New York, helping to push it higher. From "Evaluating the Impact of Online Influencers on Retail Property Rent—A Case Study in New York City," February 2019. Both sources are from *Gothamist*, "Native New Yorkers on TikTok Are Pushing Back Against the 'NYC Influencer' Trend," December 23, 2021.

Sarah Schulman, from *The Gentrification of the Mind* (University of California Press, 2013).

Claudia Rankine, from *Just Us* (Graywolf Press, 2020).

PART TWO

CHAPTER 2: EMPTINESS GIVES PERMISSION

Rebecca Solnit, violent gift, from the interview "Falling Together" in *On Being with Krista Tippett*, originally aired May 26, 2016, re-aired March 19, 2020.

Anthropause: See Christian Rutz et al., "COVID-19 Lockdown Allows Researchers to Quantify the Effects of Human Activity on Wildlife," *Nature Ecology & Evolution* 4 (2020).

E. B. White, from *Here Is New York* (The Little Bookroom, 1949).

Mary Oliver, from the poem "Don't Hesitate," and Langston Hughes, from the poem "Luck."

Weegee, from *Naked City* (De Capo Press, 1945).

Nora Ephron, from "The Boston Photographs," *Esquire*, 1975.

Susan Sontag, from *Regarding the Pain of Others* (Farrar Straus & Giroux, 2003).

Plagues have a disinhibiting effect, from Andrew Sullivan, "A Plague Is an Apocalypse. But It Can Bring a New World," *New York*, July 21, 2020.

Rebecca Solnit and Kathleen Tierney on elite panic, from Solnit, *A Paradise Built in Hell* (Penguin, 2009).

In Finland, from "Finland: Europe's Quiet Success in Covid-19 Fight," *Euractiv*, November 4, 2020.

CHAPTER 3: JUST BEFORE THE REVOLUTION, A CERTAIN ATMOSPHERE ARISES

Samuel Delany, from *Times Square Red, Times Square Blue* (NYU Press, 1989).

Neuhaus: See Ulrich Loock's essay, "Times Square: Max Neuhaus's Sound Work in New York City," *Open!* online, November 1, 2005.

Walt Whitman, "I too am not a bit tamed, I too am untranslatable . . . barbaric yawp," from "Song of Myself."

Giorgio Agamben, from the chapter "On the Uses and Disadvantages of Living Among Specters" in *Nudities* (Stanford University Press, 2010).

Lucy Sante, from "Bass Culture," in *Maybe the People Would Be the Times* (Verse Chorus Press, 2020).

Walkman Effect: See Shuhei Hosokawa, "The Walkman Effect," *Popular Music* 1 (1984). The Walkman "listener seems to cut the auditory contact with the outer world where he really lives: seeking the perfection of his 'individual' zone of listening."

Lillian Hellman, from her memoir *Pentimento: A Book of Portraits* (Little, Brown, 1973).

Herbert Marcuse, all quotes are from *Eros and Civilization* (Beacon Press, 1955).

David Wojnarowicz, from *Close to the Knives* (Penguin, 1991).

Cathy J. Cohen, from "Punks, Bulldaggers, and Welfare Queens: The Radical Potential of Queer Politics?" *GLQ* 3 (1997). She further writes, "I envision a politics where one's relation to power, and not some homogenized identity, is privileged in determining one's political comrades. I'm talking about a politics where the *nonnormative* and *marginal* position of punks, bulldaggers, and welfare queens, for example, is the basis for progressive transformative coalition work." Feminist scholar bell hooks also saw the broader potential of *queer* as a "self that is at odds with everything around it and has to invent and create and find a place to speak and to thrive and to live," from the talk "Are You Still a Slave?" The New School, May 6, 2014. For more on Black people occupying a non-normative position, see philosopher George Yancy on whiteness as *the transcendental norm*, "that according to which what is nonwhite is rendered other, marginal, ersatz, strange, native, inferior, uncivilized, and ugly," from *Black Bodies, White Gazes* (Rowman & Littlefield, 2008).

Toni Morrison, from *What Moves at the Margin* (University Press of Mississippi, 2008).

Christina Sharpe, from *In the Wake* (Duke University Press, 2016).

PART THREE

CHAPTER 4: THE PHASE OF BREAKING

Saidiya Hartman, from *Wayward Lives, Beautiful Experiments* (W. W. Norton, 2019).

Fuck 12: The term might have started in Atlanta, from the radio code 10-12, or from the TV show *Adam-12*, but its origin is ultimately uncertain.

Frantz Fanon, from *The Wretched of the Earth* (Grove Press, 1961).

Vicky Osterweil, from *In Defense of Looting* (Bold Type Books, 2020).

CHAPTER 5: QUEER NEGATIVITY: NOT GAY AS IN HAPPY, BUT QUEER AS IN FUCK YOU

Sara Ahmed, all quotes are from *The Promise of Happiness* (Duke University Press, 2010).

Tim Dean, from "The Antisocial Thesis in Queer Theory," *PMLA* 121, no. 3 (May 2006).

Mari Ruti, from *The Ethics of Opting Out* (Columbia University Press, 2017).

Heather Love, all quotes are from *Feeling Backward* (Harvard University Press, 2009).

Mariana Ortega, from "Hometactics," in Gail Weiss et al., *50 Concepts for a Critical Phenomenology* (Northwestern University Press, 2019).

Susan Stryker, from "My Words to Victor Frankenstein above the Village of Chamounix: Performing Transgender Rage," *GLQ* 1, no. 3 (1994).

Michael Warner, from *The Trouble with Normal* (Free Press, 1999).

CHAPTER 6: THE COP IN MY HEAD

"Cop in my head": Brazilian theater director Augusto Boal hypothesized "The Cop in the Head" as an internalized oppressor. Why do many people not dare to participate in political actions? He answered, "Because they have cops in their heads. They have internalized their oppressions." See "The Cop in the Head," *The Drama Review* 34, no. 3 (Autumn, 1990). The slogan "Kill the cop in your head" was popular during protests in the summer of 2020.

Newbold Morris and the jazz musician: "from the Bronx" is from the *New York Times*, April 11, 1961, and "undesirable" is from Ted White, "Balladeers and Billy Clubs," *Rogue*, August 1961.

Christopher Bollas, from "Normotic Illness," in *The Shadow of the Object* (Columbia University Press, 1989), and "Normopathy and the Compound Syndrome," in *Meaning and Melancholia* (Routledge, 2018).

Michel Foucault, "a model of social relations," from *The Birth of Biopolitics: Lectures at the College de France 1978-1979*, trans. Graham Burchill (Palgrave Macmillan, 2008).

Philip Mirowski, *Never Let a Serious Crisis Go to Waste: How Neoliberalism Survived the Financial Meltdown* (Verso, 2014).

Foucault, "faceless gaze," from *Discipline and Punish*, trans. Alan Sheridan (Vintage, 1977).

Foucault, "If power is exercised too violently," from *Foucault Live: Collected Interviews, 1961–1984* (Semiotext(e), 1989).

Pierre Bourdieu, from *The Logic of Practice* (Stanford University Press, 1980).

Foucault, "agitations, revolts," from *Discipline and Punish*.

Frank B. Wilderson III, from *Afropessimism* (Liveright, 2020).

CHAPTER 7: TO BE OF USE

Jia Tolentino, from "Ask a Sane Person: Jia Tolentino on Practicing the Discipline of Hope," *Interview* magazine, July 8, 2020.

Emmanuel Ghent, "Masochism, Submission, Surrender: Masochism as a Perversion of Surrender," *Contemporary Psychoanalysis* 26 (1990).

CHAPTER 8: THE RETURN OF REVANCHISM

Claudia Rankine, "to imagine herself a rescue": From *Situation 11*, a short film by Rankine and John Lucas.

Stephen J. Mexal, "The Roots of 'Wilding': Black Literary Naturalism, the Language of Wilderness, and Hip Hop in the Central Park Jogger Rape," *African American Review* 46, no. 1 (Spring 2013).

Neil Smith, from *The New Urban Frontier: Gentrification and the Revanchist City* (Routledge, 1996).

Lee Edelman, from *No Future: Queer Theory and the Death Drive* (Duke University Press, 2004). In his earlier paper "The Future Is Kid Stuff" (*Narrative* 6, no. 1 [January 1998]), the sentence made it clear that the Child is symbolic: "fuck the social order and the figural children paraded before us as its terroristic emblem."

"Poor children, children of color . . .": The normative Child, says Katherine Bond Stockton in *The Queer Child* (Duke University Press, 2009), is the one who must be safeguarded, the one who, "as an *idea*," is "likely to be both white and middle-class" because "[i]t is a privilege to need to be protected—and to be sheltered—and thus to have a childhood."

CHAPTER 9: A QUEER LONGING FOR RUINS AND MUD

For this chapter, I took much inspiration from Fiona Anderson's book *Cruising the Dead River: David Wojnarowicz and New York's Ruined Waterfront* (University of Chicago Press, 2019).

Andrew Holleran, "Nostalgia for the Mud," in *The Christopher Street Reader*, 1983.

Herbert Muschamp, "Nostalgia Tripping in Times Square," *New York Times*, August 25, 1996.

Michelle Tea, "Times Square," in *Against Memoir* (Feminist Press, 2018).

Helmut Illbruck, *Nostalgia* (Northwestern University Press, 2012).

I am pro-nostalgia, but I also like *solastalgia*, a word conceived in 2005 by environmental philosopher Glenn Albrecht, who called it "the pain experienced when there is recognition that the place where one resides and that one loves is under immediate assault . . . a form of homesickness one gets when one is still at 'home.'" It can be caused by climate change, war, gentrification. From "Solastalgia," *PAN: Philosophy, Activism, Nature* 3 (2005).

"constant enemy . . .": From a letter from Eugene Brieux, used as a preface to Emile Augier's *Four Plays* (Knopf, 1915); the line "romantic ideas of redemption through love" is from the play.

Henry James, *Italian Hours* (Heinemann, 1909).

Rose Macaulay, *The Pleasure of Ruins* (Thames & Hudson, 1964).

CHAPTER 10: NEW YORK FUCKIN CITY

"disorderly persons . . .": From Minutes of the Common Council of the City of New York, 1675–1776, vol. 4.

Michael C. Philipp and Laura Lombardo, "Hurt Feelings and Four Letter Words: Swearing Alleviates the Pain of Social Distress," *European Journal of Social Psychology* 47, no. 4 (June 2017).

CHAPTER 11: QUEER TIME

Jack Halberstam, from *In a Queer Time and Place* (NYU Press, 2005).

Elizabeth Freeman, from *Time Binds* (Duke University Press, 2010).

"grow sideways": See Katherine Bond Stockton in *The Queer Child*: "I coin the term 'sideways growth' to refer to something related but not reducible to the death drive; something that locates energy, pleasure, vitality, and (e)motion in the back-and-forth of connections and extensions that are not reproductive."

Carl Jung on chthonic: See *Man and His Symbols* (Aldus Books, 1964), in which he describes it as dark, earthly, maternal, feminine, deep, unconscious, belonging to the underworld.

Jessie Kindig, from "We Keep Us Safe," published online at *n+1*, July 8, 2020.

Jack Halberstam on imagined violence, from "Imagined Violence/Queer Violence: Representation, Rage, and Resistance," *Social Text* 37 (Winter 1993). June Jordan, "a place of rage," is from a 1991 film by the same name by Pratibha Parmar.

Angela Davis on trans, from *Dream Defenders, Sunday School: Abolition in Our Lifetime*, a Zoom discussion posted to YouTube, June 23, 2020.

CHAPTER 12: YOU WANTED THE 1970S, YOU GOT THE 1970S

Elijah Anderson, *The Cosmopolitan Canopy: Race and Civility in Everyday Life* (W. W. Norton, 2011).

"whiteness and wealth are properties": See Cheryl Harris, "Whiteness as Property," *Harvard Law Review*, June 1993.

CHAPTER 13: MOVING OUT IN MOUNTAINS

"widening gyre," taken from W. B. Yeats's poem "The Second Coming."

PART FOUR

CHAPTER 14: I WOULD PREFER NOT TO

A Met for New Yorkers: When I asked the ticket seller for the breakdown, he told me that New Yorkers made up 75 percent of the visitors that day (it's usually only 30 percent) and another 20 percent were from the local tri-state area.

Rebecca West, from *Black Lamb and Grey Falcon* (Viking, 1941).

Margaret Kohn, *Brave New Neighborhoods: The Privatization of Public Space* (Routledge, 2004).

Fred Moten, from *The Undercommons* (Autonomedia, 2013).

CHAPTER 15: HAUNTOLOGY

Mark Fisher, from *Ghosts of My Life* (Zero Books, 2014).

Sara Ahmed, from "A Phenomenology of Whiteness," *Feminist Theory* 8, no. 2 (2007).

Melanie Klein, from "Notes on Some Schizoid Mechanisms," *International Journal of Psychoanalysis* 27 (1946).

For more on anasuromai, see Catherine Blackledge, *Raising the Skirt: The Unsung Power of the Vagina* (Weidenfeld and Nicolson, 2020).

CHAPTER 16: ONE WEEK IN NOVEMBER

Weathering: See the work of Arline T. Geronimus, starting with "The weathering hypothesis and the health of African-American women and infants: evidence and speculations," *Ethnicity and Disease* 2, no. 3 (Summer 1992).

CHAPTER 17: GOOD OLD BAD OLD NEW YORK

"The symbolic Vaginal": See my writing as Griffin Hansbury, "The Masculine Vaginal: Working with Queer Men's Embodiment at the Transgender Edge," *Journal of the American Psychoanalytic Association* 65, no. 6 (2017).

Erin Pineda, from *Seeing Like an Activist* (Oxford University Press, 2021).

Mike Davis, from "The Embers of April 1992," *Los Angeles Review of Books*, April 30, 2012.

Martel Pipkins, from "'I Feared for My Life': Law Enforcement's Appeal to Murderous Empathy," *Race and Justice* 9, no. 2 (2017).

PART FIVE

CHAPTER 18: BACK TO NORMAL

Sonya Renee Taylor, from her Instagram page, April 2, 2020: "We will not go back to normal. Normal never was. Our pre-corona existence was never normal other than we normalized greed, inequity, exhaustion, depletion, extraction, disconnection, confusion, rage, hoarding, hate and lack. We should not long to return, my friends. We are being given the opportunity to stitch a new garment. One that fits all of humanity and nature."

Boring dystopia: A Facebook group, and a concept, started by Mark Fisher in 2015. I like Elle Hunt's description (from *The Guardian*, August 6, 2018): "the bland, mildly coercive signs that abound in late-stage capitalist society, which foster a vague sense of isolation or unease."

Molly Crabapple, from "Molly Crabapple on New York City Before—and One Day, After—COVID-19," *Literary Hub*, online, February 5, 2021.

Comrade Josephine, as embodied by philosopher Luce de Lire, from "Full Queerocracy Now! Pink Totaliterianism and the Industrialization of Libidinal Agriculture," in *e-flux Journal*, 117 (April 2021).

Sara Ahmed, from *The Promise of Happiness*.

For more on the micro-expression of contempt, see the work of psychologist Paul Ekman: www.paulekman.com/universal-emotions/what-is-contempt/.

CHAPTER 19: KILLING THE VIBE

Arundhati Roy, *Financial Times*, April 3, 2020.

The Business District Recovery Initiative: Regarding pressure from real-estate developers, the *Post* reported that Bill de Blasio "caved to pressure from special interests including the Times Square Alliance and the 34th Street Partnership, as well as Vornado Realty Trust, Brookfield Properties and the Related Group, developer of the Hudson Yards complex" (April 20, 2021). NYPD Commanding Officer Steven Hellman is quoted from the Manhattan Community Board 4 public meeting, streamed live, June 2, 2021. The "retaking of Manhattan" is from CBS2 New York, April 22, 2021.

CHAPTER 20: REBELLION IN WASHINGTON SQUARE

Broken windows: Kelling and Wilson introduced their theory in the article "Broken Windows," in *The Atlantic*, March 1982. Since then, several researchers have challenged and debunked the theory. Daniel T. O'Brien, a professor at the School of Criminology and Criminal Justice at Northeastern, has recently led the charge. Writing in the *New York Daily News* (May 26, 2019), O'Brien outlines his research and states: "the consensus across the literature is that the relationships proposed by the broken windows theory are untrue. Disorder in a neighborhood does not in fact lead to people living there being more likely to commit crimes, either violent or not. . . . What it does do is create antagonistic relationships with communities, engaging cops in what feels to many people on the receiving end like low-level harassment."

Themis Chronopoulos, from *Spatial Regulation in New York City* (Routledge, 2011).

For more on the origins of the "quality of life" offenses and the NYPD response, read the source: "Police Strategy No. 5: Reclaiming the Public Spaces of New York," a memo from the New York City Police Department, 1994. Downloadable from the U.S. Department of Justice's virtual library.

On the crime rate: It's complicated. The NYPD's CompStat database shows that overall serious crime (the "Major 7") reached a record low in 2020. While crime rose again in 2021, the increase was comparable to the slight bump between the years 2011 and 2012—when the city was considered to be very safe. Shooting incidents and gun-related homicides have increased markedly during the pandemic. This is not a New York phenomenon, however; it's a nationwide trend, occurring in cities and small towns across America, where the state of Montana has seen the largest percentage increase. Questions about crime during the pandemic will surely occupy criminologists for years to come.

Lincoln Quillian and Devah Pager, from "Black Neighbors, Higher Crime? The Role of Racial Stereotypes in Evaluations of Neighborhood Crime," *American Journal of Sociology* 107, no. 3 (2001).

Claudia Rankine, "Space," from *Just Us.*

Stono Slave Rebellion: South Carolina's Negro Act of 1740 explicitly banned enslaved Africans from the "using or keeping of drums, horns, or other loud instruments, which may call together or give sign or notice to one another of their wicked designs and purposes." See John Jeremiah Sullivan's article "Talking Drums," *Oxford American*, online, November 19, 2019.

Foucault on illegalisms, from *The Punitive Society: Lectures at the College de France, 1972–1973*, trans. Graham Burchell (Palgrave, 2015). See also Delio Vásquez, "Illegalist Foucault, Criminal Foucault," *Theory & Event* 23, no. 4 (October 2020).

CHAPTER 21: BETWEEN THE WAVES

"the force that drives the flower," taken from the Dylan Thomas poem "The Force That Through the Green Fuse Drives the Flower."